To Byran
from
Bessie

Suite in Four Movements

an autobiography

by

ERIC COATES

foreword by

IAN LACE

Thames Publishing
LONDON
1986

Text ©1986 Austin Coates
Foreword © 1986 Ian Lace
Production © 1986 Thames Publishing

This book shall not be reproduced in any form, either in whole or in part, without the written permission of the publishers — Thames Publishing, 14 Barlby Road, London W10 6AR.

CONTENTS

Foreword	Page iv
SUITE IN FOUR MOVEMENTS	
Allegretto Pastorale	3
Lento – Andante – Allegretto	57
Romanza in Modo Variazione	159
Rondo	214
Index	265
Selected list of works	272

Illustrations between pages 134 and 135

FOREWORD
by Ian Lace

Regular listeners to BBC Radio's long-running 'Desert Island Discs' will know that its famous signature tune, *By the Sleepy Lagoon*, was written by Eric Coates.

In the unlikely event that I were ever to be interviewed on that programme, and was asked which book I would take with me to my desert island, I would reply unhesitatingly — this one!

I first read *Suite in Four Movements* when I was in my late teens and discovering the world of music. Since then I have read it many times, always with the same enthusiasm and enjoyment, which is something rather special, for I rarely re-read other composers' lives.

Suite in Four Movements is not only a delightful and often witty story about a gifted composer and a charming, happy, well-adjusted man, it is also an invaluable historical record of what life was like as a student of the Royal Academy of Music, and a player in concert and theatre orchestras and chamber music ensembles in the early years of this century. We learn, for instance, much about the infamous deputy system which blighted British orchestras at that time, and much about the styles of such conductors as Henry Wood, Beecham, Nikisch, Mengelberg, Elgar, Debussy and Richard Strauss.

The idea for a new edition of *Suite in Four Movements* evolved after I produced a half-hour programme for local radio based on Eric Coates' many associations with the county of Sussex. The programme included interviews with Stanford Robinson, Teddy Holmes of Coates' music publishers, Chappell's, and the composer's son Austin Coates, author of books on the East, who lives in Hongkong.

The concept of this new edition was that it should be expanded to include some words of appreciation from those who knew him, a list of works, some pictures not included in the original edition, and biographical details about the remaining years of Eric Coates' life not covered in *Suite in Four Movements*.

The original autobiography covered Eric's life up until 1953, when this book was published. He died just four years later, on December 21, 1957. During those latter years he composed one of his most popular works, *The Dambusters March*, and there were one or two notable concerts. Austin Coates sent me the following description of the highlights of that period:

> 'One occasion I shall always remember was his appearance at a Promenade Concert at the Royal Albert Hall on a Saturday night in August 1956. Malcolm Sargent was the conductor, and the second half was to consist of my father conducting his *Four Centuries' Suite*, followed by Sargent conducting a work by Tchaikovsky.

Sargent had not heard *Four Centuries* before the rehearsal that morning. Just before lunch he asked my father if he would mind if the items were reversed. My father came home so worried that he was in a mood not to conduct. He could not understand why Sargent should interfere with the programme.

Just before the second half that evening, a Tannoy announcement said the works were to be reversed. Sargent conducted the Tchaikovsky, after which he brought my father in with a flourish.

All went well to start with, but the orchestra was tired, and *Four Centuries* is a very demanding work. In the valse, the leader, faced with that appallingly difficult violin solo, fluffed badly. I thought to myself, 'How on earth are they going to get through the fourth movement?' (Rhythm: 20th Century).

When that movement began, my mother and I were getting pretty nervous. Then, when the tenor saxophone entered, the audience laughed. Jascha Krein, who had been specially engaged with two altos from his saxophone team, was so shocked he nearly dried up. There was a moment when the work very nearly collapsed. Outwardly, my father remained entirely cool, and avoided looking at Jascha Krein, who somehow mastered himself and went on.

Again, at the point of the trumpet phrase played 'in the hat', there was a laugh. Although it was a very warm evening, my mother and I were, by this time, stone cold and perspiring with anxiety. The trouble with laughs from the audience is that you can never tell whether it is a laugh of ridicule or amusement.

By the end of the work I had reached a stage where I didn't mind what happened. I had somehow cut myself off.

Well, there was no clapping. Instead, they were banging on the boards, waving their arms in the air and yelling at the tops of their voices. Even in the more sedate tiers they were on their feet cheering, and in the gods they were yelling and waving. The noise was deafening. I have never before or since seen such an extraordinary scene in a concert hall, and it went on unabated while my father took two calls, at the end of which the principal violin said something to him. Amid the uproar it was impossible to hear a thing, but by lip-reading I could see the principal was saying, 'Eric, you've got to . . .!'

So, in defiance of BBC rules — they were on the air — my father took up his baton (immediately dead silence) and conducted the fourth movement again. This time, Jascha Krein, realising the audience was with him, not against him, and the orchestra having recovered from *their* nerves (make no mistake, they had been worried too), they gave a magnificent performance, far better than the first. And the same incredible scene took place a second time. Deafening uproar. And again, it went on unabated while my father took two calls. For an awful moment I thought he might have to do it a third time. But he had a wonderful way with an audience. He made a very simple gesture, which without need for a word, said, 'Now, I'm going home. So must you.' They cheered him till the last instant they could see him. The moment he was lost to view the cheering stopped, like turning off a tap, and they were all rumbling home.

Then, a few days later, on his 70th birthday, there was the concert by one of the BBC orchestras and broadcast from the Albert Hall, Nottingham. The hall was packed, with people sitting and standing all round behind the orchestra; some of them who could not get foot-room were even clinging to the organ pipes. When I pointed out this last point to him, he said, 'Yes, when I go to Nottingham I do draw quite a crowd.'

On one occasion I came back from Hongkong and found him turning out electric lights all over the place. I asked him why on earth he was doing so. He said, 'It's this terrible income tax. If I write another *Sleepy Lagoon* I shall be ruined.' I thought of this when he wrote *The Dambusters*.

Many people, particularly those connected with the Royal Air Force, have asked me why he included such cheerful, light-hearted music in a march with a solemn theme. The answer is he was thinking of the experience of Arthur Bliss when the latter wrote the music for the 1930s movie *Things to Come*, based on the H G Wells story. Bliss was given the script, and meticulously wrote the music for it. A special set of tubular bells had to be sent from Leningrad to get one of his effects. When it came to the final editing, large sections of the movie were cut. Something like 183 pages of Bliss' music were not used. Nor were the tubular bells. Bliss was understandably upset, told my father about it, and my father never forgot it.

When Associated British Pictures (ABP) asked him to write the music for *The Dambusters* he refused, though he had enjoyed reading the script. A great deal of persuasive argument had to be brought to bear, notably from Teddy Holmes of Chappell's, to make him change his mind. He finally relented to this extent. He said, 'I'll give you a five-minute concert march, and leave you a free hand to use it as you like in the film.' Which Leighton Lucas admirably did.

ABP arranged for my father and mother to see a run-through of the movie, but when they got to the studios the sound-track had not arrived, so they saw the film silent. They were so moved by it they felt certain it would be a success, and brushed aside ABP's apologies. I think one of the things that appealed to him most about *The Dambusters* was when he was told about the first performance of the film in Paris, when a British military band played on the pavement outside the cinema, and the march brought the traffic on one side of the Avenue des Champs-Elysées to a halt.

When I was last with him, in the autumn of 1956, he complained once or twice of crystals in front of his eyes, going up and down. At the Norwich Festival of, I think, 1957, he could not see his way clearly from the artists' room to the rostrum, and they had to put him on course through the desks. Then he was all right.

His last appearance was conducting a performance of another film march, *High Flight* — not a film of much worth — at the Royal Festival Hall in November 1957. Shortly afterwards, he and my mother drove to their country home near Bognor, and in a very rare moment, he asked my mother to drive. Then, on 17th December, in the middle of the night, he cried out to my mother — 'Phyl!' (his last word). He had a massive stroke, and was paralysed. My mother managed to get a doctor at 3.30 a.m. and shortly afterwards an ambulance took him to the Royal West Sussex Hospital at Chichester. He never re-gained consciousness, though technically alive for three days. He died on 21st December 1957.

High Flight, his last work, had a very strange ending, almost premonitory, though of this he would have been quite unconscious. He played it over to me on the piano in the autumn of 1956, but only roughed out the ending. I did not hear the orchestral ending till after his death, and was then struck by those last peculiarly constricting chords, as if the heart was going to burst. Then comes the final note, which is not a chord but a staccato octave from top to bottom of the orchestra. It's so quick as to be impossible to analyse, but if you examine it on paper, you will see that only one composer in the world could have written it adjusted that way. As Stanford Robinson once said, you had only to see a chord of C major written for orchestra, and you could tell at a glance it was Eric Coates.'

Within half an hour of the event, the BBC was announcing throughout the world, and in dozens of languages, the death of 'the uncrowned king of light music', and it was said that perhaps no composer had ever provided music to suit the public taste so unerringly for such a long time. A span of fifty years lay between his first song success in Edwardian times and his last orchestral works.

One's overall impression, reading this book, is that Eric Coates was an essentially happy person, full of *joie de vivre*. Austin Coates confirmed that this was so. He told me:

'Yes, that's absolutely true, although at home we noticed how calm and extremely well-ordered he was. For instance, he couldn't settle down to write music until he was properly dressed in the morning, complete with tie and Harris Tweed coat — and, perhaps, a Turkish cigarette. He was very formal at home and incredibly tidy. If I left a book lying around anywhere, there would be quite a lot of remonstrances to follow. But he was very easy to live with.

Eric Coates had a marvellous sense of humour, as Teddy Holmes of Chappell's, was quick to point out. He told me:

'In the early days, Chappell took over the symphony concerts at the Queen's Hall to promote their ballads and orchestral and instrumental publications. They inaugurated the famous Chappell Ballad Concerts, at which many great singers and instrumentalists appeared. They also created the New Queen's Hall Light Orchestra, which was originally conducted by Henry J Wood and subsequently by Alick

Maclean, a fine but volatile conductor. Apart from providing a great contrast in programme content, one of the principal reasons for the creation of the orchestra was to perform the works of Eric Coates, Haydn Wood, Roger Quilter, Percy Fletcher, Montague F Phillips and other up-and-coming English composers.

Eric used to tell the story of Maclean stopping the orchestral rehearsal and saying, 'Tympani, I want the accent — bum-titty-bum-titty-bum.' During the replay, Maclean again stopped the orchestra, and said, 'Tympani, I want the accent — titty-bum-titty-bum', to which the tympani player responded (to the delight of the orchestra), 'Excuse me, Mr Maclean, but do you want the accent on the Titty or the Bum?'

Teddy Holmes went on to remember:

'Eric lived for many years in the Regent's Park area and it was his habit to walk down to Bond Street, and if we didn't see him in Chappell's by 11a.m. we used to wonder what had happened to him. He used to say that during those walks he had many of his musical ideas — even to the extent of scoring in his mind so that, when he returned home, he could sit down and write out a full score.

'When Eric was illustrating a new work on the piano, he had a marvellous facility of singing the various inner counter-melodies, and he could imitate a clarinet or oboe quite beautifully. He used to say that in his early days, he had to play so many dull viola parts that he made up his mind that every instrument — including the cinderella instrument of the orchestra, the viola — should have an interesting part, and that is what makes his orchestrations so colourful.'

Teddy Holmes also remembered that Eric was a fine viola player and in his early days, as a professional musician, played in the orchestra at the Savoy Theatre for the first revival season of the Gilbert and Sullivan Operas. Although a very modest man, he enjoyed telling the story about the members of the orchestra having a competition to see who would be the first player to play an entire score from memory, and how he won.

When I was preparing material for the local radio programme, I travelled to Buckinghamshire to meet Eric Coates' widow, Phyllis (shortly before she died) and his sister-in-law, Mrs Elfrida Joan Freeman. They told me that, although he and Phyllis liked to dance the night away at the London night spots, he was essentially a private person, preferring a quiet evening at home with a few good friends rather than a hectic round of parties..

They also confirmed that he enjoyed conducting his own music and had very decided views on the subject. He liked his music to be taken at brisk and lively tempi — he frowned on those conductors who made it sound slow and stodgy: there was nothing like that about him.

Eric Coates frequently conducted his own music. When I asked what he was like on the rostrum, Stanford Robinson, who must have conducted more performances and made more recordings of Eric's music than any other conductor, said, 'He was very good. He was always neat and immaculate and, of course, having been an orchestral player himself, he did not bully the orchestra; but he was always in control.'

Another conductor of Eric Coates' music, Sir Charles Groves, wrote of him: 'Eric Coates was a gentle and quietly-spoken man but his music crackled with vitality. He could write tunes and could clothe them in the most attractive instrumental colours; not for nothing had he been Henry Wood's principal viola in the Queen's Hall Orchestra.

'He did not, as far as I know, aspire to writing symphonies or oratorios like two of his famous predecessors, Arthur Sullivan and Edward German; he knew what he could do and he did it superbly well.

'Someone once said that the marches of Sousa would make a man with a wooden leg step out; a man would have to have a wooden heart not to respond to the music of Eric Coates.'

Probably one of the most graceful trubutes was when Sir Adrian Boult celebrated his 50 years of conducting at the Royal Albert Hall and, after a great ovation, he played as an encore, *The Dambusters*.

What is not quite so well known today is that Coates composed a large number of songs. Speaking of these, Mrs Stanford Robinson, who sang many of them under her professional name, Lorely Dyer, said: 'I always enjoyed singing Eric's songs. They had a lovely vocal line and gave one every chance to colour one's voice. My favourites were, *Fairy Tales of Ireland, Bird Songs at Eventide, I Heard you Singing* and, most of all, *Green Hills of Somerset.*'

In his early years he was much influenced by Edward German. During the 1920s, Eric Coates developed a distinctive style which embraced his own use of the newly-introduced American syncopated idiom. Indeed, he was the first European composer to treat this new style seriously, and successfully integrate it into symphonic writing.

When he adopted syncopation, the music critics of the heavier press ignored him, but it never seemed to concern him. 'After writing the *London Suite*,' he once said, 'I moved from the music page to the news page, and it was one of the moves I have never regretted.'

From time to time he was asked for a new march by persons or organisations he felt he couldn't refuse — for example, when Athelstan Popkiss became Chief Constable of Nottingham and asked for a march for the City of Nottingham police. Coming from an old friend and his native county, it was an inescapable request. The result was *Men of Trent*. Strangely enough, when these requests were made, within a few hours, sometimes in less than an hour, tunes would come into his head.

Inspiration sometimes came to him in the most unusual places. A certain pillar box in Harley Street, for instance, is said to have inspired one of his marches.

For over 27 years Eric Coates' march *Knightsbridge*, from his *London Suite*, introduced BBC Radio's 'In Town Tonight'. And it was not the only long-running programme that used Coates' music. His march *Calling All Workers* was the clarion call for the thousands of 'Music While You Work' programmes broadcast during the hard days of the war. *Halcyon Days (Elizabeth Tudor)*, from the *Three Elizabeths Suite*, opened and closed BBC Television's immensely popular serialisation of Galsworthy's 'The Forsyte Saga'. These were just a few of the programmes that were enhanced by Coates' music, which seemed to give them a special cachet and perhaps a touch of magic, because thay all seemed to be successful. Indeed, 'Desert Island Discs' is still with us.

There is one story, which Austin Coates told me, that will not be found in this book, and it brings this introduction full circle. It is the story of how *By the Sleepy Lagoon* came to be composed – and in a way it is a typical example of Eric Coates' rich imagination and interesting and impressive working methods.

Austin said: 'It was inspired in a very curious way and not by what you might expect. It was inspired by the view, on a warm, still summer evening looking across the "lagoon" from the east beach at Selsey towards Bognor Regis. It's a pebble beach leading steeply down, and the sea at that time is the tremendously deep blue of the Pacific. It was that impression, looking across at Bognor, which looked pink – almost like an enchanted city with the blue of the Downs behind it – that gave him the idea for the *Sleepy Lagoon*. He didn't write it there; he scribbled it down, as he used to in pencil at extreme speed, and then simply took it back with him to London, where he wrote and orchestrated it.'

But the story of Eric Coates is *Suite in Four Movements* told by the best possible author – Eric Coates himself. Perhaps it will become your Desert Island choice?

Ian Lace
Haywards Heath
January 1986

FIRST MOVEMENT

ALLEGRETTO PASTORALE

"SPEAK well back in your throat, Eric, and remember you are descended from the Welsh Kings." With these words, delivered in a deep aristocratic voice, my Aunt Eliza Anne gave me to understand that there was a danger of my acquiring a Nottinghamshire accent which she felt might be derogatory to the prestige of my mother's side of the family—evidently my father did not count.

Alas! I have never been taken for a king, though I have at one time or another been mistaken for a barrister, a doctor, a head-waiter and a bathing-attendant. I hasten to add that the head-waiter in question was undeniably good-looking, though I am not so happy about the bathing-attendant. One thing is quite clear: I have never been taken for a composer. The reason for this may be that I wear my hair short; cannot work unless properly dressed; dislike being late for an appointment; dislike even more being kept waiting for one; make a point of always being in good time for a theatre, a cinema, a train or a plane; in fact, I am what one might call orthodox.

Aunt Eliza Anne's declaration that we were descended from the Welsh Kings was greeted with derision by us children, much to the disapproval of the older members of my mother's family, who, true to their Victorian upbringing, took the whole thing very seriously. Whether there was any truth in our being of royal lineage I cannot say, for when in later years I considered taking up the matter of my ancestors on my mother's side, my brother Gwyn, although believing that there was truth in it, laughingly deterred me by saying it were better to leave well alone, and then proceeded to tell me the story of the man who, after having paid a large sum of money to investigate the history of his forebears, paid a larger sum to have the matter hushed up. So perhaps it may be wise to let my ancestors sleep on undisturbed in the shadow of the Welsh mountains, leaving me to dream my dreams of kingly descent, of Llewellyns and Glendowers and Castles in Wales, while the truth about the family who once upon a time dwelt on the Welsh border remains safely hidden in the dust of some royal tomb.

August 27th, 1886, was an important day for me, for at four-thirty in the afternoon, while the rest of the family was at tea, I descended on the Coates *ménage*.

My father was a well-loved and respected doctor in a small flourishing mining town situated on the railway which still connects Nottingham with Mansfield, in the centre of the Nottinghamshire coal-fields.

My earliest recollection of my father is of someone of whom I was greatly in awe. In later years as I grew up I came to appreciate his sterling qualities and he was to become one of my closest friends. He was an autocrat in the house, the only person ever having the temerity to stand up to him being my wife when still in her teens, and I think my father rather liked it; he had a fiery temper allied to a delightful sense of humour, the latter seeming to be a kind of apology for perhaps having said an unnecessarily sharp word under slight provocation. Dogs were his passion, and he had a remarkable knack of picking out a winner, bulldogs being his strong point. He was a keen amateur photographer, in the days when taking a photograph was a serious business; the possessor of a charming light baritone voice and no mean performer on the flute. He was always alluded to affectionately by his poorer patients as "t' little doctor" and he had the reputation of being the most upright man in Hucknall, both in his bearing and in his dealings.

My mother came from just over the Welsh border where her father reigned in supreme and unchallenged authority over his large family and still larger straggling flock, his castle being an old and draughty rectory standing back from the road, midway between Usk and Raglan. My grandfather was a man of iron will and impeccable morals—I think his creed must have been *fear* of God rather than *love*, for he certainly put the fear of God into his children, judging from the tales my mother used to tell me of her brothers being soundly thrashed every week for the sins they were sure to commit later on. His daughters he guarded in a manner which was comparable to the keepers of an Eastern harem, not even trusting them to the care of a chaperone. My mother was never allowed into Monmouth for a music lesson without her father accompanying her (even sitting in the room throughout the session), and on the occasions when she went to her dancing class it was only his personal dignity which prevented him from taking part in the routine to see for himself whether the steps she was learning were strictly within the bounds of propriety. I heard dark rumours from a roundabout source that one of my aunts (the only religiously-inclined one) once disappeared for over a week to find out for herself what the outside world was really like, forcing her sisters to depths hitherto unknown in their efforts to conceal from their father her non-appearance at meals. Can you not imagine the flutter of excitement when the truant returned, and the suppressed expressions of envy which met her account of her unmaidenly behaviour and the pronouncement that she had had a *lovely* time?

I never knew my mother's parents, but used often to stand before the portraits which adorned the walls of the dining-room, trying to imagine what they could have been like, these two figures of the past, particularly my fearsome grandfather. The only grandparent I knew was one on my father's side, and how clearly I can recall sitting on the old man's knee and playing ridiculous games with him, much to the annoyance of my father, who had misgivings as to my grandfather's playful influence undermining the parental authority. The fact that my grandfather was three times Mayor of Henley-on-Thames was a never-ending source of childish romancing to me and many were the imaginary stories I wove around this exciting figure. Once, he donned his chain of office specially for me; this was indeed a thrilling moment, for I had only seen this emblem of authority in the picture which hung over the mantelpiece, and to be able to touch this magic chain with my small podgy hands was as exciting to me as being whisked away on a magic carpet.

My mother, who had made a runaway match with my father, was everything that a mother could be and my first recollection of her is of someone to whom I could always turn for comfort in my troubles. She was dark and slim when I first remember her, with features not unlike those of my grandmother on my father's side. Kind; loving; tolerant; with a keen sense of humour, a pretty voice, an exceptional talent for the piano; and a ministering angel when I was ill. She could be strict, though I rather fancy this was not easy for her where we children were concerned, and the confidence I placed in her was such that I would readily submit to a beating from her and would turn up promptly at the appointed time for its execution, though perhaps at the back of my mind I felt confident that her smacks would not be so effective as my father's. Him, by the way, I would never allow to touch me. He and I certainly had one or two battles together, but it usually ended in my being despatched forthwith to the Official Place of Punishment, my mother's bedroom. My father was secretly thankful to be able to avoid these tussles, as it did not sit well on the autocrat of the house to be seen tearing helplessly round the garden in vain pursuit of a very agile youngster, who in those far-away days was a pastmaster in the art of eluding. I know how silly I have felt when, in later years, I tried to enforce law and order upon my own son, when very small. One has to find other means than corporal punishment for the educating of the young, and the old saying, "Spare the rod and spoil the child", does not seem to work today.

I was the youngest of a family of five. My sisters (of whom there were three) and my brother were all musical but, fortunately for my father and mother, not musicians. I think I must have been what they call in the Midlands an 'odd' little boy. I am sure I must have been an aggravating little boy on occasions, and can well believe the stories which my sisters tell about my youthful outspoken opinions and my sometimes all-too-pointed allusions to the shortcomings of my elders. I remember, at the age of six, being in the drawing-room when a lady guest was asked to sing. Having my own views as to the quality of the lady's voice, I crossed over to my mother and said in a determined way: "You know, my dear, we can't stand this. . . ." I was hurried from the room.

* * * * *

It was the advent of Pen Peyton that started the trouble. The Peytons were old friends of my mother's side of the family, Sir Richard Peyton being at that time lucratively employed making beds in Birmingham, by which I mean all the etceteras that go to the inducing of a good night's rest. I believe the spring mattress was one of his inventions. Now in those far-away days nobody in 'trade' was received in the best circles, and as I had repeatedly heard members of my mother's side of the family speak with deprecation of anyone who was not in the Royal Navy, or the Army, or the Church, it was a never-ending source of wonderment to me as to how Aunt Eliza Anne (of the deep aristocratic voice) was able to reconcile herself to numbering among her friends a tradesman, and a bedmaker at that—but no matter. My first impression of Pen Peyton was of a man with a gargantuan appetite for Pontefract cakes and cigarettes, for he ate these horrible little liquorice medallions by the dozen and smoked cigarettes by the hundred. His having come from London led me to suppose that perhaps all people from this remote region ate and smoked in this astonishing manner, for at that early age London, to me, was a very far-away place indeed where, I was told by my nurse, "things happened". What she meant by this dark pronouncement I was never quite sure, unless it had something to do with liquorice and cigarettes. Nottingham was about as far as I could possibly conceive making a journey to—in those days the fourteen miles there and back was something to think about and was only undertaken under pressure of extreme necessity. The idea of London conjured up in my mind spending days and nights, or even weeks, sitting bolt-upright in one of those uncomfortable, badly-sprung, third-class carriages which made up the rolling-stock of the Midland Railway—even the first-class was nothing to boast about. I often wondered why this antiquated railway did not call in the services of Sir Richard Peyton to do for these bumpy carriages what he had done so admirably for beds. However, I was soon to discover that the rapid consumption of Pontefract cakes and the never-ending inhaling of cigarettes were an advantage, for the many journeys which, in consequence, my small legs made to the local sweet-shop in Watnall Road were the means of my being able to spend the welcome penny tip on one of Mr. Burrow's marvellous ice-creams. And what wonderful value they were, though perhaps I was specially favoured by being "t' little doctor's" youngest.

The trouble before-mentioned was a queer-looking black box which was included in Pen Peyton's, to me, luxurious luggage. This box fascinated me from the start by being so uncomfortably like a small coffin, and I was certain there was something sinister in it and even went so far as to imagine that it might contain the remains of someone who had eaten too many Pontefract cakes and smoked too many cigarettes. To my credit, I must say that I kept my suspicions to myself and awaited my opportunity. This came sooner than I expected, and in a manner which took the wind out of my sails—not that I wished to incriminate my friend in any way, but you must admit it *would* have been exciting to have been the means of producing a corpse at one of the parties which took place in the drawing-room on Sunday evenings after Evensong. We had finished supper—I say we, because I had been allowed to sit up specially to hear the principals of our local church choir, of which my father was the choir-master, perform some glees in our drawing-room after the Service. To my astonishment, Pen Peyton was taking part in the proceedings, in what capacity I could not imagine, and when the significant-looking black box was produced, my excitement knew no bounds. Nevertheless, from that moment my hopes about the corpse were dashed, for surely Pen's manner was far too calm and casual, pending such a *dénouement* as that? No, I felt I must have been wrong about the corpse—the box probably had something to do with some form of magic—yes, that was it, a conjuring outfit. Pen had by now placed the black box on the piano and was fingering the lock—how I wished he would hurry up and open the thing, coloured handkerchiefs, rabbits and all—my heart was beating strangely fast, even though I was certain there was no corpse. Pen had opened the lid of the box now and was taking something out with his left hand—'Hurry up', I was thinking, as my heart pounded more than ever—and there in his hand was a small shining, wooden thing—a violin! I must say that at first I was a little disappointed —somehow or other I simply could not associate Pontefract cakes and cigarettes with the violin—but my chagrin was forgotten when, for the first time, I heard the silvery notes of the instrument. From that moment I had no peace and I fear my father and mother had no peace either, for I worried and worried until out of sheer self-defence my father procured a tiny little fiddle from out of the window of the music and cycle shop in High Street, owned by John Munks.

How well I recollect my first violin—it was very, very small, not much more than a toy (I could not have been much more than six years old at the time) and of a bright red and yellow colour. To me it was the most beautiful thing I had ever seen. Another visit to Mr. Munks in High Street brought forth a violin tutor, by one Henry Farmer of the Music Emporium of the same name in Nottingham, a local composer of some renown, whose *magnum opus* was a cantata entitled 'Christ and His Soldiers'. (I was to come face to face with this effort later on. It was an awful work.) With the aid of this praiseworthy book I soon began to find my way about my beloved violin and in a very short time I was treating my admiring family to simple tunes, even some of my own making. Then came the 'Lady of the Violin'—for the moment I cannot remember her name—a local violiniste and teacher who took upon her shoulders the responsibility of giving me my first lessons. Months of practising followed, interspersed with lessons, jumbled up with my first attempts at the piano under the tuition of my mother. Those were exciting and eventful days and were only spoilt by the arrival of Miss Hobbs, who was called in to see that we children did not grow up altogether ignorant, that is of reading, writing and arithmetic. I could not bear the new governess, she was so cheerful and, among other things, would use old English words to bring home a point, some of which shocked us inexpressibly. 'Stench' for instance, probably an excellent word in its day was, I thought, hardly a nice word for a lady to use, but it appeared that she was equally shocked at our alluding to Judy, the bulldog, as a well-bred 'bitch'. But how could she have expected us, the children of a dog-fancier, to lower ourselves by talking about a 'lady-dog'? The idea was ridiculous. Another aspect which irritated us even more was the way in which my father's various dogs were always spoken to as a 'nice girl' or a 'nice boy'. "And does the little girl want to go for a lovely walk?" would rouse us to white-hot fury. I am afraid we must have been a dreadful handful and I wonder that Miss Hobbs did not give notice after the first term. I believe she was an excellent governess, and when I met her again in my late teens I realised what a charming and clever woman she was and did my best to make up for my behaviour when she first came to Tenter Hill.

Life at Tenter Hill was a busy affair from then onwards. Daily lessons with Miss Hobbs; practising the violin and the piano in my spare time; walking in the fields with the bulldogs; taking little presents of tobacco to the gypsies who camped near the old well; playing games by the brook where the kingfisher lived; fishing for tadpoles; scrambling down the quarry on the Annesley Road; hunting for lizards in Sandy Lane; watching the men at work constructing the new railway which was to run from London to Manchester and riding in the cab of the fussy little tank-engine which took the coal from the pit-mouth to the Midland Railway junction between Hucknall and Nottingham.

Then there was the occasion when I was held by my brother over the side of the great pit-shaft which went down four hundred and fifty yards into the bowels of the earth. I remember his strong hands lifting me up over the wall which surrounded this bottomless-looking pit and his telling me not to be afraid and not to mind looking down. Needless to say I did look down, but I was frightened.

Sometimes my brother and I would go late at night into the hot engine-house when the engines were silent, to hear the music made by the thousands of crickets which made their home there. You had to go at night, for the roar made by the machinery in the daytime was too much for them, and you had to tread very quietly so as not to frighten them. I can still see the engine-house with the shadows of the winding-drum thrown by our oil-lamps on the hot damp walls, and my brother and myself peering about in the dark corners to see if we could catch one of these queer little creatures. Although you could hear them in their thousands, you could never see one, let alone capture one. Then there was rat-hunting with the dogs and I can vouch for it that a pit-bank is an ideal place for this kind of sport.

Then came the installing of our first telephone, and I remember what an impression this miraculous aid to communication made upon me. It was one of those awkward instruments cast in one piece, ear-phone at one end and mouth-piece at the other, with a spring in the centre which had to be depressed before you could make yourself heard. And if your ear happened to be near your mouth, as mine was at that early age, and your fingers were not a match for the spring, then any conversation was only undertaken with extreme difficulty. This one-piece spring-actuated telephone receiver started a vogue in home-made telephones among the younger members of the Coates family, beginning with a couple of pill-boxes and a long piece of string, the former pilfered from my father's surgery. This gave way to the more modern and long-distance carrying-power of the common garden hose, my father having pointed out to us that the string-and-pill-box method was more than useless as a means of communication and that we could hear one another better by talking normally. The hose-pipe was excellent because with this you could carry on a conversation with an unseen friend round the corner, which impressed me greatly until one day my brother Gwyn, conveniently out of sight, connected his end of the hose to the garden tap and turned the latter full on. This somewhat put the damper on amateur telephony, as far as I was concerned, until I discovered, quite by accident, that you could talk down the hand-basin upstairs in the bathroom to anyone who did not object to going down on his hands and knees in the garden below and pushing his head between the spout and the drain to listen. I usually managed to take up my position overhead, for the simple reason that I could thus satisfy my innate desire for comfort by taking a chair and carrying on a conversation in comparative ease with the huddled-up figure of my companion below, oblivious of the fact that drains were connected with an unpleasant complaint called diptheria. The day my father came along and caught us, and the painful things which followed, made me resolve to confine my telephonic attentions to the real thing, ear-phone, mouth-piece, spring and all.

Then there were the occasions, the very rare occasions, when my father took me out in the trap visiting his patients. I did not enjoy these outings, as I was always nervous when my father, going into some house or other, left me alone with the pony. I could *not* learn to manage the little thing and was terrified lest it would run away with me. I dared not tell my father I was frightened for I knew he would laugh at me, notwithstanding the fact that it had already taken the bit between its teeth on more than one occasion. So I had to sit and wait nervously, holding tightly to the reins and praying for the moment when my father would reappear, hoping all the time that I should be returned to my home intact. One day, however, one of these outings was the means of a very unusual and novel experience. It was a lovely Sunday morning in the middle of the summer, a soft breeze was blowing and we were driving back from seeing one of the staff at Newstead Abbey. As we came up a small rise towards a railway bridge on the outskirts of Hucknall we heard a voice calling out anxiously: "Are we going right for Mansfield?" My father pulled up and we looked about for the speaker, but could see no one. Once again, from a slightly different point, the voice, this time more anxiously: "Are we going right for Mansfield, *please?*" And there it was, a balloon, drifting just over our heads, with two men leaning out of the basket, shouting and waving frantically to attract our attention. My father, quickly taking in the situation and noting the course the balloon was taking, shouted up: "Yes, straight on," just as if it were an everyday occurrence to give navigational directions to balloonists. With a wave and a "Thank you" the two men threw out some ballast, at which the balloon narrowly escaped catching-up the pony with some rope-ends, rose rapidly and was soon caught in a stiff breeze which carried it north-west away over the sunlit fields. During luncheon, on our return, my mother asked my father if there were any news of interest and he replied: "Nothing much, except that we put a couple of aeronauts on the right road to Mansfield." I looked open-mouthed at my father. How *could* he dispose of such a breath-taking adventure in such a matter-of-fact way?

Sometimes when my father was in one of his best story-telling moods, when he was not over-tired from nocturnal visits with his pony and trap to some out-lying hamlet to deliver some woman of her 'first' (and his sleepless nights on this account were frequent), I would get him settled comfortably in his old rocking-chair in the room where he kept his files, fill up his pipe from the stone tobacco-jar from which my sisters supplied the gypsies, get out the whisky and soda, and wait for results, which were always forthcoming and never disappointing. Perhaps he might begin by talking about photography, and he would show me the wonderful photos he had obtained of the colliers actually working underground. He had to get special permission from the owners of the mine to take these photographs, and many were the precautions necessary to ensure that the workings were free from gas, so that my father could use flashlight powders to obtain a well-exposed negative. You must remember that this was before the days when the electric Sasha flash-bulbs were thought of. What was so wonderful to me was that these pictures, taken with a stereoscopic camera, stood out in perfect relief when seen through the 'viewer'. I very much doubt if any photographer to-day could have improved on my father's work, notwithstanding the tremendous advance made in this branch of art with the innovation of the large-aperture wide-angle lens, the focal plane-shutter and the ultra-rapid film and plate. After I thought I had dwelt long enough over these fascinating underground pictures, I said politely: "Please tell me about when you were a young man." And well-plied with tobacco and whisky, and with a cushion under his head, my father began to talk about the Hucknall he knew when he first set up house with my mother in Watnall Road. Those must have been days to remember, and none too pleasant to have lived in, I should think. Terrible and bloody fights with bare fists up at the boxing booth on the common, sometimes fights to the finish, unless the police got wind of the affair and arrested the pugilists (not a pleasant job to take two muscular giants into custody under the nose of a hostile crowd); cock-fighting in the depths of some unholy cellar where you could only gain admission by being 'in the know'; plying fowls with neat brandy and making bets on the course the inebriated creatures would take; fearful scenes at the local public-house at closing time on Saturday nights, when the carousers objected to being turned out before they had got through the week's earnings and the 'chucker-out' had to show what stuff he was made of, which usually resulted in horrifying consequences to the 'chucked'; hair-raising stories of strikes at the local collieries; the occasion when the manager was attacked by a mob of infuriated workers and the windows at his house smashed to pieces with sticks and brickbats; stories of special police being drafted in from Nottingham to quell the rioters. Even I can remember seeing some 'blacklegs' being taken round Hucknall on a dray drawn by strikers. It was not a pretty sight to see these men trying to shield their faces from the stones, potatoes and eggs, which came at them from every direction. This particular strike became so violent that the police had to call on the Sherwood Foresters to stand by as a precaution.

When I come to think of it, we were never afraid of these men when the spirit to disrupt law and order took them, for, being children of the doctor, and "t' little doctor" at that, we were always treated with affection. I have even known us bustled out of the way by the strikers themselves, when they thought we were too near the danger-zone. I always had, and still have, a weak spot for these underground workers—they are a fine body of men, kind-hearted and, tackled in the right way, usually open to reason. Of course, there are many hotheads among them, but these are usually youngsters with an eye to the main chance and with nothing to lose through organising a rough-and-tumble. The older men, those with domestic responsibilities, are a decent, hard-working, saving and studious lot. I have spent many happy hours with them in their homes and have always found them, besides being courteous, excellent company and able to talk on a diversity of subjects with surprising authority. Music seemed to come naturally to them—in my own town, for instance, we boasted in later years an excellent choir, an orchestra, a male quartet which made quite a name for itself in the Midlands and a first-class brass band which brought home many a coveted prize from competitions about the country. The story goes that after carrying off a first prize at Leicester, the band returned home with a silver cup, but without the soprano cornet. They were in a fix, as they had another important date to fulfil a couple of days later and without this necessary solo instrument they were stuck. Urgent telegrams were despatched, trains were searched, waiting-rooms and cloak-rooms scoured, but no soprano cornet. Things looked bad. There was nothing to be done but call a special rehearsal and see if a little 'writing-in' into some other instrumental part would overcome the difficulty. Sharp at ten o'clock on the next morning, the band assembled in the yard at the back of the public-house next door to the police station, at the bottom of the hill leading down from our house, and the rehearsal started, and so did the trouble. Could the bass-tuba play his opening solo? The bandsmen were horrified at his fruitless efforts to get that bottom note and saw their glory of yesterday being turned into mockery to-morrow. The bass-tuba unable to play, and the pride of the band, the soprano-cornet soloist, without an instrument.

Things certainly looked black, and the things the men said were even blacker and quite unprintable. Another and a more determined 'go' at that bottom note resulted in a sound something between a groan and a hiccup. At last, the embarrassed virtuoso, filled with wrath at his inability to produce a musical sound, turned the instrument upside down and shook it with all his might. To the astonishment of the gaping crowd of bandsmen, *out fell the little soprano cornet.*

However, the most extraordinary tale of all, which my father vouched for as being absolutely genuine, was the one of the man who became tired of his wife and put her up for auction in the Hucknall Market Place. Evidently the bidding did not become lively, for she was knocked down for the sum of five shillings. Who knows, perhaps she was expensive at that! So Hugh Walpole's dramatic story of the human sale in his fascinating *Rogue Herries* is not so far-fetched after all.

How clearly I can see my father puffing away at his pipe (such deliciously sweet-smelling tobacco) and sipping his whisky and soda and trying to make up his mind whether he would indulge in another story; leaning back in his old rocking-chair with his feet propped up on a conveniently placed foot-stool; sometimes imagining he heard the surgery bell and interrupting his story to listen for a brief moment. And then my mother's voice from somewhere far away upstairs: "Harrison! do you know it is nearly ten o'clock and that child ought to have been in bed hours ago?" And so to bed and to dream of prize-fighters, illicit auctions, strikes, insurrections, gaming, and extraordinary operating-theatre tragedies. And how hard my father worked!—holidays were practically out of the question during his early days in Hucknall, for building up a practice was an all-time job, and there were five of us to provide for. A day off now and again, however, was managed, provided great secrecy was observed. A careful look through his visiting-list first of all, and then a hurried calculation as to whether we could catch the ten o'clock train to Nottingham. Just ten minutes to go, and so, laden with camera, slides, plates and tripod, my father and I were hurrying down the hill to the Midland Railway Station, like two naughty boys playing truant from school. The journey to the station being safely negotiated without any untoward incident, we were soon in our seats in an empty carriage, full of apprehension lest my father should be called out of the train at the last moment to attend some case or other at one of the collieries. On one occasion our outing was interrupted by the station-master at the next station down the line calling: "Is Doctor Coates on the train? There's been an accident at No. 1 Pit!"—and back we had to go. But this time we were taking no chances and had made sure of a fast train to Nottingham. We waited impatiently—two minutes passed: the train was before time. Would we never start? At last a great banging of doors, the guard waved his flag, a whistle from the engine and— we were off! Ten minutes to wait on Nottingham Station, and then off again on the single-track to Southwell.

Southwell—what a delightful old-world place, completely unspoiled, and a paradise for the photographer with an eye for an unusual picture. A lovely Cathedral—small perhaps, but what it loses in quantity it makes up for in quality. As he looks through the grating of the gate which leads down to the old paved path, the West Door with the twin towers above is the first thing which strikes the visitor. Whenever I go up to my native Nottinghamshire to-day, I always make a point of motoring over to this old Cathedral town to look through the iron grating to see if my first impression still remains—and it always does. And so we arrived at the Minster, my father and I, handed over the permit to the verger, and the whole of the lovely interior was ours to do with as we would—photographically speaking, of course. The view-point chosen, the camera set in position, the sheath drawn from the slide and the shutter opened, we then repaired to the Saracen's Head to have lunch while the picture was registering itself through the tiny lens on to the specially slow plate at the back of the camera. The local chemist advised about an hour to obtain a correct exposure at such-and-such a lens aperture, and so we were able to eat the admirable meal set before us without haste and to enjoy it to the full.

The Saracen's Head always interested me on account of its associations with Charles I—I believe he stayed the night there prior to riding out to Newark and being taken prisoner. The proprietor, as a gesture to old customers like my father and myself, showed us with pride the fine four-poster which stood in the low-ceilinged bedroom over the dining-room, where the ill-fated monarch spent the last night of his freedom. On this particular day Southwell was thronged with visitors—it was market day. All sorts were there: farmers with their dogs; villagers from outlying hamlets; clergymen with their wives; old women with large baskets; young women with small baskets; little children clamouring at their mothers' skirts; and the local policeman very much in evidence, regulating the slow-moving traffic, which included all kinds of transport, from wheel-barrows to smart little dog-carts. What a crowd and what a din!

The lunch, which we ate in company with the more affluent of the locals, was over. A last drink of that delicious sparkling cider (I could not waste *that!*), and my father and I pushed our way out of the crowd, on to the hotel steps, crossed the road, and were soon wending our way down the well-worn flagstones of the path which led from the old iron gateway to the West Door of the Minster. The West Door—a perfect example of Norman art and a delight to look at; I do not believe there is a finer specimen to be found anywhere. As a matter of fact, this old Cathedral is full of lovely Early English and Norman carving, some most unusual, such as the cluster of stone leaves which, if you examine them carefully, will be found to contain on the underside of the leaves tiny stone pigs. There is also a very fine lectern fashioned out of an eagle of pure gold, which golden bird was salvaged from the bottom of the lake in the grounds of Newstead Abbey during dragging operations, where it had been thrown by the monks of Newstead to prevent its falling into Cromwell's hands. I remember how disgusted the verger was on the occasion of his showing a party from Hucknall over the Cathedral. He was about to eulogise over the beauties of the golden eagle lectern when a plaintive and extremely unpleasant female voice called out from the rear of the party: "I don't want to see no blooming *duck*, I want my *tea!*"

Once again the camera was set up for another shot, this time the view of that portion of the Cathedral containing the famous lectern. This was my opportunity to explore on my own, while my father sat on one of the stone seats in the grounds near the ruins of the Archbishop's Palace, adjusted his monocle, smoked a cigar and made elaborate calculations in his notebook on exposures and so forth. The old pulpit with the golden reading-desk always interested me, on account of the latter having come from the romantic home where Byron wrote so many of his poems. This was my first port of call and, climbing up the circular steps and making myself comfortable on a large foot-stool, taking care at the same time not to get into the field of the camera, I settled down for a nice long think about my hero. . . .

'So we'll go no more a'roving
So late into the night,
Though the heart be still as loving
And the moon be still as bright.'

What kind of a man could he have been to have written anything so lovely?

I must have sat for quite a long time on my foot-stool, much longer than I knew, for my day-dreams were interrupted by my father's voice enquiring of the verger if he had seen a small boy wandering about the building. This was my cue to reveal myself, and also time to pack up the camera and the accompanying paraphernalia and repair once again to the Saracen's Head for a tea consisting of bread and butter (masses of it), freshly boiled eggs, lettuces, radishes, an assortment of jams, cakes (masses of these, too), and a large plate of strawberries with an even larger jug of cream. When I think on these things to-day I wonder whether I must have been dreaming; but it was no dream—and did I enjoy myself! Even my father forgot his slightly enlarging figure and gave himself up to the delights of the moment. And then the journey home through the cool of the evening—two very happy people, having spent a wonderful day together doing nothing that mattered (always the best kind of day to look back upon). I do not know how it happened, but I always seemed to be my father's companion whenever he managed to steal an hour or so from his consulting-room. Perhaps it was because I did not mind helping him with his camera, which, as I have already said, was a very bulky affair; or perhaps it was because I was so thrilled at being taken about by anyone so important as my father that I never minded where we went, what we did, how long we took to get where we did or how long we took to do what we did when we got where we were.

Football matches never interested me and never will, but it was well worth while going to one with my father to see him called out by the referee to attend a casualty on the field. How proud I was to watch that small upright figure hurrying across the ground to the little knot of men bending over a prostrate player on the grass, who, on seeing my father, quickly made way for him to attend to the injured footballer; and when a voice from the crowd called out: "It's t' little doctor! We shall soon have our Fred on his feet again," 1 nearly burst with pride. Then it might be Southwell again, to have another shot at a picture which had not been very successful —one photograph was spoilt by an old lady who sat for half an hour making her devotions right in the line of the camera-lens, with the result that she registered herself on the plate *nearly*: by *nearly* I mean, you could see *through* her. If she had sat another half-hour all would have been well and she would have made a perfect still-life subject. However, the old lady had her uses, for besides making a good excuse for another outing to Southwell, she went down to posterity as 'the ghost in the Minster'. Then there were visits to local dog-shows, my father acting sometimes in the capacity of judge and sometimes as competitor.

A dog-show in those far-away days was a thing to be seen to be believed. Arguments in the ring, quarrels amongst the competitors, faking of points and even attempted bribery of the judges, to say nothing of bitter fights among the exhibits themselves. It was quite an education to watch the competitors, especially the women, 'arranging' their precious charges in the ring in order to show them off at their best before the judge. A favourite dodge was to place the dog carefully on the ground, particularly in the case of a bull-dog, and 'arrange' the animal's front legs wide apart, so as to give the effect of broad shoulders (an important point in the correct make-up of this breed, and one of the signs of a thoroughbred), and then to see the expression on these ladies' faces as the judge carelessly picked up the hopefuls by the scruff of the neck and dropped them to the ground again to see what the dogs' natural position really was. The results were often disconcerting. Some of the things which happened at these shows about the countryside were often unexpected, and perhaps one amusing episode which might have had disastrous consequences is worth the telling. It was during the evening, when the dogs were safely back in their private boxes in the tent at the back of the judging ring. They were left here on show for an hour or so, in order to give visitors an opportunity of having a look at the winners close up, and also for the owners to be able to discuss the various points of their respective animals and to criticise the findings of the judge when they felt they had not been fairly treated. I remember how delighted I was to see our own little Hucknall Prince sitting in his stall, laughing all over his great, broad face with the slobber pouring out of the folds of his chops. He certainly had something to laugh about, for over the barred door it said: 'Hucknall Prince, 1st prize and Special. Owner, Dr. W. Harrison Coates, Hucknall Torkard'. My father and I were wandering round the tent for a few minutes, before starting for home, when suddenly there arose an uproar from the direction of Prince's box. Furious barkings, then the screams of an animal in pain, followed by shouts of: "Get him off," "Hit him on the head," "Bash the door in," "Where's Doctor Coates?" "Fetch the doctor" —everybody shouting at the same time and all the dogs in the place raising their voices to add to the general uproar. Hurriedly making his way to the scene, my father was confronted by a furious little man who turned out to be the owner of the dog in the next box to Prince. "Your dog has attacked mine and made a nice mess of him." The man was so excited that it was quite a minute or so before my father could get any sense out of him. He gathered at last that the dog, which happened to be another bulldog, but by no means a thoroughbred, had pushed its tail (the length of which, my father had discovered from the judge, had been the cause of his not having won any honours in the ring) through the bars of the grating separating the two dogs. Now Prince objected to dogs, especially those without pedigree, poking parts of their anatomy into his private apartment and, taking the law into his own hands, had bitten off the offending end. The unfortunate affair was so ludicrous, apart from its element of tragedy, that my father and the crowd which had gathered round the two exhibitors could scarcely control their laughter. The owner expostulating, my father trying to soothe the man, only made matters worse. At last my father lost his patience, and after making it quite clear that the animal had no right whatsoever to push its tail through the bars and had only got what it deserved, he finished up by saying: "And confound it, man, your wretched dog is now in a *class!*" which it was. As any dog-fancier knows, a long tail in a bulldog is nothing more nor less than a crime, and no owner should exhibit a dog with such a fault. Now, my father had started a vogue in bulldogs in Hucknall, but the trouble was, they *would* have long tails. Could they get a pup like my father's famous Prince? No! And so the local barber, Mr. Oakden, divided his time, very profitably, between cutting hair and cutting off bull-pups' tails, and (I shudder to state) not with his scissors, but with his teeth!

After the passing of dear old Prince, my father seemed to lose interest for a time in bulldogs, until one day he saw the advertisement of an auction of a house and effects in Doncaster, among the sundries being 'one bulldog'. So on the morning of the sale my father stole a day off from his practice and took the first train to the town of the church with the leaning spire, and there among the household effects, furniture, piano, pictures, etc., was a dejected-looking little bulldog, tied up to a mangle, moping for his late master and wondering what all the racket could be about and wishing the whole wretched affair would come to an end so that he could return once more to that comfortable kennel outside the kitchen door. Poor chap, he little knew his home had already been broken up for firewood. My father's heart went out to the neglected fellow and, quickly wending his way through the throng which crowded the room, he spoke a few kindly words to him. The dog's dull eyes lighted up immediately and he pushed his wet nose into my father's hands with a sigh of relief. From that moment he knew he had found a friend. The journey home in the train was eventful. In those days no animals were permitted in the compartments and all dogs had to be placed in the care of the guard. As soon as my father approached the rear of the train in search of this worthy, the dog, sensing what was to come, became awkward, and refused to budge. My father persuaded, cajoled, entreated, but to no effect. The arrival of the guard on the scene only made matters worse— the dog became nasty and showed fight—and then the trouble began. By this time my father and the guard were joined by the station-master—more cajoling, persuading and finally threatening. This was the last straw! The little dog went 'berserk', flew at the guard, who retired hurriedly into the van, then he turned on the station-master, who, forgetting the dignity of his profession, managed to dodge behind a luggage trolley. Finally he stood in front of my father in a protective position, glaring dangerously at the crowd of porters and passengers who had collected. Through all this manœuvring my father had managed to keep his hold on the lead, but I think he must have paid a heavy price for his determination, if the tale he told us of his pirouettes and final collapse on the platform was true. By this time the train was long overdue to start and the situation was, to say the least of it, embarrassing. A hasty consultation among the station staff, the guard and the engine-driver, resulted in my father being placed in an empty first-class carriage, complete with dog, who, the instant he knew the guard's van was out of the question and that he was to be allowed to remain with his newly-found friend, became perfectly docile. The dog's passion for my father grew as the days passed and he followed his master on all the occasions when his visits were made on foot, sometimes even attempting to run after the trap until he became 'winded' and realised that long trots along country lanes were not in keeping with a bulldog's build—then he would sit on the steps outside the surgery door and wait patiently for his master's return.

I can remember at one time not being allowed out at night without my brother, and in any case we were always accompanied by one or two of the bulldogs as escort. Tramps and footpads abounded everywhere. One particular spot I often used to visit when I grew older and was the proud possessor of my first bicycle, was on the old turnpike road which wound from Nottingham to Mansfield, the road which was known by the country folk as the 'ramper'. At the bottom of the hill beyond the turning on the left for Kirkby-in-Ashfield, on the right of the road near a wood, half concealed by long grass and weeds was a lonely spot where, if you sat very still, the rabbits would come out of their holes in the sandy bank and sit around and about or play their games in the sun. Here was a little crooked stone with the name 'Beth Shepperd' roughly engraved upon it. There was no date; probably the unkind elements had washed this away many years before. It was a pathetic monument to the little girl who had been set upon and murdered by highwaymen on her way back from market, after having sold her simple wares. Poor Beth Shepperd—and all for a few paltry shillings. In the towns it was just the same. Nottingham, for instance, was no place at night for nervous pedestrians and even in the daytime certain quarters were better avoided if you wanted to remain in possession of your money. In Narrow Marsh and Broad Marsh, down by the canal, the police patrolled in twos and threes. Often, while taking a short cut through this forbidding district when time was short for the last train to Hucknall, I have seen battles between the police and the gangs which frequented the dark alleyways which ran crisscross about this unsavoury place. The police were mostly picked men, none under six foot, numbering amongst them many amateur heavy-weights, and I can assure you they were needed. Saturday night just after closing time was the hour to go down into Narrow Marsh if you wanted to see life in the raw and were not afraid of being mixed up in some terrific brawl. I confess I normally kept to the main thoroughfares, giving the excuse to my brother, when he twitted me over taking such care of myself, that it was only my violin I was thinking about. Election times, of course, were a good excuse for all kinds of lawlessness, and the extremes to which some of the rowdies went were unbelievable. Nottinghamshire, at that time, was Liberally minded, and any Conservative candidate who had the temerity to challenge the local Divisions was manhandled in the most savage manner. One candidate, driving out to Hucknall from Nottingham, was stopped on the road by a mob of unruly colliers, dragged out of his carriage and kicked, the horse unharnessed and allowed to run wild and the carriage smashed to pieces. Notwithstanding my father's own political views (he was a staunch Conservative), we all of us liked the M.P. for our Division, John Edward Ellis, owner of some of the collieries in the district. He was a fine-looking old man with an aristocratic head and bearing, and many times he passed the time of day with the little boy in the train on his way into Nottingham for his violin lessons.

My father's illness came as a shock to us all, for up to that time we had never known him have a day in bed. Driving out in all weathers, rain, snow and fog, did not seem to affect him in the least; he refused to use a closed carriage of any kind and when the motor-car made its appearance on the roads he said he preferred to have a conveyance which got him to his destination on time. The first motor-car was certainly not the most reliable of machines, so I think there was some sense in that. Over and over again my mother did her utmost to persuade him to invest in a more weatherproof kind of vehicle, but her words were of no avail and he persisted in driving out uncovered, no matter what the weather, and I can vouch for it that driving along the top of the Annesley Hills in winter is no joke—six hundred feet up in a north-easterly gale in these parts is something to talk about—but my father did it once too often and for the first month or so things looked serious. A 'locum' was engaged to take over the practice and, fortunately, besides being an excellent doctor, he turned out to be a very nice fellow. Coming from St. Thomas's Hospital, London, meant that he had a good deal in common with my father, who always looked back upon his own days there with affection.

The weeks which followed were anxious ones indeed, and the house had to be kept very quiet—such a change after the busy routine which had existed for so long. No more outings to football matches; no more dog-shows and no more expeditions to Southwell; uncomfortable days and worrying; never again must my father go without a holiday—he had learnt his lesson. We children, of course, always spent a month at the sea every year; sometimes it was

Skegness on the Lincolnshire coast near-by, and sometimes it was to stay with Aunt Eliza Anne of the deep aristocratic voice, who lived in a pleasant house among the pinewoods at Southbourne near Bournemouth, surrounded by retired Admirals and Indian Army Colonels, a sprinkling of Baronets and several Honourables. Aunt Eliza Anne, on our rare visits to her, although never completely forgetting our royal heritage from the Welsh Kings, would become almost normal. She and I, I soon found out, had similar tastes, for during our first holidays with her I discovered that she was an excellent pianiste, besides playing the 'cello in an amateurish way. Many were the pleasant hours I spent with her in her old-fashioned Victorian drawing-room, listening to her renderings of my favourite intermezzi and valses by Brahms and Chopin, interspersed with some Grieg or some Chaminade, both of these latter composers being very much to the fore at that time. Then there were visits in the evenings to the Winter Gardens to hear Dan Godfrey and the Municipal Orchestra, followed by bathes in the moonlight after the couple of hours spent in the stuffy concert-room. Hot days on the beach; lunch on the pier; trips to Swanage and round the Isle of Wight on the paddle-steamers from Bournemouth, and on one very special occasion to see the Grand Fleet off Weymouth.

And all this time my father had been scanning his visiting-list, attending to accidents at the collieries, going to bed wondering whether the night-bell would disturb his slumbers at some unearthly hour, and knowing, at the back of his mind, that he ought to have a holiday, practice or no practice.

Nine months in bed is a long time, and to an active man like my father it must have seemed like nine years. The danger was past, and now it was just a matter of convalescing for a month before going to North Wales for a long-needed change of air. The 'locum' had been a great success, both with my father's patients and with the family at Tenter Hill—yes, it was quite in order for him to stay on another six weeks while the much-looked-forward-to holiday was in progress. And so, early on a sunny July morning, my father and mother and I were standing on the Midland Railway Station waiting for the train to take us to that lovely Welsh watering-place, Barmouth, and, who knows, perhaps to find some of my royal Welsh ancestors. This was the beginning of many holidays for me with my parents, for when in later years I left Hucknall my father always arranged for his vacations to coincide with mine.

We stayed in a little house in the High Street looking out to the Mawddach Estuary on one side and to the sea on the other (I was to stay in this same house many years later under very different conditions). After having settled ourselves in, the first thing to be done was to see about hiring a pony and carriage to take my father out each day, so Mr. Hughes was engaged to come daily from ten in the morning till one, and on special occasions for longer. My father was in his element—photographs were taken by the dozen and developed by the local chemist, in strict contradiction to my father's usual practice, for at home he always saw the plate through from start to finish. Old Hughes, our constant companion on these delightful excursions, was very interested in my father's camera, and it was amusing to hear him hold forth, in his lilting Welsh accent, on his ideas of art. After all, he had cause to consider himself an authority on the subject, for had not a Mr. Landseer stayed in the little cottage which he and his wife shared on the Harlech road, in order to sketch the famous Welsh cattle? To our horror, he told us that this Mr. Landseer, when he left, presented him with a number of unfinished pencil sketches which he eventually sold to an American lodger (who evidently knew what he was buying) for a few shillings. "After all," he said, "they were of no value, whatever, and look you, indeed, who wants to sketch cows?"

And so the lovely holiday drew to a close. One more walk on the sandy beach to have a final sniff of the sea, and then to go round the town saying good-bye to my newly-made friends. There was the girl at the stationer's who had tried so hard to teach me to speak Welsh; and old Captain Griffiths who piloted the little steamer each day through the rapids under the bridge which spanned the Mawddach, up to Dolgelley and back, and who presented me with a model of a sailing-ship which he had made out of sea-shells and which remained for many years my most treasured memory of the first holiday with my father and mother; there was the old boatman who used to bring us freshly-caught turbot for our tea; there were Griffiths, Williamses, Hugheses, Morgans, Evanses, Pryces, Joneses in plenty, but I regret to say, not a trace of my forebears the Llewellyns and Glendowers.

As a parting treat, my father had arranged for a landau to come for us the day before we were due to leave for home, to take us over to Harlech for the last time. It had rained during the night and the morning came up hot and misty with the promise of one of those perfect days which you associate with early September. An early breakfast was followed by much activity on the part of my father, loading up slides in his changing-bag, testing the shutter of the camera to see if it were functioning properly and attending to all the hundred-and-one details which are so important for obtaining a good picture. Meanwhile, my mother and Mrs. Jones were discussing the all-engrossing problem of that evening's supper. No sandwiches or ginger-beer bottles were needed this time, for we were making the Castle Hotel at Harlech our temporary headquarters for the day and intended to have both luncheon and tea in that excellent establishment. The landau arrived early and about ten o'clock we were trotting leisurely down the High Street past the Cors-y-gedol Hotel towards the Harlech road. The mist had cleared by this time, and as we ambled along the road which winds its way along the mountain-side above the sea, distant hills came into sight across the blue waters of Tremadoc Bay. It was like a fairy-land, and it took my father all his time to refrain from telling the driver to stop every moment in order for him to take a picture of the lovely little corners which kept coming into view. Harlech was reached about noon, and while my father pottered about the old town with his camera, my mother and I made our way up the steep path to the castle. Having settled her on a seat on the battlements overlooking the wide expanse of meadow-land, hundreds of feet below, which stretched for miles along the magnificent bay to Portmadoc, just visible in the distance, with Snowdon rearing his head high into the sunlit sky beyond, I explored every cranny and nook of this imposing old fortress, from the highest tower to the deepest dungeon, until it was time for lunch. And so we returned once more to Hucknall with the memories of brown mountains, sparkling sea, rushing waterfalls, quaint little churches, quainter little villages, and with the pretty upward lilt of the Welsh speech sounding in our ears. It had been a marvellous holiday and, best of all, my father was a different man and able to return to his work with renewed vigour.

* * * * *

I never think about my holidays with my parents without calling to mind the various 'locums' who took up temporary residence at Tenter Hill. There was usually a certain amount of risk attached to the business of handing over my father's large practice to a stranger, however good the references may have been, though I must say that, barring the episode of the doctor who managed to get through my father's entire stock of morphia and cocaine, and the elderly gentleman who drank himself almost incapable in the surgery, on the whole my father was fortunate. Some of the 'locums' who came to the house, especially those of the dignified type, had rather a thin time, for my two younger sisters had a flair for taking it out of anyone who did not possess what they considered to be a sense of humour. One 'locum' in particular (I remember he was bald and extremely serious) got on the wrong side of my sisters and I should imagine the poor fellow must have praised the day when his term of office ended and he was free to shake off the dust of Tenter Hill, never to return to it again. It was inviting disaster for anyone not popular with these two members of the household to hope for any sort of peace unless safely locked in the surgery. Who would wish to stay in any house with the risk of having water poured on to his head from an upstairs window, particularly if he were bald and were incautious enough to take up his stand outside the front door while two young demons waited about overhead for him to come into line with the jug so conveniently balanced on the edge of the window-sill (and my sisters, having practised beforehand, were not wanting where accuracy was concerned, their prowess with the jug being notorious). It was not only the 'locums' who came in for it, for now and again my sisters turned their attentions to the Church dignitaries of the neighbourhood, and the curate, a frequent caller at Tenter Hill, was just the right subject for baiting. I remember this young clergyman, after the evening service one Sunday, telling us over supper that he thought there was far too much bad language used among his parishioners and he was determined to put a stop to it, in fact he had made up his mind that if ever he came across anyone using language which he considered to be out of keeping with his religious views he would tackle the wrong-doer on the spot and make an example of him in public. This was too good an opportunity to pass unchallenged and the next Sunday evening saw my sisters, outside the front gate, locked in loving embrace (Dorothy in normal attire and Meta in raincoat and bowler hat, pulling at an evil-smelling pipe), awaiting the arrival of the castigator of the foul-spoken inhabitants of Hucknall. The curate's tall figure loomed up in the gathering darkness, and the demand for a kiss from a high-pitched female voice, answered with a husky, "Shut yer mouth or the bloody parson will hear you," was obviously heard but passed unnoticed. Over the supper which followed this illuminating revelation of the weakness of the Church, the trend of the conversation left no doubt in our curate's mind that he had been badly 'had'. My sisters' exploits were not only confined to 'locums' and curates, for on one notable occasion I was persuaded to have my hair curled. At the time I thought, in my innocence, that my sisters wished to improve my otherwise ordinary appearance, and the idea of having my hair crimped as magnificently as that of the stable-boy appealed to my sense of vanity so greatly that I submitted to the heated hair-tongs with alacrity, only to discover that, notwithstanding repeated hair-washing, for some unaccountable reason the horrible waves remained with me until they grew out. Up till that time I had had no idea how slow this hair-raising business was, for it had always seemed to me previously that I was for ever being told to "Go to the barber and have that stuff taken off!" However, I got my own back on them the night I planted a metal elephant with hinged legs inside a box under one of their beds and retired to the safety of my own bed, holding tightly to a length of string attached to this holy animal, and waited breathlessly till my sisters were fast asleep. The piercing screams which greeted my ears from the other end of the house when a pull on the string brought the metal beast to life were as music to my ears, but they were nothing compared to the pandemonium which followed the animal's ultimate rush out of the box, over the floor and along the passage to my bed. My sister Dorothy seemed to be the ringleader where any mischief was on foot, Meta being a good second, and myself, as the youngest, being more or less of a 'stooge'. It was Dorothy who dared Meta to dare her that she would put a match to the curtains in my mother's bedroom. How in the world the house escaped destruction I do not know, for it was only by a miracle that the three of us were able to extinguish the conflagration that followed.

We three had two things in common, the first being an insane desire to pull the communication-cord in any train in which we happened to be travelling, and the other an even more idiotic urge to throw our tickets out of the carriage window, especially if they were season tickets and we were going through a tunnel. This latter desire on one occasion became so strong that we literally had to cling on to one another to prevent the other from disposing of this most valuable piece of cardboard. Railway carriage doors also held some strange fascination for us and we were continually wondering what would happen if we opened one while travelling at speed, until one day we succumbed to the temptation (in a tunnel), forgetting all about season tickets and communication-cords in the excitement of the moment, and discovered to our horror that the rush of wind prevented us from closing the door again. We pulled up at the next station, feeling very frightened, and swore to the station-master and the crowd of porters who had gathered round that the door had blown open on its own. The incredulous looks on these gentlemen's faces showed us all too clearly that they did not believe us, and visions of lifelong imprisonment in Bagthorpe Gaol stared us in the face, until it was proved that we were the Railway Doctor's children, and only then were we let off with a caution and told not to do it again. Was it not Rudyard Kipling who said one could come to no harm if one made one's friends among cabbies and policemen? To this I would add stationmasters and porters.

* * * * *

As this is supposed to be the autobiography of a composer, perhaps it is about time I started to talk about my musical activities. Music had always been part of my life, every day an hour or so having been put aside to be devoted to scales and arpeggi and simple showy pieces of the de Bériot type, and also for putting down on paper my home-made melodies. I must have wasted reams of music paper writing out these childish thoughts, and some of the experiments I carried out in my excursions into the world of orchestration were enterprising enough, if perhaps not altogether dignified. 'Florodora' was all the rage at that time, and besides having heard Leslie Stuart's tuneful music at the Theatre Royal, Nottingham, I was able to listen to some of the numbers at will through the medium of the forerunner of the modern gramophone, the phonograph. I can still hear that squeaky voice announcing the item, followed by a thin scratchy orchestral rendering of 'Tell me, pretty maiden'. One particular bar in this pretty sextet always attracted my attention on account of the accompaniment having an appealing descending chromatic passage in the 'cello which I was not able to find in the vocal score. This annoyed me very much and I decided to make an arrangement myself of this piece of music (with the object of including the fascinating 'cello part) for the instruments I had at my disposal, through the co-operation of some of the local musicians with whom I had struck up acquaintance in the town. After much cogitation and after having worn the tiny wax cylinder threadbare, and after a great deal of manuscript paper had been quickly scribbled upon and as quickly torn up, I completed a score of Leslie Stuart's 'Tell me, pretty maiden' for two violins, one viola and two 'cellos. The separate parts were then copied and hurried calls made at the bank to enlist the services of 'Mr. Bowler who played the viola' and Mr. Howitt who lived near the bridge (made famous by the balloon episode), and who was an amateur 'cellist. Aunt Eliza Anne was staying with us at the time, and I was looking to her to supply the bass part, for she had fortunately brought her 'cello along with her. I was rather worried about my aunt's abilities and had carefully given her nothing technical to play, confining her part to pizzicato notes on the open strings where possible, and a holding-note now and again, always in the first position. At last the fateful evening came round, and soon after eight o'clock we were all sitting at our places in the drawing-room ready for the 'try-out'; myself leading; Dorothy, the youngest of my sisters, second violin; Bowler the viola; Howitt first 'cello, and Aunt Eliza Anne second. The arrangement started off quite nicely and continued satisfactorily up to the moment of the celebrated 'effect'. Poor Aunt Eliza Anne was doing her best and was looking terribly worried in doing so. Now anyone with musical experience at all knows how the most lovely of passages can be thrown completely out of gear if the bass part is not correctly played—well, it happened! My lovely 'effect' was ruined. After three hopeless attempts by my aunt to control that stiff right arm and stiffer left hand, the blood rushed to my head, I lost my temper and with marked effect used some language I had recently acquired from a collier who had slipped on some orange peel outside the surgery door. My father came in at this moment and ordered me to go to my room at once. This I did, but not before I had finished my vocabulary and hurled the greatest insult known to dog-fanciers, at my father—"You *mongrel!*" I was boxed on the ears. So ended my attempt at forming my own orchestra.

The building of the new organ at the parish church was the next event which commanded my attention, and I spent many hours wandering about the church watching the men at work assembling the intricate parts of this unmanageable-looking monster, and at the same time picking up quite a number of adjectives new to me.

The opening of the new instrument was a grand occasion for the church people, for was not the great Sir Frederick Bridge making a journey all the way from London to demonstrate the remarkable capabilities of both the organ and himself as organist? Quite candidly, I was not impressed with Frederick Bridge as an executant. He played dull pieces in a dull manner and was not even entertaining. I vastly preferred our Mr. John Munks (the organist of the Congregational chapel and owner of the famous music-shop in the High Street) from a playing point of view, and from an angle of pure entertainment the regular organist at the parish church itself, who, during a burial service, inadvertently slid off the organ seat and in his efforts to disentangle himself from the pedals gave us a realistic impression of a thunderstorm.

Going to church, to us children, was more of an entertainment than a devotional business. We were too young to trouble ourselves about 'souls', being much more interested in seeing how many acid-drops we could stick on to the back of the old lady in front during the prayers, and waiting for the inevitable moment when she rose from her knees and the sweets dropped about the pew with delicious clicks. Then there was always the excitement of watching and listening to the trombone player who had been taken out of the Hucknall Brass Band and recklessly placed in the front pew in order to give encouragement to the faltering congregation. There was one glorious day when he laughed down his instrument accidentally and brought the service to a stop. Then there was the time when the choir-master (who also happened to be my father), after having blown his nose, tucked back yards of his neighbour's surplice into his pocket in mistake for his own pocket-handkerchief; and the pin which my sister Meta stuck into the air-cushion of the 'old lady of the acid-drops' and the unforgettable hiss of escaping air which preceded the disappearance from view of the unhappy victim. Is it to be wondered at that we children behaved badly in church when one Sunday morning the parson went so far as to take advantage of the absence on holiday of Mr. Abel Smith, the Nottingham banker of Papplewick Hall, by announcing the text of his sermon as: "And there was no smith in the land"?

* * * * *

Two great events, the Boer War and the death of Queen Victoria (especially the latter) made a deep impression on me. During this disastrous South African affair I firmly believed that the world was on the verge of coming to an end, and the death of the old Queen confirmed my fears. I shall long remember the horrifying headlines which appeared each day in the papers about disastrous defeats; colossal victories; not enough ships; not enough men; not enough guns; too much red-tape; not enough red-tape; and ridiculous cartoons showing President Kruger complete with fantastic top-hat and even more fantastic beard, as against imposing and magnificent pictures of the British Bulldog draped in Union Jacks.

But the thing which stands out in my mind the most clearly is the song specially written by Sir Arthur Sullivan in collaboration with Rudyard Kipling to raise funds for the war (a clever way of getting more income tax out of you through the collections which always followed a performance, under the cloak of Charity, a ruse which is still resorted to to-day, although they put up your income tax at the same time). Even at that tender age I could not see what there was to shout about, let alone collect about, over either the words or the music of 'The Absent-minded Beggar'. If anything, I thought the music was worse than the poem. I remember my disappointment on hearing this song for the first time at a charity concert in the Town Hall of my native Hucknall, and I felt, even then, that surely the writer of such melodious and popular comic operas could have given us something better than this laboured effort.

The Boer War was bad enough, but the death of Queen Victoria was, to me, a catastrophe of the first magnitude, and the entire population of Hucknall going into mourning for the old lady did not improve matters. Black hats; black gloves; black ties; black shoes; black stockings; and, where an entire suit or costume was too expensive, black bands round the arms. Black everywhere. It was awful. Funeral services, funeral hymns, tolling of bells (I remember wondering whether those dreadful parish church bells would ever reach the end of those mournful eight-six strokes), shops closed, even the doors of the public-houses remaining shut, and everyone either walking about on tip-toe or whispering together at street corners. The End of the World had definitely come. Even my treasured bicycle looked far too bright and I was wondering whether I ought not to drape it with crêpe. But the days passed and the funeral was over, and before we knew where we were everything seemed to have been forgotten and we were looking forward to the Coronation of our new King. Well, I thought, so much for the fickleness of human nature. I was not old enough to know of the existence of the old French salute: "Le Roi est mort—vive le Roi!", or possibly I might have understood what seemed to me to be nothing more nor less than extreme callousness.

* * * * *

But to get back to my music. I had now come to the stage when better tuition was needed, so my father, after having made exhaustive enquiries as to who was the best violin teacher in Nottingham, placed me in the care of Georg Ellenberger, a qualified exponent of the method of the great Joseph Joachim, whose favourite pupil he had been when a young man in Berlin. Ellenberger was a naturalised British subject (though I always suspected that his heart was really in his old home in Cassel) and had married a charming lady, the daughter of an old and respected Nottingham family. I believe there was a great deal of opposition to the marriage at the time and for some years the couple were ostracised by the bride's parents. The idea of their attractive daughter lowering herself by marrying a musician, and a German at that, was going too far, and so the newly-weds, for some years, went through a difficult phase. By the time I came under Ellenberger's wing the scandal had blown over and he was being sought after by all those mammas in the county who wished to find the ideal professor for their precious daughters. For had he not married into one of the best families in Nottinghamshire? And so the reputation of the favourite pupil of the great Joachim grew day by day and his large and well-to-do clientèle was augmented by the arrival one morning of a little twelve-year-old boy from Hucknall, with a black wooden violin case, an assortment of violin pieces and a mother to act as accompanist for the ordeal to follow. Yes, I certainly showed promise, but of course much that I had learnt would have to be undone. For one thing, my bow-arm was not good—thank goodness he did not criticise my intonation or my rhythm, that was something! By the time the interview had come to an end I confess I was feeling a little crestfallen, and my mother was studying with alarm a formidable list of music which had to be bought from a Mr. Waterfield, the music-dealer in Nottingham with whom I suspected the maestro had a private understanding. Viotti, Fiorillo, Kreutzer, Bach, Spöhr, Beethoven, Brahms, Mozart, Joachim, Wieniawski, Vieuxtemps—a formidable list indeed. And so, back to the station, calling at Waterfield's on the way (where the bill was so heavy that my mother was forced to open an account—this made a deep impression on me) and spending the time on the homeward journey wondering what my father would say when he heard of the fifteen guineas a term, the enormous music bill, and the suggestion that he ought to put me under a Dr. Ralph Horner to get me acquainted with the rules of harmony, etc. My father came up to scratch, and it was forthwith arranged that I should have two lessons a week with Ellenberger and one with Dr. Horner, and as this would mean three journeys to Nottingham each week I was raised to the dignity of being a first-class season-ticket holder on the Midland Railway. Why first-class, goodness knows, unless it was that my parents sensed my antipathy (even at that early age) to travelling third. The next step was a visit to Dr. Horner, who lived with his wife in a pleasant house in West Bridgford, a suburb of the city, and after a breezy interview with the little professor I found myself coming out of Henry Farmer's establishment, the possessor of a concise book on Harmony by Dr. John Stainer. The worthy little Doctor of Music impressed me immensely on account of an uncontrollable stammer and a habit of running his hands unexpectedly through his short, bristly, white hair and sending little clouds of dust flying about his shoulders. The effect with his back to the light was astonishing. I was soon to discover that this diminutive musician was a teacher without rival and, what was more important to me, he had a heart of gold and treated me like a grown-up. Georg Ellenberger and Ralph Horner —when I look back upon my young days I can see what a great deal I have to thank these two kindly musicians for. Ellenberger, besides imparting to me the impeccable Joachim style, introduced me to his beloved Great Masters. To him, of course, Germany was the only country which ever produced music. I could not argue with him about this, for up to that moment my musical training had not gone much further than short, easy, showy pieces by composers who are today, fortunately, dead and forgotten. The concertos by Beethoven, Brahms, Joachim's 'Hungarian', Ernst, Paganini, Spöhr, Wieniawski, Vieuxtemps, Mendelssohn, Bruch, and the Bach unaccompanied sonatas, went hand-in-hand with technical studies in which that all-embracing book by Kreutzer played a great part. As I improved in my playing I was admitted to the quartet classes, which took place in the softly-decorated room facing on to the park. My first experience in this direction was of Mozart's G Major Quartet, in which I was responsible for the 2nd violin part. Mrs. Ellenberger, who was quite a proficient viola player, was sometimes called in to take over the tenor part and on very special occasions Ellenberger himself would lead, to give us a practical demonstration of the correct rendering. The viola in those days, as every musician knows, was greatly neglected, unlike today, when there are so many fine exponents of this instrument, thanks to the activities of Lionel Tertis and William Primrose.

My lessons with Dr. Horner were just as much a delight. He was very strict at first and would not allow me to put any of my young ideas down on paper. No! I must work hard at my harmony and my counterpoint and my canon and my fugue, and then we would see. And so I worked hard at my exercises and harder at my violin, while at the same time I composed on the quiet. It was difficult to do this, as my father, who knew that Horner was adamant about my not writing, would keep turning up at unexpected moments and catching me in the act of playing over some melody or other on the old Brinsmead. Using the soft pedal was out of the question, for the piano-tuner (who flourished under the ridiculous name of Giggle) had put this out of action years ago, and so I was forced to play with one ear on the piano and the other on the door. Poor father, he was only anxious for me to make as much headway as possible and did not wish me to waste my time. He little knew that my melody-making excursions, allied with the stolen hours I spent playing through the lovely songs of Grieg, Schumann and Schubert, the valses of Johann Strauss and Waldteufel, the operas of Massenet (my special favourite being 'Manon'), all borrowed from the music library in Nottingham, and plodding through the pianoforte accompaniments to the violin concertos I was learning (with the fascinating orchestral indications) were later on to be of such immense value to me. So I practised when my father was within earshot and continued my illicit studies when he was not. I regret to say that my mother aided and abetted me in these underhand practices, probably because she knew intuitively that it was good for me, up to a point, to discover in my own way how music was made. As I progressed with my fiddle-playing my lessons with Ellenberger became more and more interesting. There were more difficult concertos and studies and more advanced ensemble classes, and even my little Doctor of Music (Ellenberger liked Dr. Horner well enough and respected him as a teacher, but, being a German, he was never able to reconcile himself to that musical degree) was encouraging me, at long last, to take him examples of my writing. It was hard work for a small boy who was not over-strong, and sometimes I think it might have been better if I had not gone at it with such enthusiasm. Two violin lessons a week, each lesson being followed by a couple of hours' quartet-playing, and one long lesson with Dr. Horner, meant three whole mornings and afternoons having to be taken out of the time given to my practising and my writing. Practically the only time I ever sat down was to busy myself with some involved contrapuntal problem or to make some experiment in orchestration. The rest of the day, except for the necessary meals, was spent walking round and round the dining-room table practising my fiddle—a habit I was never able to cure. It must have been exasperating for my family, now I come to think of it, but except for being turned out by my father one day and told to go and practise elsewhere because I was wearing out the carpet, they put up with my eccentricities without a murmur. If it had not been for the bicycle with which my father and mother presented me one birthday, I firmly believe I should have become very ill.

I think the machine was a means resorted to by my parents to get me away from my music. At any rate, it had the desired effect, and from then onwards I divided my time between practising and composing and exploring all the lovely winding roads and lanes in which Nottinghamshire was so rich. To start off early in the morning with the sandwiches my mother had prepared for me safely tucked away, with a bottle of home-brewed ginger-beer in the holder underneath the saddle, almost before the sun had cleared away the morning mists, and to know that I had the day before me to wander where I would! How I loved these little lanes with their dusty scent; to see the clouds gathering for another shower; to smell the roads after rain; to hear the cuckoo in the woods across the fields; to see the lark winging up into the still blue sky; to hear the rumble of distant thunder; and if I remained very still, to catch the sound of a far-away train labouring up the incline on the Mansfield line; to shelter under the branches of an enormous oak while the storm spent itself, and then to sit down on my waterproof cape to eat my lunch, conscious of being miles and miles away from anywhere and not a soul knowing my whereabouts; and then again to smell those intoxicating summer scents which always seemed to be a mixture of wet roads, new-mown hay and wood-smoke; to watch the steam rising from the little lane as the sun reappeared from behind the storm-clouds; and then to take out my trusty ordnance map and see to what other places of enchantment I could find my way before the next shower. Hardly a soul would I meet, unless it were sometimes a tramp making his weary way to the next workhouse, and these nomads were scarcely what one could call company, trudging along silently with downcast eyes as they did. These people of the roads were interesting to watch especially when they were in company with another—never would they walk along together, always on opposite sides of the road, and you could never catch them holding any sort of converse, though I suppose they must have had some means of communicating with each other, probably by signs. And then came that spot on the road where, especially after rain, you could see nearly the whole of this lovely county, and here I would stand my bicycle up against a tree and scramble up on to the bank at the side of the road where the view was best and look out on to the landscape which stretched away into the blue distance. Not a sound could I hear—even the birds were having their afternoon rest, and the little cool breeze which followed after the storm had completely dropped. Far away on the horizon I could see a train wending its way slowly through the countryside, but even this made no sound. The silence was complete. Here I would sit and think, and try to grasp the meaning of this wonderful thing called 'nature'. If only I could understand this lonely yet friendly feeling which seemed to permeate my entire being and everything around me! I little knew that on the hills around Elstree, a hundred and thirty miles away to the south, there was a little fair-haired girl, whom I was to meet some years later, doing exactly the same thing.

Later on I was to be joined by a companion on these voyages of discovery, for my brother, Gwyn, having saved up a few pounds out of his allowance, had presented my mother with a modern tricycle—a Humber. She had secretly hankered after having a bicycle, but my father considered it unseemly for a woman of her age to be seen careering along Papplewick Lane on two wheels in full view of the natives. I could never quite understand what difference the third wheel made, but for all I knew it may have given tone to the proceedings; so a tricycle it was. To-day, when I see old ladies of between seventy and eighty punting about on their bicycles doing the daily shopping, I cannot help but think that my father must either have grossly under-estimated my mother's capabilities or over-estimated her dignity as the wife of the most prosperous doctor in Hucknall; and, besides that, I cannot see where the question of age came into it, for she must have been well under fifty at the time.

By this time my two younger sisters were also owners of a 'safety', but my eldest sister, Gladys, said she would rather die than make an exhibition of herself in front of the inhabitants by mounting such a ridiculous-looking machine (I do not know whether she preferred the look of the ancient 'penny-farthing'—the contraption with a huge wheel in front and a tiny wheel behind. I must say I would have liked to have seen her mount that!) I think it was that 'mounting' which deterred her, for had she not witnessed her sisters' wild career down Aden Lane, frantically and helplessly clutching the handlebars in their vain endeavour to keep their balance, before the inevitable crash into the dusty ditch ahead? Aden Lane, by the way, just behind Linby Colliery, joining Papplewick Lane with Linby Lane, was the bicycle-learners' joy. It was protected on either side by a high hedge, thus hiding the victim from the vulgar gaze, and the thick dust which covered the surface of the road acted as an admirable shock-absorber for the 'fallen'. The only danger was the ditch with the nettles—I became far too well acquainted with this particular ditch during my apprenticeship.

The rides I enjoyed most were those in company with my mother. She, like my father, seemed to have something specially in common with me, and I think that being the youngest may have had a good deal to do with it. Much to my annoyance, I was alluded to by my sisters as my father's and mother's 'little Benjamin'. I expect I deserved it, for I am quite sure I was a spoilt little wretch. At any rate, when I was not alone during my expeditions, you may be certain that I was either with my father or my mother, with the former on foot or by train, with the latter on my bicycle. They were delightful days exploring with my mother the beauties of Sherwood Forest, where the oaks are so old that they give the impression of shrivelled old gentlemen stretching up their withered arms in supplication. Every corner had some association or other with the romantic Robin Hood—Robin Hood's Caves, Robin Hood's Stables, Robin Hood's Larder—every moment one expected to hear the sound of a horn and to see this gallant outlaw galloping at the head of his band of followers through the wooded glades—Will Scarlet, Little John, with the lumbering Friar Tuck bringing up the rear on a pony far too small for him—and the lovely Maid Marian. What a romantic story and what surroundings to set it in! Cool streams finding their rambling way across green fields made greener by the water which, in places, ran unchecked over the grass; little old stone bridges; stepping-stones; majestic avenues; forgotten unused grassy tracks; and brooding over this vast stretch of wooded country, Welbeck Abbey, the home of the eccentric old Duke of Portland.

Yes, Nottinghamshire was very lovely in those distant days and even to-day certain parts of it remain unspoiled, and in those quarters which have suffered through that menacing thing called 'progress' the memory of their one-time loveliness still remains in the hearts of those who knew them as they used to be. Welbeck Abbey, Newstead Abbey, Rufford Abbey, Southwell Minster, Newark Castle, Wingfield Manor, Hardwicke Hall, the Fosse Way, Icknield Way, Ermine Street, the remains of a Druid's Circle at Blidworth, the Hemlock Rocking Stone beyond Nutthall—all these and many other historic places were within cycling distance, and in my holidays and when the weather did not look too threatening my mother and I used to make the most of them. If we felt we were not up to a long day's ride, especially if it were hot, we would cycle over to Hazleford Ferry on the Trent, about ten miles across country, and have a picnic under the trees on the well-wooded bank of this pretty river and watch the tugs pulling the heavy barges up-stream through the rapids, on their way from Newark to Nottingham. We usually chose the spot where the current was swiftest, as it was exciting to see those sturdy little vessels just managing to shepherd their charges into the slower-moving stream ahead. Sometimes, when there were two or even three barges in tow, it did not seem possible that they would ever get through. Then my mother would take the opportunity of having her customary afternoon nap while I sat near-by and kept the flies from bothering her by smoking a cigarette.

About this time my mother and we children were invited by my Religious Aunt to spend some of the summer holidays with her at Usk. Aunt Marjorie lived in a comfortable Victorian house, with a pleasant garden leading down to the river, near the old stone bridge which carries the road across on its winding way to Newport. I enjoyed my visit on the whole. The picnics; Maurice the butler (whom Aunt Marjorie would address as 'Murris'); the cat which caught fish in the river by gently putting its front paws around them and lopping them out; and the old relic of a tricycle, a model of a bygone age with two large wheels in front and a small wheel behind, the rear wheel being the one used for directing the course, which was controlled by a Heath-Robinson contraption on either side of the saddle—these attractions made the holiday worth-while. But I was annoyed at having to take my violin with me, for this meant that I had to amuse the guests in the drawing-room after dinner, while 'Murris' handed round the coffee. As a matter of fact, I liked 'Murris', for he allowed me to help him make the sparkling ginger-beer which accompanied us on our picnics. But I objected to playing my fiddle to a crowd of, what I considered to be, gaping idiots who would persist in talking all the time. To tell the truth, I was dying to have a 'go' at the antiquated-looking machine which lived in the stables, and my only chance was after dinner while my Religious Aunt was busily engaged entertaining her guests. My aunt must have looked extraordinary seated on her tricycle, and I believe she used it regularly, but, alas, I never had the good fortune to witness her in full sail. We were all a little in awe of the lady—she was so large, so expansive, so grand, so condescending, so supercilious, though I expect she had a good heart. Snob, I believe is the word. She had a most unpleasant way of throwing her head back, slightly closing her eyes and addressing you as if you were a small kind of worm—to say you felt only six inches high was exaggerating. One point in her favour, at any rate so far as I was concerned, was that she had a delightful mezzo-soprano voice, and to hear her sing the old, simple songs, such as, 'I shot an arrow in the air', and 'I remember, I remember the house where I was born', brought a lump even into my throat. She was, besides being a snob, a confirmed Christian Scientist. My father's opinion of her was unprintable but, he being a doctor, it was justifiable. My aunt was civil to my father but nothing more, and to see them together was a comedy, and between the two my mother had a difficult time trying to keep the peace. I forgot to mention that my aunt was the widow of a wealthy Irishman, which explains what seemed to me, at the time, an extravagant mode of living.

Those Monmouthshire picnics, for instance, were indeed luxurious affairs—so different from our simple outings at Hucknall. Carriage and pair, coachman and butler and a small 'buttons' made me think we might be having lunch at Buckingham Palace, instead of being seated round an improvised table with a snowy-white cloth, high up on the slope of Sugar-Loaf Mountain.

How my aunt put up with us I cannot imagine, for I am sure we children must have behaved very badly, and to give her her due, she showed no signs of disapproval, whatever she may have said about us to my mother when we were safely tucked up in bed and 'Murris' had locked up for the night. I was not sorry when the day came to start the long and tedious railway journey back to Hucknall, although I was sorry to say goodbye to the lovely Welsh Mountains. What would I not have given to have been there alone with my bicycle! But we were now in the stuffy railway-carriage, slowly crawling over the Welsh border with all that romantic country receding into the distance behind us and with the unpleasant prospect of half-a-dozen changes ahead.

* * * * *

It was pleasant to be home again with all my belongings around me, especially my much-missed bicycle. My fiddle, at that moment, I almost disliked; it had been the most awful nuisance in the train and I swore a solemn oath that on no account should it ever accompany me again, aunt or no aunt, and it never did. The end of holidays is always an unhappy time, I think, nothing seems right— I missed the deferential attentions of my friend, 'Murris'. '*Master Eric*', this, and '*Master Eric*', that! So bad for me, but so pleasant! If it had not been for my bicycle I think I should have tried to drown myself in the Leen, but recollecting that it was not more than a couple of feet deep at the most, I got my beloved machine out and spent all the next day riding as hard as I could and as far as I could into the heart of the country and away from people until I came to the spot overlooking my lovely county and, scrambling up to the top of the bank at the side of the road, settled down for a long, long think. After a while that warm, friendly, lonely sensation, as if someone were trying to say something to me, crept over me again and I began to think that perhaps life was not so bad after all, and, giving up the idea of finding a river deeper than the Leen to end things once and for all, I mounted my trusty bicycle and made my way home contentedly through the sweet-smelling autumn twilight.

* * * * *

About half-way through the term, Ellenberger asked me if I would like to join a special quartet he was forming to play on Friday evenings at his house. The maestro himself was going to lead, I was to be second violin, Mrs. Ellenberger viola, and a local musician, Fred Hodgkinson, the 'cello. Of course I was delighted to have the opportunity of studying the Great Masters under such conditions, and to have the privilege of being admitted into the 'Inner Circle'. And so it was arranged, and the trains between Hucknall and Nottingham saw me more frequently than ever.

I usually left my home after what we call in the Midlands a 'high tea' (it took me years to break myself of this old custom, but to-day I can fortunately pass that magic hour without a pang) and arrived at my professor's house just as they were finishing their dinner ('high tea' in the Ellenberger *ménage* was not considered 'the thing') and in time for a very acceptable cup of coffee. A cigarette, and then, the stands arranged and the music set out, the evening would begin. A quartet of Haydn's and then some Brahms; a quartet of Mozart and then again Brahms; a quartet of Beethoven's and yet again Brahms; it did not matter which of the Masters was omitted from our practices provided it was not Brahms. I am sure these delightful evenings were responsible for my love of Brahms to-day, especially his quartets, quintets and sextets and, finally, the Clarinet Quintet in B Minor. I have cause to remember this work in particular, for it was to be the means of great changes for me in my musical career. Ellenberger had for a long time been endeavouring to find a local clarinettist who was willing to spend an evening playing the Brahms Quintet 'for love'. Now, I wish to state quite clearly that I am not criticising clarinet players as a body, and I am sure there are artists to-day who enjoy playing for the love of it, but in those days clarinettists were far too often of what I call the 'beery' type. You would find them in the interval at any orchestral concert playing nap on a beer-barrel, or some such other type of receptacle, in the evil-smelling band-room under the stage. And would they play their clarinet for nothing? Certainly not! It was bad enough anyhow, playing professionally. Now do you wonder that there were few really good clarinet players, when they were so mercenary? But, one day, Ellenberger met a charming old clergyman, the rector of some parish on the Fosse Way, outside Nottingham (I cannot recall his name, but perhaps that may be as well), who considered himself a clarinettist of some ability. It was too good to be true. And so one Friday evening Fred Hodgkinson and I arrived at the charming house in Burns Street to find the reverend gentleman already installed with the maestro and his wife, and beaming with goodwill. Everyone was very happy. Evidently the dinner had been beyond reproach, and excitement over the impending performance of the Brahms Quintet ran high. Once again the stands were arranged (five this time), the music set out, the chairs placed in position, one more cigarette and a last cup of coffee, followed by much tuning-up of instruments, and then Ellenberger raised his bow and the two violins began that lovely introduction to one of the Master's greatest achievements in chamber music. I can recall the scene even now. The pretty drawing-room with the soft-coloured lamp-shades, the soft-coloured curtains, the soft-coloured rugs on the parquet floor; an effect of pastel blue throughout. Even the pale blue night outside seemed in harmony, with the garden showing a misty blue through the open french windows. A large standard-lamp in the centre of the players, throwing a pleasant light on to the music and five very serious people intent on the work in hand. At the entrance of the clarinet I realised that all was not well. A quick glance at Fred over the top of the music-stand—but he was absorbed in a technical passage; and then an alarming 'quawk' from the old clergyman. He had blown what is known among orchestral players as a 'goose'—an unearthly note in the high register of the instrument, due to faulty lip-pressure. Again I looked across at Fred and unfortunately our eyes met. Ellenberger and his wife appeared unmoved—this made matters worse, as far as the 'cello and the second fiddle were concerned. Another unearthly 'goose' followed by another and yet another (all the notes sounded like 'geese') finished the proceedings. Hysterical attempts on the part of Fred and myself to prevent ourselves from laughing merely brought us to the verge of complete collapse; we cried, silently and helplessly, and nothing could stop us. The music ceased. The Ellenbergers were furious—at the time we did not know whether their fury was directed at the old clergyman for his 'quawks' or at us for showing such deplorable lack of self-control. But what could they have expected? To see the old boy with his eyes standing out of his head, sucking at the mouthpiece of his clarinet and vainly trying to keep the thing in order, was ludicrous beyond description. Fred and I had him in full view, so we knew. Murmuring something about the keys having seized up through the instrument's lying for too long in its case, the old fellow closed his music, saying he would like a little longer to practise before playing the work again ensemble. By this time we were feeling sorry for the old man, for he had really taken it very well, and now that our mirth had subsided we both felt ashamed of ourselves for our display of bad manners. Apologies were duly made, strong drink was forthcoming, and after half a dozen glasses of good old port, our clarinettist was laughing at himself.

And so the Clarinet Quintet in B Minor by Brahms was put on one side, until one day Ellenberger discovered that the clarinet part had been arranged (I believe by the composer himself) for solo viola. Mrs. Ellenberger was not up to it—what did I think about having a try to see if I could play it? So, with my father's consent, I called on my friend, Mr. Waterfield, to find out if he had a viola to sell. He had—several. An hour or so was spent in the little room over the shop, trying over this instrument and then that, and at last Waterfield, who was an excellent judge, suggested a Testori. It was rather on the small side, but he thought it wiser to wait until I had had some experience before going in for a full-length instrument. The next thing was a bow—and after a great deal of searching about in dusty drawers and cupboards in another little room at the back a beautifully-balanced bow by the famous Tourte was produced. This Tourte bow is still in use to-day, along with a larger and very remarkable viola which I procured from a brother artist when first I came to London. Both of these have now been given by me to one of the viola players in the London Philharmonic Orchestra, who lost his outfit in the disastrous fire which destroyed our beloved Queen's Hall in 1941. The little Testori passed out of my hands many years ago. I don't expect my old friend Waterfield is alive to-day, though when I used to go up to my old home to visit my parents when first I came to London, I usually managed to find the time to call at the little music shop in Goldsmith Street to talk over old times.

He was a character, with dark, shaggy hair; played the viola with tremendous gusto; was very excitable and a great talker; with a fund of interesting anecdotes about the artists who dropped in now and again to buy some strings or some rosin, or to bring in a bow to be rehaired. Ysaye, Kreisler, Thibaud, Kubelik, John Dunn, Willy Hess, Emile Sauret, Maurice Sons, the members of the Bohemian String Quartet, the St. Petersburg String Quartet, etc. etc., names without number, knew the little temperamental artist at one time or another. I never tired of sitting in his back room (only his most intimate callers were admitted here) listening to his musical stories of how so-and-so played such-and-such a passage on the G string and how so-and-so could never master that down-bow staccato passage in such-and-such a concerto, and so on and so on.

My taking up the viola opened up a new field for the Friday nights in Burns Street, for now the added wealth of all the quintets and sextets was at our disposal. After tackling the solo part in the Brahms Clarinet Quintet we turned our attention to the G Major Quintet for two violins, two violas and 'cello; then followed the F Major; and calling in another of Ellenberger's pupils we settled down to the sextets by the same composer. I think my favourite of these Brahms works, bar the Clarinet Quintet, will always be the G Major Quintet with its fine viola solo in the slow movement. After we had exhausted the string chamber music a pianiste was enlisted, and we explored the beauties of both the Schumann Piano Quartet and the Piano Quintet and, after that, the magnificent Piano

Quintet by Dvorák. I could write pages about these works, but no words of mine could possibly describe the joy it was to me to have the privilege of being introduced to them by such an artist as George Ellenberger.

About this time the maestro started a series of Subscription Chamber Concerts at a hall off the Derby Road and the Friday nights' ensemble was at last to show what it could do in public. The hall was packed and the reception was enthusiastic. It was my first public appearance with my master and I was conscious that a good deal depended on my giving a good account of myself. Fortunately all went well, and Ellenberger did not criticise me unduly, which showed that he must have been fairly pleased; he was always grudging in his praise of me, as though he were afraid I might become swollen-headed. Personally, I think you can carry this kind of thing to excess, for I feel a little praise now and again hurts nobody, and where should we be if we never received any encouragement? This was the only thing about Ellenberger which might have had harmful consequences, had I stayed with him for too long. How different from my first days at the Royal Academy of Music in London with Lionel Tertis, who never ceased to encourage me and enthuse me to greater efforts. "You *can* play it, Eric!" "Don't be afraid of it!" "Play it your *own* way!" "Put your *own* personality into it!" "That's more like it!"

My next step was to gain orchestral experience, so I joined a newly-formed amateur String Orchestra run by a local organist and conductor. He was a mild-looking, intellectual man with fair, longish hair, wore pince-nez, had a marked lisp and an irritating habit of waving his arms about when he spoke. He had acquired a young and attractive wife (astonishing how some pretty women fall for the most unexpected) and I suspect that this had something to do with the large number of young men who presented themselves for inclusion in his orchestra. I remember his evincing some surprise at the numerous applications he received from unknown, aspiring male musicians—really, Nottingham must be more musical than he had imagined. He was really a very good fellow, but I always had the desire to stick a pin into him.

There seemed to me at that time to have been a great dearth of music for the String Orchestra medium, for our conductor resorted to inviting local talent to send in works for performance; up to that moment we had been restricted to Grieg's Holberg Suite, and the Serenades by Tschaikowsky and Elgar. Here was my long-awaited opportunity and, backed up by Dr. Horner, I submitted, a 'Ballad for String Orchestra' which I dedicated to Georg Ellenberger. It was an unambitious, youthful attempt, and it did not come off too badly. I remember how Fred Hodgkinson, who was playing principal 'cello, pulled my leg over the minute directions in the 'cello part—'espressivo', 'sonore', 'legato', 'flautando', 'marcato', 'glissando' and so on—intimating that I might have left something to the artistic discretion of the performer: "After all, Eric, we're not *all* fools!"

My time throughout the term was now fully occupied. Besides viola lessons and ensemble classes with Ellenberger, composition with Dr. Horner and the String Orchestral rehearsals, my father allowed me to join the Nottingham Sacred Harmonic Orchestral Society, which gave three or four concerts yearly in the Albert Hall. It was good experience for me and I met most of the amateur and professional orchestral players in the county in this way. H. Lyell-Tayler, the violinist, used to conduct the rehearsals, which were held weekly in a large room in the Mechanics' Institute, the concerts themselves being directed by Henry Wood (specially engaged for the season), who also took over the final rehearsal, Lyell-Tayler then taking his place at the first desk as principal violin. Lyell-Tayler was a fine-looking man, over six foot I should say, and correspondingly broad, good-looking in a flashy way with tremendously long flowing grey hair. To see him fully arrayed in his fur-lined coat with huge beaver collar covering a perfectly-fitting dress-suit, adorned with snowy-white shirt-front and diamond studs, his beautiful crop of hair carefully waved round his shining silk hat, made you understand why he had earned for himself the nickname of 'lion-tamer'. He was an excellent trainer (of an orchestra) and spared no effort in preparing the ground as much as possible for our Mr. Wood. He was also a first-rate leader, a bit showy perhaps, but that was only in keeping with his personality. He was extremely kind, took an interest in everything and everybody and was always ready to be of assistance.

Mr. Beard of Birmingham (the father of Paul Beard, the violinist) was the principal viola. I felt greatly honoured at being placed at the first desk with him and did my best to please him by always turning over the pages without interfering with his bow or getting in his line of vision—not always an easy thing for a beginner, however simple it may appear from the front. We became good friends and I learnt many helpful orchestral 'tips' from him. Fred Hodgkinson was there, of course, and many others with whom I soon became friendly. It was invaluable experience for me to be able to become acquainted with the numbers of specially-engaged instrumentalists who came all the way from Birmingham, Manchester and London to see the concerts through. I took every opportunity to talk to them about the capabilities of their respective instruments and even went so far as to pluck up my courage, when I knew them better, to ask them to demonstrate certain passages. They were a kindly lot and I have a great deal to thank these first friends for. They never appeared tired of answering the countless questions I fired at them, whatever they might have been feeling, and many were the happy and interesting half-hours I spent with them in the band-room during interval-time, while the trombone player or the horn player showed me how *not* to write for his instrument. Meeting all these professional musicians fired my enthusiasm to try to become one of them myself and, as I had for some time been chafing to earn my own living, the idea occurred to me to write to Dan Godfrey, then the Musical Director to the Bournemouth Corporation, to ask him if he could find a place for me in the Municipal Orchestra. Yes, by all means, but did I play some other instrument besides the viola, as all his men were obliged to be double-handed on account of having to play in the Military Band on the pier each morning? And so my father, acting upon the advice of Fred Warren, the principal flautist in the Nottingham Orchestra and one of my newly-found friends, bought me a modern Boehm flute, and once a week I made a journey to West Bridgford to take lessons from my new master, who lived only a few doors away from Dr. Horner. My progress with this cheery musician was a little slow at first, but after a few weeks of practising the correct lip-pressure and making myself acquainted with the fingering, I was soon at the stage when I was able to tackle the first Kuhlau Duets for two flutes. Here my father came in unexpectedly handy, and, after a great deal of persuading, his old rosewood practically keyless instrument was taken out of its box, carefully dusted and warmed up for action. I shall never forget, as long as I live, the practice which followed. My father took upon himself to look after the second part, which was merely accompaniment and not technically difficult, while I was responsible for the more showy first. There we were, sitting opposite one another, my father swearing every time his drooping moustache interfered with his blowing, saliva dripping out of the ends of our respective instruments, and just as things were progressing reasonably, the surgery bell would ring. By the time the patient had taken his leave, the second flute had to be warmed up all over again and it was several minutes before we could get down to business once more. My father, as I said some time ago, was quick-tempered and, at times, very impatient. Unfortunately it was times like these that caused this impatience to show itself long before it had really had a fair trial, and after the rebellious moustache had found its way into the mouthpiece half a dozen times and had been removed with much bad language and placed furiously in position again and everything seemed to be about to go along smoothly—one of the keys jammed, and the unnecessary force my father put into the releasing of the recalcitrant hinge pulled the flute in two. In future my practices were severely solo.

My activities with the flute, however, did not go further than making me conversant with the wood-wind side of the orchestra, for I did not take advantage of Dan Godfrey's kind suggestion that I should write to him again when I considered that I was in a position to say I was proficiently 'double-handed'. My experience with the flute, and the lessons which I received from my friend, Fred Warren, stood me in good stead and were invaluable in later years when I started to write seriously for the orchestra. Phrasing, tongueing, double-tongueing, triple-tongueing, flutter-tongueing and all the technicalities which are so opposite to those of the string section which I already knew so well, were mastered through ardent practice, and I was soon to find out that I could apply my knowledge to certain instruments in the brass section as well. It is an absolute necessity to have at least one instrument at your finger-tips, preferably a string instrument, before you can hope to write with authority for the orchestra.

Most of the famous composers of orchestral works have had some kind of orchestral experience; by this I mean actually playing in an orchestra, not merely serving as its director. No amount of conducting, or orchestral score-reading, or even reading any book devoted to the art of orchestration, will ever produce a composer. I do not think I can mention the name of a single director who has become a composer in the truest sense of the word. Too much conducting of other musicians' works destroys the individuality or originality of thought which might perhaps have existed in the beginning. You will find that all conductors can do is to launch out in some glorified arrangement of another man's work. Not that I am deprecating their efforts in this direction (although I think that some of them are in bad taste), for the world of orchestral music has been much enriched in this way by such famous conductors as Beecham, Weingartner, Hamilton Harty, Seidl and Stokowski. And here I will take the risk of running the gauntlet by including Henry Wood, although I think it will be wiser to draw a veil over his 'Fantasy on British Sea Songs'.

* * * * *

After I had been playing in the Nottingham Orchestra for some months I received an intimation from the Directors that I was to be given a small fee for my services. Up to that time my father had been subscribing half-a-guinea per season for me to have the privilege of being allowed to sit next to Paul Beard's father; but now I was to receive the large sum of one guinea for each final rehearsal and concert. I cannot say this disbursement went very far, for by the time I had paid for my lunch and fortified myself later on in the day with a substantial 'high tea' before the evening concert, there was not much left over for investing. Anyhow, I felt that I was a professional at last. Small engagements now began to come along, thanks to the recommendations of my brother orchestral players. Could I play in the 'Messiah' on Boxing Day at Mansfield? Was I free on such-and-such a day for the 'Elijah' at Sutton-in-Ashfield? Could I go up to Chesterfield for a special performance of 'Hymn of Praise'? At other times it may have been an Orchestral Concert, and I can vouch for it that some of these 'dates' were pretty tough when I say that I was expected to make my viola sound like the whole of the viola section of the B.B.C. Symphony Orchestra. 'Tannhauser' Overture with one viola! The conductor who could, alas, only beat four-in-a-bar, was extremely short-sighted and wore a dicky which persisted in flying out of his waistcoat in the Venusberg section revealing a bright red shirt underneath. At the height of the excitement this dicky shot up so high that it knocked off his glasses and forced him on to his knees underneath the rostrum, blindly and hopelessly hunting for his property. Observing his plight, I came to the rescue and with great difficulty managed to extricate the glasses from a hole in the woodwork of the improvised platform, during which process we bumped our heads together violently. It was quite some time before either conductor or viola was seen or heard.

* * * * *

During the Christmas and Easter holidays I used to take advantage of the visits of celebrated artists to the Albert Hall, Nottingham, to keep myself *au fait*, as well as possibe, with what was going on in the musical world outside Hucknall. Richter with the Hallé Orchestra; the incredible performance of Bach's unaccompanied sonatas for violin by the young Kubelik, which made me feel very dissatisfied and inclined to discontinue bothering any more about the fiddle, until I transferred my place of practice to the bathroom, which enhanced my tone (never mind about the technique) and cheered me up a little; Eli Hudson, that amazing flautist; Sousa and his band, with the 'wizard of the trombone', Pryor (I suspect there are many trombone players to-day who could play Pryor off his feet, but in those distant days the trombone was looked upon as nothing more than an instrument for supplying the bass notes, and a necessary evil at that); Smetana's 'Aus meinen Leben' Quartet played by the original Bohemian String Quartet, and I remember the thrill I experienced when the viola player, Oscar Nedbal, turned over the first two pages of his part and deliberately faced the audience to deliver himself of the dramatic first theme (my friend Arnold Bax quotes this very instance, in his delightful autobiography *Farewell my Youth*, as being one of the things which stand out in his mind). Then there were exciting journeys by the Sunday League Trips from Nottingham to London (four shillings and threepence return) to pay my half-crown to sit behind the orchestra to hear Fritz Kreisler make his début at the Queen's Hall in the Beethoven Concerto; I shall always remember his fine figure standing at attention while the orchestra played the Introduction and the deliberate way in which he raised his violin into position before he started the well-known opening ascending octave passage—and what a performance! I remember also the grudging praise of this consummate artist by my master, Georg Ellenberger, who was inclined to criticise the characteristic first finger of the right hand, which seemed to have nothing whatsoever to do with the remaining fingers. Then there was the Joachim String Quartet playing the Brahms Clarinet Quintet with the famous clarinettist, Muhlfeld: I was disappointed with Joachim, for, although his style was impeccable, he was cold in his playing and somewhat out of tune, and I remember thinking that perhaps a little more vibrato might well have covered up this lack of intonation. As for the clarinettist, he may have played the work according to the Brahms tradition, but his tone was in keeping with the rest of the ensemble, which was poor, and his rendering, to me, seemed inartistic. 'L'après-midi d'un faune', with the Queen's Hall Orchestra under Henry Wood, was my first introduction to the great French composer; I had never heard music written on the tonal scale until then and the impression I received, on this first hearing, was intoxicating. I had no programme, and the name Debussy would not have meant anything to me if I had, but this strange, lovely music opened up a hitherto unknown realm which I spared no effort to explore to the utmost.

* * * * *

It was a carefree kind of life, living comfortably at home with my family; taking an odd engagement here and there; working up the scanty viola repertoire for Ellenberger; writing fugues for Dr. Horner; practising Kuhlau for Fred Warren; and, when I could persuade her to evade her onerous household duties, playing over some such work as the Hans Sitt Viola Concerto with my mother in the drawing-room. Occasionally I went into Nottingham of an evening to spend an hour or so at the Theatre Royal, where I sat in adoration while Gabrielle Ray, Zena Dare, Gertie Millar, or Marie Studholme charmed a packed house. At other times I laughed hysterically at the absurdities of Huntley Wright, Little Tich or Dan Leno. I never tired of exploring the endless passages and caves which lie beneath the houses in the old quarters of the city, which Charles Peace was said to have made good use of in his attempts to evade the Law. And then back to my practising and my writing.

What did the future hold for me? I was determined to take up music as a profession, but my father was apprehensive, for he knew what a precarious kind of life musicians led and what difficulties they encountered in trying to make both ends meet. Alas, matters were not improved by our local bank manager who came in one evening to Tenter Hill to go through some accounts with my father. Over the cigars which followed, Vine Hall asked my father what he proposed to do with me. Surely he was not thinking of letting me try to make a living out of music, for the boy would never make a success of it. He then brought home his point by quoting several instances of Nottinghamshire musicians who had never got further than being local celebrities. No, no—music as a career was out of the question. Why not put me into a safe job in the bank, starting as a clerk with a certainty of a rise after five years and with the prospect of becoming a branch manager and one day retiring on a pension? Of course I would be allowed to continue with my music as a hobby, but I would not be permitted to accept engagements professionally, the rules of the Management prohibiting this. Yes, the bank was the thing—a nice safe job. The conference went on far into the night, leaving my father very shaken, and to say I was shaken was under-estimating my feelings. My heart sank at the thought of my freedom and my music being taken from me. Then, after a long and anxious discussion with my mother, to which I was not admitted, my father, to my dismay, decided to act on Vine Hall's advice, and our bank manager thereupon began to make tentative enquiries as to vacancies on the staffs in the branches of the bank about the county. I protested vehemently that I was no good at figures, but my protests were useless and I was becoming more and more depressed. The timely arrival of a letter from

Gloucestershire, inviting me to stay with W. H. Harding, one-time curate at Hucknall and friend of the family, now vicar of Churcham, put out of my head for the time being, at any rate, the horrible subject of pounds, shillings and pence, and the even more horrible prospect of having to try to master that nightmare of all nightmares, figures.

* * * * *

I was met at Oakle Street Station by old Dobbs, the gardener, and shepherded across the fields to the Vicarage, standing surrounded with trees near the church, which faced on to a duck-pond and some pretty, old-fashioned cottages and a farmhouse, the whole commanding an extensive view of the Cotswold Hills on the one hand and the distant Welsh Mountains on the other. My stay with Harding at the comfortable old Vicarage, which was the first of many visits to follow, was one of the pleasantest holidays I had experienced. I knew, from the moment I met old Dobbs at the station, that I was going to enjoy my stay, and by the time I had been welcomed by my friend, unpacked my bag in the pleasant bedroom looking across the orchard to the fields and the distant mountains, become acquainted with the housekeeper and Bob, the fox-terrier, I already felt I was at home. My friend's housekeeper, besides being an excellent cook, was a past-master at the art of cutting sandwiches, which accomplishment stood us in good stead when a picnic was called for on the occasions when Harding and I set off on our bicycles to visit those parishioners who lived nearly a day's journey away. I enjoyed accompanying my friend on these outings and becoming acquainted with this lovely Gloucestershire which, had it not been for the glimpses of the Malvern Hills and the Welsh Mountains, might have been my native Nottinghamshire. Dinner was always awaiting us in the cool dining-room on our return, and afterwards we would sit in the garden in the warm evening among the sweet-smelling night-scented stock, talking over old times while Bob scratched about in the scrub looking for rats, and the bats flitted around our heads, the owls called to each other in the woods and the moon came up slowly over the old church tower—Harding with a cigar, me with a cigarette, and both with port. I felt very mature.

On Sunday mornings I always sat in the special pew reserved for the vicar's guests and did my best to live up to the standard which Harding expected of his parishioners by refraining from laughing when the old lady behind me sang 'Onward Christian Soldiers' in a high, tremulous voice, on one note. Dobbs, on these days of prayer, acted in the official capacity of organ-blower, and it was only on going behind the scenes one morning when Harding was trying over some new hymn that I realised the weight of the responsibility which rested upon the shoulders of the humble supplier of wind. The story came back to me of the organ-blower who, after the parson had given his short recital at the conclusion of each Sunday evening service, said, with much satisfaction: "That was a grand concert we gave this evening, sir!" "*I*, John, not *we!*" reproved the parson—then came the fateful evening when, in the middle of a moving passage, the organ mournfully petered out and a voice was heard coming from somewhere in the bowels of the instrument, "Now, sir! Is it *I* or *we?*"

* * * * *

Gloucester Cathedral saw us more than once during my visit, and it was here I made the acquaintance of Dr. Herbert Brewer (later Sir Herbert Brewer) and was taken up into the organ-loft to be initiated into the mysteries of manuals and stops, and of how he had to anticipate the choir and allow for the take-up of the organ by playing a trifle ahead of the singers, which seemed to me to be an almost impossible thing for any sensitive musician to achieve with satisfaction. No wonder the famous lecturer I heard in later years in London made the statement that there were *two* schools of accompanists, those who anticipated the artist and those who followed. Up to that moment I had always been led to believe that the true art of accompanying was for the opposing forces to act simultaneously. I remember my friend, Frederick Kiddle, after having played for a somewhat uncertain singer in a very difficult aria at Queen's Hall, coming up to me and asking me if he had acquitted himself all right, and on my confessing I had not noticed the accompaniment at all, he said: "You could not have paid me a greater compliment."

* * * * *

I loved staying with my friend at the old Vicarage—he was one of the easiest of men to get along with—and I never tired of wandering round the garden or lying lazily in the hammock in the orchard, listening to the drowsy humming of the bees or perhaps to the impending thunderstorm moving across the distant mountains. These were the days I loved; uncertain days; hot, stormy days; the days which made you feel that Nature was carrying out her plans strangely near to you and that at any moment you might be on the verge of comprehending something of this great mystery; the days which started in storm and ended in quiet, when every tree and flower seemed to be alive with busying, tiny creatures, and the sound of raindrops dripping gently on to the wet leaves or the sodden gravel outside the front door made you wonder whether it were safe to venture out to watch the grey owls teaching their little ones to fly in the twilight of the woods across the fields.

And then my dreams might be rudely awakened by the clanging of the front-door bell announcing one of the church workers, or perhaps it was a present of some grouse from Harding's neighbour, Sir Hubert Parry. The latter would be the cue, after dinner, for my friend and me to settle down in a couple of deep chairs in the drawing-room to discuss, in the soft lamplight, through the medium of the old harmonium, our favourites in music. Did I know Parry's 'Blest Pair of Sirens'? How did I like Elgar's new work, 'The Dream of Gerontius'? And so on and so on. And then Harding would pull himself up out of his chair and play some of his favourite hymn tunes, and I, in return, would play him some Edward German, some Tschaikowsky, or some Grieg, and sometimes even a selection from the musical comedies of Lionel Monckton or Paul Rubens was included in these joint recitals. Then my host would ask me about my ambitions. Was I going in for music as a profession? Had I considered teaching music? Why did I not get my father to let me go up to the 'Varsity and work for a Doctor's degree? It would be so useful when applying for a post. What did my father think of my chances of making a success as a musician? What did I think of my chances myself? What did I think! If only I could be allowed to go in for music, but, at that moment, everything seemed set against me. The pleasant drawing-room became misty and in its place I saw Vine Hall, closeted with my father, waxing eloquent on the advantages of a banking career—and my heart sank within me. I had already heard that our bank manager had warned my father I should end my days ekeing out a miserable existence in some music-hall if he were foolish enough as to let me take up music as a profession. The bank loomed ominously near.

* * * * *

My stay at Churcham came to an end all too soon, and my regret at having to take my leave of four such good friends was considerable. I say 'four' because, besides my host, there were the housekeeper, old Dobbs and Bob the fox-terrier, who had more than done their share in making my stay at the Vicarage such a happy one, and I honestly believe they were even a little sorry to say goodbye to me. I just had time for one more stroll round the grounds before breakfast; a last look from my bedroom window at the distant mountains; down the three worn steps for a last look at the old flagged kitchen; a last look at the Cotswolds from the little church; a last look at the duck-pond, the cottages and the farmhouse, and here I was, seated alone in a first-class carriage (an extravagence which has never left me) with my suitcase beside me, my bicycle safely tucked away in the guard's van, and with dear old Dobbs's parting words ringing in my ears as the train moved slowly along the platform: "Goodbye, Surr; come back again soon."

* * * * *

It was our wretched Vine Hall who, thinking he was acting for the best, had caused all the trouble, and now it was a case of either taking up the post which he had unluckily found for me in a bank at Ilkeston or following Ellenberger's advice and going to study in Berlin, or going up to the 'Varsity, which was the course urged by my friend at Churcham. It was a difficult problem; with Vine Hall assuring my father I would assuredly die in penury if I went on with my music professionally; Ellenberger warning him I would end my days playing in theatres if I did not go to Germany (to give him his due, to him the bank idea was unthinkable); and Harding insisting that two or three years at Cambridge was the obvious and only possible course to take. Dr. Horner, fortunately, adopted a neutral attitude over the whole affair, for if my parents had had a fourth agitator to contend with I firmly believe that, out of sheer desperation, I should have been sent off forthwith to mess up the banking accounts of the unfortunate inhabitants of Ilkeston. My father and mother and I thereupon met in council to endeavour to thrash the matter out. Germany came first on the list—quite definitely I did not want to go there. My parents agreed that the idea was not a good one, for my eldest sister, who had studied the piano for several years in Berlin, had, on her return home, never touched the instrument again —so Berlin was ruled out.

Next came the 'Varsity—no, I would far rather get down to trying to earn my living at once. Look at my brother, Gwyn—he had had the opportunity of going up to Cambridge, but had preferred to start immediately on leaving school to study the workings of the colliery and, because his heart was in it, had made a success. Why could I not go up to London? I could have a shot at it and, at any rate, I should soon know whether I was going to make a success or not. The idea of going into a bank was becoming more and more intolerable—I could never make a 'go' of clerking, with my hopeless inaptitude for figures, whatever Vine Hall might say. Had my father forgotten the day when he was forced to take me away from school on account of these very figures getting me down to such an extent that I was quite ill?

Yes, figures certainly never were my strong point and even today I am compelled to make calculations on my fingers, which makes any sort of addition beyond ten somewhat complicated unless I resort to the not altogether convenient expedient of calling on my toes to help me out. I must admit, however, that I once had a compliment paid me in this respect by the Editor of the London *Daily Express*. It was the occasion of a caricature of myself which appeared in the *Daily Express* with the label underneath: 'Eric Coates, famous composer, who started life as a bank clerk.'

I wrote to the Editor pointing out the inaccuracy of his statement and the following neat correction appeared in the next day's issue of his paper: 'It seems that I paid composer Eric Coates an unintentional compliment when I said that he had once been a bank clerk. He chides me gently in a letter, which concludes: "Knowing my complete inability to add two and two together correctly, you can imagine how flattered I am by your statement. I am afraid no bank would ever have given me a job." Mr. Coates is unduly modest. He can handle notes better than any bank clerk.'

* * * * *

They say it is always darkest before the dawn. Just then, hot from the Royal Academy of Music, London, came Fred Hodgkinson, to have tea with us at Tenter Hill. How I blessed the thought that had prompted me to ask him over, for his enthusiasm about his experiences in London was infectious. We were all infected, even my father. "Doctor—you *must* let Eric go up to the Royal Academy of Music. Get him with Lionel Tertis for the viola and Frederick Corder for composition. If you don't let him go to London he will end his days arranging the music-stands for Georg Ellenberger!"

Lionel Tertis and Frederick Corder! How marvellous it would be to be taught by the viola player who was being talked about as being the greatest living exponent of the instrument! And Frederick Corder, who had had so many well-known composers through his hands!

Matters now rested with my father. It was a difficult decision for him to make. London, or the bank on the road to Derby. The latter a certainty and the former an unknown quantity. And so for some days my fate hung in the balance and I spent a miserable week wandering about the country lanes on my bicycle thinking of ledgers and banking-accounts and stocks and shares and all the hundred and one horrors associated with money. I was far too depressed to think about music, in fact I had more or less made up my mind that, so far as my viola was concerned, it was the end. And anyhow, what chance had I against people like Vine Hall who, with the best intentions, seemed determined to prevent my father from allowing me to continue with my music? I had got to the state when I would quite cheerfully have jumped into the River Trent at its deepest when my father came up to scratch and, despite opposition from all the 'Vine Halls' in Hucknall (and there were a great number), decided to send me up to London to study at the Royal Academy of Music, with the condition that if I had not shown signs of making a success by the end of a year I was to return to Hucknall to take up the post which, Vine Hall had assured him, would be waiting for me. The River Trent, the bank in Ilkeston and even my trusty bicycle were all forgotten in my relief at the turn events had taken. I could have burst with excitement.

Many letters passed between Hucknall and London during the next few weeks and I was in a fever to be off. At last the day came for me to pack my bag and take my leave of my good friends in Nottingham (the serious Georg Ellenberger, the kindly Ralph Horner, the cheery Fred Warren, the enthusiastic Waterfield) and finally, of my beloved family.

* * * * *

As I sat in the train bearing me south through the pleasant Nottinghamshire countryside, away from the scenes of my happy carefree childhood to unknown adventures in the great metropolis, my thoughts turned to the modest bank on the road to Derby. How blessed I was to have been spared the dismal prospect of having to spend the rest of my life adding up other people's money incorrectly and how fortunate for the bank manager to have had such an escape!

* * * * *

EXIT THE BANK! ENTER HOPEFUL MUSICIAN WITH SMALL VIOLA CASE AND BIG IDEAS.

SECOND MOVEMENT

LENTO—ANDANTE—ALLEGRO

SECOND MOVEMENT

LENTO—ANDANTE—ALLEGRO

IT was in the pleasant, sunlit room on the first floor, looking down on to Tenterden Street, Hanover Square, that I first met that great musician, Sir Alexander Campbell Mackenzie, the Principal of the Royal Academy of Music. I had been more or less over-awed when I climbed up the stone steps to the front door of the old building, but these emotions were as naught compared to those I experienced when I was ushered by the general factotum of the Academy into The Presence. Of medium height; stoutish, with a marked stoop; eyes which gleamed mischievously at you through pince-nez perched at such an angle that they looked as if they might fall off at any moment and a massive forehead topped by one of the greatest heads I had ever seen. When he spoke, you felt as if you were miles away on the Scottish moors (and I am quite sure *he* did!), for his accent was broad indeed and he appeared to delight in it. When he smiled, which was often, it was as if the sun had suddenly come out from behind a cloud; when he did the other thing, which I was to find was equally frequent, it was wise to beat a hasty retreat and hide in some convenient spot where his wrath could not reach you. His sense of humour was of the keenest and when he laughed he literally laughed all over. At other times his fury, which was a wonder to behold, would leave him completely speechless, but this incoherence seldom lasted for long, and after a few caustic remarks his face would relax into one of his seraphic smiles and his wrath would be forgotten. He had an unpleasant habit of walking round and round the room when interviewing you, which had the effect of making the interviewed feel at a disadvantage. I dread to think what would have happened if you had dared to follow him round. Professors and students alike feared to cross his path, but to me he was the kindest and most understanding of men, and all the years I knew him, up to the time of his death in 1935, it was my privilege to be called his friend. Harpists, singers and modern music were his abomination.

* * * * *

It was the early autumn of 1906. I had come carrying my viola and armed with my latest efforts in composition, which included three settings of poems by Robert Burns for soprano and orchestra.

After having played my piece on the viola, accompanied by Welton Hickin, at that time the official accompanist to the Institution, I nervously took my precious manuscripts out of the small viola case already referred to, (the Hopeful Musician with Big Ideas already beginning to feel rather small,) and placed them on the piano. Sir Alexander's sharp eyes immediately lighted on his fellow countryman's name, and the settings of the verses by the one-time plough-boy were the first chosen for hearing. My heart fell, for there was no singer. There was nothing for it but to play the melodies on the viola, and so, as I screwed up my courage and prayed that the accompanist would be able to read manuscript, the performance began. How Welton Hickin would have laughed if he could have read my thoughts at that moment. The first song—no comment; the second and then the third. A long pause. Was I going to be admitted as a student? Perhaps the Principal thought I was no good. I felt like picking up my viola and my wretched manuscripts and making a bolt for it. And then Sir Alexander, peeping at me over the pince-nez with which I was to become so familiar, delivered judgment: "Ye shall take composition as Principal Study and viola as Second Study." A good deal of argument followed about this.

Sir Alexander was evidently pleased with my playing but I think my having set Scottish poems to music had touched him. I pointed out how important it was for me to earn my living as soon as possible and also told him about the bank which was waiting for me if I did not make good in London soon.

He agreed with me about the viola being the best bread-winner at the moment and finished up by saying: "We'll give ye the best start we can. Ye shall have Lionel Tertis for viola, Hartley Braithwaite for pianoforte and Frederick Corder for harmony and composition. But, mark my words, young man, ye'll start as a viola player but ye'll end up as a composer!"

There was no doubt that my innocently having set Robert Burns's 'My Love is like the red, red rose' to music had stood me in good stead.

*   *   *   *   *

My place of residence was up a long, dark flight of stairs over a haberdashery store in the Kilburn High Road, where my pseudo maiden-aunt and old friend of my mother's family lived in state with a neat little maid and a large, very spoilt spaniel which answered to the misleading name of Tiny. My aunt was kindliness itself and very well-meaning, but the responsibility of having a young man under her roof rested so heavily on her shoulders that I was soon to discover my every movement being watched. She was delicate almost to the point of frailty and loved being waited on. When she took her walks abroad she donned a poke-bonnet, large black stole, immaculate white kid gloves and shining high boots. She was musical, but her quotations, being rarely accurate, were disturbing.

* * * * *

In an atmosphere of sweet-smelling potpourri, with the sounds of the traffic far below in the street coming gently through the open windows, we drank weak China tea out of old and priceless teacups and consumed dainty sandwiches and thin slices of home-made cake, while we talked about the doings at Tenter Hill and I delivered to my hostess the many personal messages from my family. At the end of the ceremony, which was prolonged, I was invited, as a great gesture, to smoke one cigarette. I was then introduced to my bedroom, a comfortable little room at the back, looking out over the chimney-pots to the trees round about West Hampstead. There was a disquieting Tin Affair in the yard at the base of the building outside my window, which turned out to be a kind of church hall where on Fridays, on my retiring early to bed after a heavy day at the Academy, fearful sounds of 'revelry by night' disturbed my slumbers. I blush to confess that I collected a little store of ammunition in the form of pebbles, to drop on to the corrugated roof when the rioting became too offensive. At least this had the effect of silencing the merrymakers while they searched in the darkness for the intruder.

The following morning found me seated on the top of a rickety old horse-bus, bumping uncomfortably over the cobbles of the Kilburn High Road on my way to the Royal Academy of Music for the first day of term. I can well recollect my feelings on this eventful day. A sensation of excitement tinged with nervousness and apprehension at what I was going to find. What would Lionel Tertis be like? Would Frederick Corder be as understanding as Dr. Horner? And fancy being compelled to take piano lessons! It did seem absurd, as I had no intention of becoming a pianist. And what would the students themselves think of the new arrival?

By the time I had crossed Hanover Square and the famous old house in Tenterden Street was in sight, I realised that I was not the only person carrying a case. There were dozens of them. Violin cases; viola cases; 'cello cases; small cases (obviously containing flutes or clarinets or some such wood-wind instruments); plain music cases; every kind of case. Elderly serious-looking men walking side by side with young men—probably professors with their favourite pupils, I thought. Groups of elderly serious-looking men and women—probably all professors. Tall girls; small girls; pale, weedy-looking youths who looked as if they could have done with a jolly good bicycle run along the Fosse Way to get some colour into their cheeks; and even one or two boys and girls not yet in their teens— and all chattering nineteen to the dozen.

As I walked for the second time up the steps and in under the old porch in company with this motley crowd, my heart, which at the best of times beats rather quickly, thumped so noisily that I was brought well nigh to suffocation. "Mr. Tertis's room? What name?" And then, having deposited my coat and hat in the men's cloakroom at the end of the long, dark passage (where I discovered to my discomfort that all the male students wore their hair short), I stumbled up the equally dark staircase to my professor's room, vowing that the next thing to do would be to find the nearest barber and have it all taken off at once. What Lionel Tertis thought of the entrance into his class of the new pupil, with his red cheeks and long hair, smelling strongly of Harris tweed, I never knew, for he kept his thoughts to himself. I was at last in the presence of the Great Master and, mercifully for me, he was alone.

What hands! What fingers! And what an enormous viola! I could not describe my first impressions of Lionel Tertis—I was in far too excited a state to notice anything except his hands and his instrument, though I remember his smile was irresistible.

My little Testori was taken out of its case and closely examined. Much too small, was the verdict. We must try and find a larger one when we can. Then my treasured Tourte bow was the next thing to come under scrutiny. Yes, that was good—well balanced. My master then seated himself at the piano and, praying that no one would come into the room while I was playing, I stumbled through some Tartini. (I don't mind admitting that he played the piano a great deal better than I played the viola!) Not at all bad. An excellent bow-arm (how pleased Ellenberger would have been) but not a very good left hand. I should have to work hard at tone production first, though, and then technique later on. Could I put up with practising nothing but slow bowings for the next month or so? I should have plenty of playing otherwise in the weekly orchestral practices. Of course I could. To please the master I would do anything. And with an encouraging smile and "That's the spirit!" I settled down to my first lesson. His tone was glorious —if only I could make my viola sound one-tenth as lovely I would practise slow bowing for the rest of my life. I could feel he was a fine teacher, but what his playing was like I could not imagine. If his technique were anything like his tone he must be an amazing artist. Perhaps before long I should have the opportunity of hearing him—probably when I was a little more advanced and it might be necessary for him to demonstrate some passage or other. I left the room just as his next pupil was arriving, and after a quick introduction, a last word of encouragement from my master and a fleeting glance at the young lady from myself I ran happily down the stairs to put my viola case away in the waiting-room. Had I time to find that barber before I presented myself, before Frederick Corder? I dared not enquire of the hall porter where I could find someone to shave my locks off, in case he should notice how terribly long my hair really was, so I pulled my hat well over my ears, pushing the offending stuff well inside, and fortunately found a policeman just round the corner in New Bond Street. In a few minutes I was seated in the chair explaining at length to the operator that I had been away for a long time in a remote part of the world where such things as barbers were unknown.

* * * * *

Frederick Corder's room was full of brainy-looking students when I nervously knocked at the door and sat down in a corner as far away from the maestro as I could. This gave me an opportunity of taking stock of the great man at a comfortable distance. He was busy going through a complicated-looking manuscript which had been placed on the piano in front of him by an equally complicated-looking youth. He did not seem altogether to approve of the effort, judging by the way in which he criticised this and criticised that.

By the time he had dealt with the complicated youth and his complicated manuscript he was becoming cynical, and the next victim went through it good and proper. My first thoughts, as I sat in my chair and watched, were of what a perfect mandarin he would have made, with his huge drooping moustache, his slightly almond-shaped eyes, his bushy eyebrows, his great bald head and the fringe of dark hair which ran round the back of his neck just above his collar. When he smiled, he gave you the impression of being more cynical than ever and his likeness to a mandarin was quite unbelievable. I was soon to discover what accounted for his critical attitude towards some of his pupils, for he detested the modern thought in music and, as many of the would-be composers who were in his care in those days were just as unpleasant to listen to as some of the young students of to-day, he must have had a good deal to put up with.

I must have sat waiting for quite three-quarters of an hour; at any rate it gave me time, besides watching and listening to what was going on between professor and pupils, to compose my one and only Limerick, which was to go the round of the Academy later on and which, I trust and hope, never reached the ears of my beloved mandarin. . . .

> There was a professor named Corder
> Who wrote a Cantata to order;
> The strain was so great
> That the hair left his pate
> Save the back, where's there's just a small border.

"Where's my new pupil?"

A friendly greeting followed by a few preliminary questions, and I was seated by the side of my professor with the manuscripts, which had stood me in such good stead with the Principal, on the piano.

* * * * *

Corder was impressed with my song-cycle, but said he would like to see me try my hand at something more ambitious and suggested my making a sketch of the first movement of a symphony for my next lesson. On my assuring him that I wanted to specialise in the lighter type of writing, he immediately began a discourse on Arthur Sullivan, which led him on to Edward German and Goring-Thomas, both of whom had been his pupils. He talked delightfully and when he was interested in his subject he waxed quite eloquent and his unusual face would light up with enthusiasm. Then he would smile his kindly smile and suggest our reading some score or other together, and out would come the published full-score of Sullivan's Overture to 'The Mikado', which we would prop up somehow or other on the piano and, he taking the treble instruments and I the bass, we would plod along contentedly until the arrival of his next pupil, at which moment he would drop his hands on to his knees, heave a deep sigh, shrug his shoulders and with a rueful expression close the music. They were delightful hours, these hours I spent with Corder.

My lessons, which were officially only supposed to be of twenty minutes' duration twice a week, became longer and longer, and it was quite a frequent occurrence to be at the side of my master for over an hour at a time. Sometimes talking, sometimes playing, another time hearing his own personal experiences with the great masters; Richard Wagner (how he used to bang out his tunes for hours on end on his little upright piano); Anton Dvorák (and his lack of personal cleanliness); Edvard Grieg; Goring-Thomas; and Edward German (who could hold on a pedal-note longer than anyone else without making it sound uninteresting).

During the first week of term, except for my three masters, the Principal, and the general factotum of the Academy, Green, I did not speak to a soul, and I felt very much out of everything. Everybody seemed to know everyone else and except for an occasional enquiring glance in my direction I might not have existed.

"You're a new student, aren't you? Viola, isn't it?"

It was a fair-haired boy with the most engaging smile who addressed me. On my admitting that I was, he said:

"Come over and have tea with me at the Blenheim Restaurant—I'll introduce you to some of the boys." My new friend took me by the arm and we were soon chatting together at a little table in the window on the first floor of what was nicknamed in those days 'The R.A.M. Students' Club'. It appeared he was studying the organ and that his home was somewhere in Surrey. We talked about our respective ambitions and I was soon telling him about my father and mother and about the little bank waiting for me on the road to Derby.

From that moment we became fast friends and many were the talks which were to follow in the sunny window looking down New Bond Street.

The Blenheim Restaurant, being so near to Tenterden Street, was an admirable rendezvous for the students and it was upstairs (where you could buy a cup of tea or coffee and a bun for a few pence at any time of the day without being frowned upon by the waitresses) that I first made the acquaintance of many life-long friends. In the spacious room on the ground floor you were obliged to order a proper meal, and as most of the population of the Academy were on the verge of bankruptcy a cup of tea or coffee and a bun upstairs was usually the order of the day. Sometimes when we were feeling unusually affluent or particularly hungry a pork-pie cut in half would be devoured with relish. These poisonous-looking slabs were known affectionately by the clientèle as a 'half-sunset', on account of the sliced eggs inside having a remarkable resemblance to the Hunter of the East as he reverts to the West at the end of the day. Half, for the very good reason that we could not afford a whole.

And so the first term passed. It was hard work, for besides my exacting studies with Corder (harmony, counterpoint, canon, fugue

—and, believe it or not, I wrote a short fugue for him every week), there were my slow-bowing exercises for Tertis (three and sometimes four hours a day), piano-lessons with Hartley Braithwaite (a sub-professor, and commonly known as 'Hartley's Marmalade'), sight-singing with Arthur Eyres and orchestral practices twice a week under the Principal. The sight-singing with Eyres was a thing to be seen and heard, to be believed. The musical dictation part was not so bad, for you were able to do this in silence, but when it came to the actual singing, it was disastrous.

To hear York Bowen delivering himself in a high falsetto voice; or Myra Hess making herself believe she was a baritone, being asked to sing a tune in the bass clef; or Montague Phillips being given a melody in such a high key that he blossomed out into a soprano; or Benjamin Dale wrestling with bass notes fathoms below his natural voice (unfortunately Arnold Bax had long since finished with such things as sight-singing classes, for I would have loved to have heard him sing); and the first horrible occasion when Eyres, after having chalked up on the board a tune covering a compass of three octaves, fixed his cold steely eyes on the new viola player and ordered me to do my worst. The exhibition which followed involved my crawling up through the bass into the tenor, then into a shrill falsetto, concluding in a piercing scream. Unluckily for me, this fantastic performance was my undoing, for from the moment that Eyres discovered that reading at sight presented no difficulties for me it became his wont to write up on the board tunes which I shrewdly suspect he had composed specially for me to demonstrate, for no publisher would ever have entertained them. At any rate, after a while, this became so obvious that when a more than usually complicated-looking affair was chalked up, a murmur would ripple round the class of "Coates—Coates!"—and sure enough, Eyres, with a knowing smile, would single me out to do my stuff.

* * * * *

The orchestral practices with the Principal took place on Tuesdays from two till five, with a welcome break for tea at four, and on Fridays from three till five. Tuesday was the 'star turn', for on that day only the most advanced students were permitted to perform to the accompaniment of a full orchestra. The Friday practices, in which a smaller orchestra was employed, were reserved for those students who were in a lower grade and from whom not so much was expected. Hence the innumerable ruses resorted to by both professors and pupils to get their names down on the list for the more important occasion, as appearing at the 'Fridays' had the result of stamping one as a mere beginner. You can imagine with what scant respect the Friday rehearsals were treated when a facetious pupil, on being asked at one of the examinations at end of term to give an example of a discord, replied, "The R.A.M. Orchestra on a Friday." The examiners were evidently in agreement with this unexpected sally and I believe the remark was long chuckled over in the Principal's room afterwards.

Green, the general factotum of the Academy, was greatly in evidence at these orchestral gatherings in the Concert Hall. Green was a character; tallish; dark, with rather soulful eyes; round shoulders; thin hair parted slightly at the side with a suggestion of a forelock; a drooping moustache; and very splay-footed, which caused him to walk with an astonishing gait something between a shuffle and a limp. His mode of address when he came to know you well was by simply quoting the first letter of your surname: 'Mr. C.' or 'Miss B.' and so on. He was a kindly fellow and, being the butt of every soul in the Academy, was fortunately slow to anger.

Being a Tertis pupil, I was allowed to sit at the first desk of the violas, playing next to the professional who was always called in to act as principal. Most of the various sections of the orchestra were led by specially-engaged players and in some cases I did not envy their jobs, as a number of the very advanced students, although not so experienced in orchestral technique as were their professional brothers, could have played their heads off when it came to the solo passages. Occasionally the leader of the orchestra would gracefully permit his student-partner to take over when a more than usually difficult solo presented itself, probably quite glad to be relieved of the responsibility. I know, in later years, how willingly I would have handed over to my colleague at Queen's Hall some of the unmanageable and unviolistic solos which I met with in many of the efforts of the so-called orchestral writers of that decade.

I found these rehearsals instructive on the whole, though I fear I derived more fun from them than anything, but on hot summer afternoons, especially when I was deputising at some of the West End theatres during the evenings, they became tedious in the extreme. The Principal was in his element at the head of the orchestra, and when he was not raging at some wretched singer or harpist who, through sheer nervousness, would keep making an entry before the beat, he would entertain the company with every conceivable kind of joke, very often at the expense of some unfortunate member of the ensemble. He had a passion for digging up unknown overtures by long-forgotten French composers or the lesser-known works by composers such as Dvorák, and would spend hours plodding through some of the duller compositions of Sterndale Bennett and Walter Macfarren. However, I was glad to have the opportunity, during these tiresome afternoons, of becoming acquainted with some of the works by my Scottish friend and I think it a pity that, in these days of so much ugly musical thought, the name of A. C. Mackenzie should appear so infrequently in our programmes.

The Principal of the R.A.M. was not an inspiring conductor, for, like most composers, his tempi were very much on the slow side; in fact, so slow would they sometimes become that it was difficult, if you entered the Concert Hall during the performance of a symphony or some such work, to come to any definite conclusion as to what movement was being played. I do not think the make-up of the orchestra improved matters, particularly in the string section, where the lack of balance was deplorable. It was a question of quantity rather than of quality. Between fifteen and twenty first violins, hundreds of seconds, six to eight violas (when you were lucky), a fair body of 'cellos and three or four 'basses. The woodwind on the whole was good, the horns fair, and the brass bad. The unfortunate percussion instruments went through a trying time, being pulled about by students whose fingers were itching to have a whack at that inviting-looking bass-drum; the kettle-drums, although presenting just as inviting an appearance as the bass-drum, wanted a bit more managing, and, besides, the tuning was such an infernal nuisance. And so, between the slowness of the Principal and the unbalanced and cumbersome body of instrumentalists, most of the performances gave the listener an impression of one of the larger denizens of the forest awakening from slumber. The composer-students generally had a raw deal when they appeared at the side of the Principal for a run-through of a new work. I can still see Montague Phillips scowling at the members of the orchestra while his cherished manuscript was being ruthlessly turned by Sir Alexander from a sparkling Scherzo into a sober Moderato, and the latter, on being requested to 'hot-up' the proceedings, turning furiously on the composer, telling him it was quite fast enough and that if he thought he was going to take it any faster he was wrong. B. Walton O'Donnell, who was later to become the conductor of the B.B.C. Military Band, at that time showing great virtuosity as both composer and 'cellist, one day brought up a song with orchestral accompaniment in which the principal viola was given one of the most intricate and sky-scraping cadenzas it has ever been my lot to meet. What he had done with the voice-part was nobody's business, though I expect the present generation would have thought nothing of it. Between the screams of the singer, the heroic attempts of the leader of the violas to master the impossible arpeggi, double-stopping and chromatic scales of this fancy-waistcoat of a solo, the interruptions from the frantic composer and the furious outbursts from Mackenzie himself, the uproar which resulted from this extraordinary foursome and the consequent dismissal from the platform of the bewildered and equally furious song-writer (who rushed wildly away as his full-score was being hurled by Mackenzie into the bowels of the orchestra), put a stop, at any rate for a few breathless minutes, to that dramatic afternoon's rehearsal. To argue with Mackenzie was more than useless, nay, it was fatal. The only thing to do was to approach him with every artifice of diplomacy that you had at your command and put yourself completely in his hands, always making your request in a low voice. After all, you cannot very well criticise the Head in front of the whole school (at any rate not out loud), which is what it amounted to.

How bored we used to become with those often dreary afternoons, so bored in fact that we almost prayed aloud that some more composers would appear in front of us, or perhaps some singer who had no sense of rhythm, or, best of all, that breaker of all rhythms (at least in those days), a harpist. Put a harpist up in front of the Principal, and we knew that in a few moments we should be 'well away' and about to hear Mackenzie deliver himself in his glorious Scottish accent on the horrors of harps and harpists in general, not to mention any music composed by any composer for this, the most ancient of all instruments. He would rave, stamp his feet, become incoherent and finally get down from the rostrum and take a stroll round the hall with measured tread, while the shivering soloist took refuge behind the strings of the object of the Principal's displeasure. I remember one such scene. After the terrible and silent promenade was over, the conductor remounted the rostrum, turned to the harpist and remarked, with a heavenly smile: "Ye know, me deer, what ye want is an india-rubber band!"

I'm afraid our Principal, through his uncertain temper, rarely got the best out of those students who showed signs of nervousness when about to begin some well-worn concerto, and I was not feeling happy at the prospect of taking up my stand one day, in full view of the orchestra, to hear for the first time and under such terrifying conditions the new songs for baritone and orchestra which I had been working at all the term.

I regret to have to confess that when the rehearsals became too much for me, in so far as boredom was concerned, a good deal of the time was spent either carrying on a whispered conversation with the girl on my left, if she happened to be attractive, or taking a welcome forty winks, or just managing to keep awake by indulging in a game I invented. This consisted of changing the musical indications in the viola parts by substituting or adding a capital B either in the place of or in front of the first letter of each word, as for instance: 'Bolto Ballegro', 'Boco Biu Bosso', 'Bit Bogen', 'Ba Bempi', 'Bas Bi Bite', 'Bon Buoco'. Some of the words I hit on inadvertently had to be hastily scratched out to avoid a riot in the viola team. If you search diligently you will find some of these 'time-wasters' in certain of the viola parts at the Royal Academy of Music until this day, and in later years, as I was happily able to introduce this B pastime into the ranks of the violas at Queen's Hall, there are still to be found a few notable examples of the System in the viola parts of the Music Library of what was once the Queen's Hall Orchestra, the earliest being those by Sir Henry Wood's one-time principal viola.

The forty-wink dodge was the most difficult to achieve, unless the piano lid were raised for the performance of some concerto, in which case you had a perfect ready-made screen to shelter you from the piercing gaze of the hazardously-perched pince-nez of the Principal. But woe betide you if the lid were lowered while you were still in a state of coma. It happened to me once, and once only. I came to, conscious of a deathly silence, to hear the Principal announcing: "When Coates condescends to wake up, we'll continue with the rehearsal."

* * * * *

My first term at the Academy was very hard work, practically every hour of the day being taken up with practising the viola, writing music, viola and composition lessons, ensemble classes, sight-singing, orchestral rehearsals and journeying up and down from Kilburn four or five times a week on the top of that jolting old horse-bus. Forty minutes twice a day on top in all weathers. On wet days, if you managed to find a place in the front seat, you received a certain amount of shelter from the driver, that is, if he happened to be of the bulky-frame type, otherwise you had to do the best you could to keep the top part of you dry by running the risk of having your umbrella blown inside-out and using the scanty waterproof apron provided by the Omnibus Company to prevent the stream from your umbrella filling the turn-ups of your trousers and running down into your shoes. To do all this with a viola case and a music case on your knees was no mean feat, and when it came to climbing down the awkward spiral staircase to the platform below, clutching the two cases and the umbrella, you ran the risk of ending the day in the infirmary. Maida Vale on a winter's morning was a veritable skating-rink and it was a common occurrence for all the occupants of the 'bus to clamber out on to the frozen road to assist the conductor in unharnessing the horses, who had been doing their best to kick the shafts to pieces while lying on the ground. For some unaccountable reason, the rules of the company did not permit the driver to leave his seat on the box, so he contented himself by shouting instructions to the sliding, struggling crowd below. On one occasion an American passenger, ignorant of the rule compelling the driver to assume a neutral attitude when the horses and the passengers came to blows, shouted up to the top-hatted coachman: "What's the matter with you? Are you waiting for an introduction to the horses?" The driver was so nonplussed at the unexpected interrogation that, to the astonishment of all, he unstrapped himself and descended. I remember that we were all considerably annoyed to think that it had taken an American to achieve this minor miracle.

Later on, when my activities commenced in a professional capacity and I was picking up a half-guinea date here and there and an occasional guinea (known in the orchestral world at that time as a 'one-one'), and I was able, when time pressed, to enjoy the comfort of a hansom-cab, my adventures in the world of travel grew apace. The old-fashioned hansom, with its folding doors which clasped you to their bosoms, the funny little trapdoor over your head through which you could carry on affectionate, or sometimes otherwise, conversations with the top-hatted Cockney aloft, and, before all, the horse with the little jingling bells hanging from the bridle—it was a pretty sight and a pleasant sound to see and to hear, these carriages of the past wending their way through the quiet snow, especially if the horse were a high-stepper and the driver knew how to show him off to advantage. The taxi-cab of today is, of course, a much quicker and in many ways a more comfortable means of getting about, but if you were fortunate enough to be in the company of someone with whom you wished to waste time, the hansom-cab, during my early days in London, left nothing to be desired. A word to the sympathetic cabby, and the little trapdoor would be discreetly closed and you could trust your friend overhead, while driving you slowly through the deserted streets, to use his own judgment as to when he thought you had been given sufficient time to say all that your heart was feeling. But I found to my discomfort that it was out of the question, besides being dangerous, to expect any kind of speed from these antiquated though fascinating relics of the past, unless the roads were dry and you were fortunate in having a good horse in front of you and an experienced driver above. I remember one wintry night when the snow lay so deep that you could not distinguish road from pavement, driving along that death-trap of all death-traps, Maida Vale, to fulfil an engagement at some private house, urging the harassed cabby to make haste if he did not want me to be late. The words, "All right, sir, I'm doing my best" were no sooner out of his mouth, than the horse, overstepping itself, slithered along the icy snow and went down, and before I knew what had happened I was pitched head-first into the snow, viola, music case and all.

As I say, it was hard work, this first term at the Academy, for at the end of an exacting day the forty-minute bus journey to Kilburn and the climbing of the seventy-five stairs to the top of the haberdashery store, where my spurious aunt lived with her neat little maid and her fat spaniel, were not conducive to settling down to a couple of hours' slow-bowing exercises with my viola or endeavouring to work out the exposition of the fugue which had to be delivered to Corder the following day. There was an old-fashioned, upright Brinsmead in the little drawing-room (where my aunt and I took tea together on Sunday afternoons—my only afternoon at home), and it was here of an evening that I played over my contrapuntal exercises and, when I was alone, tried to find inspiration from the discoloured keys and the tinkling notes of this relic of a bygone age. My aunt would sometimes leave the warmth of her fireside in the next room and brave the chilliness of the drawing-room by wrapping a shawl around her shoulders to sit at my side while I gave her an impression of some of my latest musical ideas. It was drawing towards the winter, but not yet sufficiently cold to warrant the lighting of a fire in the best room specially for me. My aunt, whenever she rang the bell for her neat little maid to come in and fill up the coal-scuttle, always thought of those seventy-five stairs which had to be climbed by the exhausted coal-man when he delivered those weighty sacks each quarter and, in consequence, the fire burnt low in the old Victorian grate before we allowed ourselves the luxury of putting on another lump.

I usually climbed up into the loft above my bedroom to practise the viola, for here I could give way to the habit of pacing round and round while I persevered with those everlasting slow-bowings. If it was cold in the drawing-room, it was freezing under the draughty rafters of this sometime box-room, and my left hand used to become so numb that it was only with the greatest difficulty that I was able to put in more than half-an-hour's uninterrupted practising without having to go downstairs into the cosy kitchen to thaw.

After I had been at the Academy for about a month I was requested to report to Mr. Hans Wessely for ensemble playing. I had already heard more than I cared for about this temperamental violin professor, and was not looking forward to the experience of being included in his class. Hans Wessely, besides being of unusual appearance, was an extraordinary man. He was an excellent teacher and had a knack of getting his pupils on in a remarkable way, but I do not think I could have put up with him as a professor for two minutes. After I had been in his room for less than a quarter of an hour I had arrived at the conclusion that his pupils must either be very thick-skinned or else completely insensitive, to be able to submit to his lack of manners, and my thoughts turned to those delightful hours with Georg Ellenberger in that pretty music-room in Burns Street. I could not help comparing my old master with the excitable creature now standing over me screaming something about, "You are *flat! Now* PLAY!" and at the same moment crushing my left hand on to the strings until it was all I could do to prevent myself from getting up and hitting him. Any newcomer to these ensemble classes was made an object of ridicule, and poor jokes were made at the expense of the unhappy victim. For some time Wessely had been carrying on a feud with Tertis, to whom he had not spoken for many months, and as I imagine Tertis had managed to have the last word, the arrival in the class of a new viola student, and a Tertis pupil at that, had given Wessely the heaven-sent opportunity of getting his own back. And so I went through a nasty time. Everything was wrong—the special fingerings I had been given by Tertis were laughed at, my intonation was criticised, my bow-arm ridiculed, my technique called that of a poor amateur. Now Wessely was evidently not a good reader of character or he would have known better than to have bullied anyone with a quiet exterior, and one morning he entered the class-room to find himself the poorer by one viola player, and as viola students in those days were scarce I am pleased to be able to state that I was missed.

The excitable creature was thereupon forced to resort to the unsatisfactory expedient of coaching one of his own violin pupils in the art of producing a viola tone out of an instrument which sounded like a violin tuned down a fifth. The news spread all over the Academy that a new student had dared to defy the rules of the Institution which made attendance at the ensemble classes compulsory, and I was expecting to be expelled at any moment, when Corder, who was the Curator of the Academy at that time, requested me to go to his room to explain my non-appearance at the class on the third floor. Fortunately I knew my master well enough to open my heart to him and I think he must have sympathised with me, although he kept his counsel to himself; at any rate, nothing happened until one morning, in the entrance hall, I ran right into the arms of my persecutor. "Ah, Coates!" (he had an unpleasant way of holding his head back and talking over you when he spoke) "Ah Coates! You do not come any more to my class, hein?" There was nothing for it, so gathering up my courage I told him that I did not like his method or his manners and that so far as I was concerned his class could go to the devil. The upshot was that the violinist with the viola sounding like a violin tuned down a fifth was dispensed with, and the Tertis pupil was gladly welcomed back. From that day all was peace in the room on the third floor and, although I never really enjoyed playing in these classes, I never let Wessely down again.

On one occasion I almost felt sorry for this ogre of the ensembles, who I feel sure was well-meaning. It was a huge, phlegmatic Scotsman, a new pupil, who had just joined the class and he was going through the usual bullying with which we were all so familiar and, being without any temperament whatsoever, he was a perfect instrument for Wessely's sarcasm to play upon. The attacks grew in intensity and ridicule was heaped upon ridicule until at last the giant Scotsman, whom we had all been watching anxiously, began to change colour. His great hands trembling, his face reddening to the roots of his hair, he rose slowly from his seat, and placing his absurdly tiny-looking violin on the piano, he turned on our professor like an angry elephant, and taking him by the scruff of the neck, shook him till we could hear his teeth rattle. I have never seen a man look so frightened. As soon as our giant let go his grip, poor Wessely rushed to the door, intimating that he was going straight to the Principal to report the assault, and ran down the stairs with the Scotsman shouting after him: "Ye can tell anybody anything ye like! The next time I'll knock your head off!" We were told later by Green that when Mackenzie heard Wessely's story, the whole situation struck him as being so ludicrous that he roared with laughter. Expel a Scotsman? Not he!

Not all the ensemble classes at the Academy were distasteful, for I spent many happy and interesting hours studying quartet-playing under the well-known violinist, Louis Zimmermann, who had been brought over from Amsterdam to take up the post of Professor of the Violin at the Institution. Zimmermann was blessed with a delightful personality allied with a keen sense of humour, and what he did not know about quartet-playing was not worth bothering about. I think we all of us loved working with this fine musician and there is no doubt that our affection for him moved us to give him of our best. His enthusiasm and his energy when taking a class through some difficult movement were an inspiration.

As I write I can see Zimmermann bending over me, his hair standing up rather straight, peering at me through those thick-rimmed glasses of his, bow in hand, ready to set the tempo. I remember how when he wished to stress a point he would lapse into a mixture of French and German. It was "von lettle bit", "von idee", or "so feen"; trying to make us understand that it could always be just that tiny bit better, with the result that it was always a good deal better. His lack of command of the English language led him sometimes into saying things which left the young ladies of the class covered with confusion. They were so very strait-laced in those days, at least some of them were, so different from the younger generation of to-day. Can you imagine one of the young male students, on being invited by the professor to take off his coat because he looked hot, refusing to do so for lack of a waistcoat underneath, and the professor's observation of "Oh, I see you have only the chemise" bringing a blush to the cheeks of the young woman of the nineteen-fifties?

* * * * *

At last the monotonous slow-bowings came to an end, and although it had been an exacting ordeal for me, I was glad I had stuck to it for all these weeks. Tertis had said to me, on that first memorable day in his room at the top of the old wooden staircase overlooking the chimney-pots at the back of the Academy, "If you will put up with it for a little time, Eric, you will not know yourself" —and I certainly did not. The difference in my tone was remarkable and I think Tertis was satisfied with the improvement, and I am quite sure he was pleased to find that his new pupil had a streak of determination in him. I sometimes wonder whether he had given me this test to see the kind of stuff I was made of. And then began the gruelling business of technique and, as facility had never been one of my strong points, I started on a period which taxed my strength and my patience to the utmost. My master's command of the viola was incredible. I had thought that no one could have possessed such a technique as, or a more beautiful tone than, Oscar Nedbal, the viola player in the Bohemian String Quartet, but the sound which Tertis produced out of his huge instrument was something the like of which I had never heard before, and as for his technique, the more intricate the passage the more did it seem as naught to this great virtuoso. I wish it were within the capabilities of my pen to describe my sensations on first hearing the glorious tone which seemed to permeate the entire room. It went from a tremendously vital, white-hot fortissimo down to a trembling, limpid pianissimo so distant that it was difficult to sense whence the mysterious sound could be coming. (Later on, I heard Tertis many times in large concert halls, and on each occasion I marvelled at the way in which he could make the softest sound carry to the farthest corner of the building. It was almost ethereal.)

Scales, double-stoppings, arpeggi, fantastically-awkward passages, up and down staccato bowings, and all taken at such a breathless pace that it was bewildering. There was a time when the viola was resorted to by violinists who were not able to comply with the standard required if they wished to obtain a good position in one of the big Symphony Orchestras, for not so much was expected in those days of the 'Cinderella of the Orchestra'. But to-day things have changed, thanks to that champion of the viola, Lionel Tertis. Tertis, no matter who may come along in the future, will always remain a great figure, for besides having been the pioneer of the viola, his untiring efforts to raise the standard of this once-neglected instrument have resulted in its having come into its own at last.

I think I said some time previously that sight-reading came easily to me, and it was just the same when applied to the viola. I could play the most difficult passage at sight almost without fault, but when it came to playing the same phrase a second time it was never as good as that first once-over. In later years I was sometimes alluded to as 'the man who never practised'. I think this appellation must have arisen through my leaving my instrument at the Queen's Hall throughout an entire season and, on one occasion, in the cloakroom at Oxford Circus Tube Station for nearly six months. The reason for this latter seemingly extraordinary behaviour was that during that period I was playing at a theatre which did not possess a lock-up cupboard in the band-room, and the station cloakroom presented me with an admirable solution to the safety problem between performances and at the same time spared me the inconvenience of carrying my case up and down from my place of residence. I am not ashamed to admit that the thought of carrying anything, anywhere, at any time, has always appalled me, neither am I ashamed to confess that this dislike of portering has not decreased with age. I knew the more I practised the worse my playing would become, so I went my way, trying not to worry (an impossible thing to achieve at any time), and spent the days and most of the nights between writing my music and hoping that providence would continue to deliver me from coming up against a solo, particularly on the concert-platform, which it might be my misfortune to be able neither to read nor to play.

Time was to show that the fates had decided to be kind to me, and in 1919, the year in which I gave up my instrument to devote my energies solely to composing, I believe I quitted the orchestral-playing world with a high reputation; which goes to show that 'the man who never practised' was lucky in that he was never found out.

My ability to play intricate passages at sight sometimes had disastrous consequences. I remember, during one of my lessons with Tertis, having given a spectacular (for me) first performance of a certain difficult passage, and, anxious to show me off to his next pupil (who had just entered the room), Tertis asked me to play the phrase again. To me it was a foregone conclusion that this next attempt would turn out a failure. It was catastrophic. I never knew what my fellow-student's reactions were to my exhibition of virtuosity but I know that Tertis was furious. . . . Although playing in public was a great strain to me, and notwithstanding that I always paid for it afterwards, I usually contrived to come up to scratch all right, but when anyone handed me a viola and asked me to play on it with a view to giving my opinion of its qualities, I was 'floored'. In my orchestral days I used to listen with envy to the display of 'fireworks' which always went on in the band-room before a concert. In those days this form of show went by the name of 'band-room technique', for the simple reason that it was often those players who roused the envy of the open-mouthed personnel of the orchestra by their feats of virtuosity in the band-room who went to pieces on the platform. I can recall the case of a certain violinist whose wont it was to put to shame all the other 'band-room technique artists' by his dazzling demonstrations in the dingy room underneath the concert platform at Queen's Hall. His dexterity was astounding and we used to gather round him, urging him on to still more daring flights of technical extravagances. In the gloomy band-room he was Kubelik, Kreisler, Heifetz, all rolled into one. Imagine the excitement when he was put down to play a concerto at one of the concerts! The performance was dreadful: gone was the debonair manner; the fluent style; the easy staccato; the rush of those amazing scale-passages; the accuracy of those silvery harmonics; and in their place stood a trembling figure, whose nervous fingers, made worse by the perspiring left hand grasping the damp neck of that mockery of a violin and the shaking right arm endeavouring to control the vagaries of that obstinate bow, feverishly and hopelessly grappled with passages which any first-term student at the Royal Academy of

Music would have laughed at. Poor old fellow. I felt so sorry for him, for he was very kind-hearted underneath all that showy exterior, but I'm afraid his 'band-room technique' had been his undoing.

My one and only achievement in this sphere was a trick, and a completely useless one at that and one which I could not use in any practical sense, and this consisted of placing my bow on the strings of my viola, contracting the muscles of my right arm and at the same time setting up an extremely rapid nervous shiver, which produced a staccato so fast that it was impossible for the fingers of the left hand to keep pace with it. Sometimes when the 'band-room technique artists' were doing their worst and the air was trembling with the vibrations set up by exhibitions of execution which would have filled Paganini's heart with envy, I would retire quietly into a corner and get going with my stunt and await developments. As sure as fate the uproar would die down and the entire band-room (with the exception of the phlegmatic trombone players, who remained seated serenely at the other end of the room and who looked upon us as a lot of congenital idiots), the entire string-section, I should say, would surge down upon me just as I decided to put my viola down. "Come on, Eric! Let's hear it! Do it with the 'Moto Perpetuo'!" and so on. "Sorry boys! Too tired!" and my viola was already back in its case. I remember how Tertis laughed when he insisted on my giving him a demonstration of that super-staccato-bowing he had heard so much about, and on my reluctantly obliging, saying: "Eric! You *are* a mad boy!"

Then came the episode of the revolver. I cannot truthfully account for the circumstances which led up to my numbering among my possessions such a deadly instrument. It was a beautiful little thing, a silver-plated automatic Colt with a chamber holding eight metal cartridges skilfully concealed inside the grip. This dangerous little weapon, lying snugly in my hip-pocket and fully loaded, accompanied me on all my adventures, and when one of the students discovered I was in the habit of going about armed, my prestige, which up to that moment had been of the lowest, suddenly mounted to quite alarming proportions.

"Can't we hear it go off?"
"What does it feel like when you fire?"
"Has it got much of a 'kick'?"
"Would it kill a man?"
"Have you ever used it?"

And so, after a good deal of persuasion, a little party of four, consisting of two violinists, one violist and one 'cellist, trooped down the narrow, winding, wooden staircase to the men's lavatory, underneath the librarian's room. Here we held council together. It was decided that three of us should remain in the lavatory, taking 'pot-shots' in turn at an improvised target consisting of certain markings on the leaden wall, while the fourth watched and waited at the top of the stairs to warn us of the approach of any Academy official. The noise which followed was deafening and I wonder our eardrums survived the concussion which resulted from the letting off of the innocent-looking little silver object in the close confinement of this underground convenience. When one of the shots seemed to approach too dangerously close on its return journey we hit on the idea of firing at an angle so that the 'come-back' of that venomous-looking little brass bullet (what was left of it) would land at the other end of the wall behind us. It worked beautifully.

Then the fun waxed fast and furious, the magazine being charged again and again, while the atmosphere became more and more contaminated by the acrid fumes from the exploded cartridges. Suddenly a shout from the top of the stairs: "Look out, boys! Here's Chapman!" Now Chapman was the official librarian to the Royal Academy of Music and we had forgotten in the excitement of the 'tourney' that he spent his days just above the lavatory, sorting out the band-parts needed for the orchestral rehearsals. I don't think we were popular with Chapman, for we had already caused him a certain amount of trouble by staging a mock thunderstorm in the men's waiting-room, using muted-strings 'tremulando' for the wind and rain, a bass-drum for thunder, removing the pendulum from the clock so that its feverish ticking gave the effect of the passing of time, and flicking the electric-light switch up and down as quickly as possible to supply the lightning. (Thereby fusing the entire electric-light system at that end of the building.) Empty double-bass cases made it possible for the storm-makers to stage a disappearance worthy of the name of Maskelyne and Devant, for when our librarian made his entrance into the field of action, no one was to be found, and the excited culprits nearly gave themselves away when he was heard mumbling to himself: "I'm sure I heard a noise somewhere."

In the case of the shooting there was no doubt about his hearing a noise, but fortunately for us he could not place where the disturbance had come from, and after a look round he retired once more to the dust of his full-scores, leaving the coast clear for the four gunmen to emerge from the depths below, smelling horribly of gunpowder.

The next morning, on arriving at the Academy, we were met by the general factotum, who, with serious mien, told us of the sousing of the charwomen when they went down into the dungeon below the library to clean up before the day's rush began. It was more than a rush, it was a deluge. A waterspout might have been a more adequate description of the jets of squirting water which greeted the arrival in the men's lavatory of these denizens of the underworld of the Royal Academy of Music. They were soaked to the skin. The engineer was summoned to turn off the water, repair the pipes, assess the damage and make his report, which ended: "Whoever done it must have bin in the possession of a very sharp hinstrument, for the 'oles was drilled as clean as a whistle." As Green quoted this illuminating statement he put his hands deep into his trouser pockets and with a meaning look produced the shell of a spent cartridge which he handed to me with the words: "I think this belongs to you, Mr. C.!" Stout fellow, Green!

I got on well with old Chapman. He inhabited a musty room off the dark passage leading to the men's waiting-room (the scene of the thunderstorm) and just over the men's lavatory (the scene of the shooting). We students must have been a terrible trial to him, judging by the number of reports which found their way to the Principal complaining of the musical orgies which took place at that end of the building. Picture someone with rather long, bushy, grey hair, gold spectacles and a large drooping moustache, poring over a table littered with piles of band-parts and surrounded on all sides by towering shelves packed to overflowing with every conceivable type of music, from the ancients to the moderns. Then you have Chapman.

Moustaches, in particular those which drooped, seemed to be always coming across my path, and the variation in their characters was noticeable. There was my father's, for instance: his was a case of a very aristocratic appendage; then there was the one owned by the general factotum of the Academy: his was leaning to the side of melancholy; Corder's was the essence of benignity; Chapman's was of the fierce type, and I am sure he needed it when attempting his chastening tactics with the unruly crowd opposite and underneath his room; and last, but not by any means least, there was the one which decorated the upper lip of one of the students of the 'cello. This exhibit was a tragedy and, besides being a tragedy, nearly caused one to its owner on his one and only appearance at one of the concerts given each Saturday fortnight in the Concert Hall.

These occasions for the demonstration of youthful talent went by the name of 'Fortnightlies' and if you had a free Saturday evening you could not spend it to better advantage than by taking your seat, preferably in the gallery, and settling yourself down to enjoy as good a laugh as you would get in any music-hall at that date. Of course, some of the turns were first-rate, especially if you were fortunate in putting in an appearance when someone like Myra Hess was taking the stage, or B. Walton O'Donnell was displaying his acrobatics on the 'cello, or Carmen Hill singing some new song by Dorothy Forster, or Clara Butterworth showing off the qualities of Montague Phillips's latest efforts in the song world, or perhaps some new chamber-music by Arnold Bax or York Bowen was being played. You had to wait sometimes for several of these 'Fortnightlies' to pass before your patience was rewarded with a real 'star turn', and when this did happen, forgotten were all the artistic performances you had been listening to; forgotten were the Myra Hesses, the York Bowens, the Montague Phillipses, the B. Walton O'Donnells and the Arnold Baxes, and your eyes were fixed on some elocutionist giving an over-realistic interpretation of Shakespearian drama, or wilting under some emotional love scene from some classic or other, or battling with Ibsen's 'Bergliot' while a tense and deadly serious accompanist tried to synchronise Grieg's lovely music with the erratic performance going on behind his back. But, so far as I was concerned, a moustache did the trick. The scene was the above Concert Hall and the time eight o'clock on a Saturday evening.

The concert was soon well under way and all was progressing smoothly. A pianiste had played her piece, a singer had got through his ordeal creditably, a violinist had come and gone. Things were progressing far too smoothly for the liking of the habitués of the gallery. Why was there not an elocutionist to liven things up for them a bit? And then a shy-looking little man with a drooping moustache came on carrying a 'cello and proceeded to settle down to give us a fairly presentable reading of a sonata by Marcello. He was really doing quite well, when we were suddenly conscious that something had gone wrong, for queer scratchy sounds were coming from the direction of the little figure bending so earnestly over his 'cello. And then a breathless whisper: "Oh, gosh! Look! He's caught his moustache under his fingers!" At first I don't think he realised what it was that was holding his head down, for the harder he tugged the tighter he pressed his fingers on to the strings. One last mighty pull, nearly upsetting the 'cello, the music-stand and himself as well, and he was free.

We were all marvelling at the way in which he carried on despite the predicament in which he found himself, and, notwithstanding the excruciating noise he made during the disentangling of his moustache from his clutching fingers, he neither lost his place nor his head. And did we give him an ovation!

I used to spend some pleasant hours among the dusty full-scores in the even more dusty library with the Keeper of the Music, sometimes helping him to sort out the band-parts for the afternoon rehearsal or delving into some full-scores to see if I could find out 'how it was done'. I would get Chapman to talk about the old students who used to come along to him to borrow some score or other to study, and I would listen to him eulogising over the qualities of Edward German, who, he said, wrote better for the flute than anybody else. Then we would both talk about German. Many a time had the famous Welsh composer dropped in to the library for a chat while he was a student at the Academy. I envied Chapman at that moment, for what would I not have done to have talked with the composer who had already given us the lovely music to so many of Shapespeare's plays: 'Richard III', 'Romeo and Juliet', 'Henry VIII', 'Much Ado About Nothing'; the dances from 'Nell Gwynne' and the fascinating 'Gypsy Suite'; and who, Corder said, could hold on a pedal-note longer than any other composer without making it sound monotonous. And Chapman played the flute! I thought there was a catch somewhere over that drooping moustache of his. Why must moustaches almost inevitably go with playing the flute? Even the great Albert Fransella was moustached, though, if I remember rightly, he had the good sense to keep his in check.

All the months I was at the Academy the only opportunity I had of entering for a competition was when the annual prize of £20 was offered for the best string quartet team, given by one Charles Rube. The competition gave the four who distinguished themselves so creditably in the men's lavatory a chance of forming a quartet, with the prime object of wresting the prize away from Hans Wessely, whose ensemble class had held the field unopposed for some years. The idea of possibly being the richer by five pounds per head gave an added zest to the enthusiastic rehearsals which took place in the room below the entrance hall. This was the room where students went through a course of deportment before being permitted to advance up to the table on the platform at Queen's Hall to receive their medals (if any) from a member of the Royal Family at the Prizegiving, which took place at the end of each Academy year. I well remember being told by old Soutar, the Deportment Professor, that I walked like a battleship, but that Montague Phillips was a perfect example of correct deportment. (I remember how we all pulled Monty's leg afterwards.)

It was a lovely room with a polished oak floor and perfect acoustics, rather too perfect in fact, for its resonance had a tendency to make you believe your tone was better than it really was. After a few preliminary rehearsals we presented ourselves before Louis Zimmermann and he seemed to think that we had a good chance. I think he was as keen as we about getting the prize away from Wessely, but he said nothing, only his eyes twinkled at us more than ever through his thick-rimmed glasses and his hair appeared to stand even more on end. We felt that it was quite time a Zimmermann Quartet headed the list and we solemnly vowed that we would get the Rube Prize away from Wessely, if we worked night and day to do it. We were definitely up against it, for not only had the rival firm entered *one* quartet, he had sent in *three*. What annoyed me especially was the fact that, owing to the shortage of viola players, the same player could enter with more than one team, and one of Wessely's violin pupils, egged on by his master, had had the nerve to take up the viola with Wessely (quite wrongly, as Tertis was the official professor of this instrument), thereby giving himself three chances of winning that coveted fiver.

I was becoming worried over the lack of 'body' in my little Testori, as it did not seem to be able to hold its own with the rest of the quartet, and I was afraid this weakness might prejudice our chances in the forthcoming competition. Then, quite unexpectedly, I was given the opportunity of purchasing an instrument from a brother viola player. A telegram was immediately despatched to my father, making an urgent request for the necessary money, and a cheque arrived by the next post. And so my little Testori went to defray the cost of my new acquisition, a viola of such strange build that when I took it in to Arthur Beare of Wardour Street to have it put in shape he was quite incoherent for some moments. When Tertis saw it for the first time he almost laughed, and on the occasion of its appearance in the Zimmermann ensemble class, proceedings were held up for quite ten minutes while it was handed round for inspection. Beare simply would not take it seriously and gave his opinion that there could not be another like it in the world, for the reason that its maker would most certainly have died of heart failure when he realised the full horror of the finished article; Tertis, at first, could not take it seriously either, and although he altered his opinion slightly when he played on it, he always regarded it with a certain measure of doubt; Zimmermann looked upon it as a complete freak and could not understand why an instrument whose structure was so unorthodox could possess such a lovely quality of tone. I remember his taking it in his hands, scrutinising it from its scroll to its tailpiece, turning it over and over, playing a few notes, turning it over and over again, plucking the strings, and then handing it back to me with the words: "Vell, my deer Meester Coates, it is *most* peculiar, but it is *vonderful!*" And so it was. Extraordinary in build—tremendously deep from back to front, with little patches let in here and there to its back and belly as if, at one time or other, it had received unkind treatment from unappreciative hands, and F holes of such proportions that it went round the profession in later years that I made use of their abnormal size to push my sandwiches inside the body of the instrument when time did not permit of a proper meal. Everywhere I went they laughed—"But it is all wrong!" "It is so fat!" "It is just like a boat!"—and then someone spread the rumour that I was contemplating a Mediterranean cruise *in* my viola. Probably from a collector's point of view it was valueless, but what did I care for those who put their instruments under glass cases merely for the satisfaction of gloating over them and telling their friends about the fabulous sums they had paid to acquire such-and-such a make from so-and-so! "And do you know, they tell me that it is believed Paganini once played on it!" How much better for some violinist to be playing on it now! Well, my much despised and nameless viola could hold its own with any of the famous makers and in some cases beat them. And so all the viola players who smiled, and jibed, and ridiculed, were silenced; but I always had the feeling at the back of my mind that, although my beloved instrument sounded so lovely, the fact that it looked so odd made them regard both it and me with suspicion.

How we four worked! Every moment we had to spare between lessons and orchestral rehearsals were taken up with long sessions in the room underneath the hall. We found that our best work was usually put in after tea, following on the afternoon orchestral rehearsal *séances* with Mackenzie. Tea has always had a magical effect on me where work is concerned, and what I call my 'broody' time follows unfailingly after breakfast and the always-looked-forward-to four-o'clocks.

The day of the competition came round at last, and at two-thirty in the afternoon we were sitting nervously outside the examination-room, listening to the distant sounds of what seemed to us like horribly brilliant performances of the test-piece coming through the closed doors. "Oh gosh! He played that bit much better than I!"—this from the 'cellist. And then I heard Wessely's viola pupil playing that nasty scale passage which bothered me so much, just as if it were nothing. By the time our names were called out we were in a dither, and I was heartily wishing I could have gone into that room as many times as my rival Wessely viola pupil; he seemed to have been dodging in and out all the afternoon.

It was no use wishing; and so, with a final: "Now then, boys, think of Zimmermann!" from the leader, we were ushered into the presence of the examiner and were soon under way. Once more we were back in the waiting-room in company with several other quartet teams, all holding unnerving post-mortems and living the test-piece over and over again. "Why did we muck up that particular bit?" "One part never came off at all!" "Confound that horrible viola passage!" "If only we could be allowed to do a repeat performance!" And then Green calling out: "Mr. C., they want to hear your lot again!" It had evidently been a 'draw' between Wessely and Zimmermann. Now for it! The 'cellist excelled himself, my little bit luckily came off all right, and, inspired by the thought of seeing Zimmermann's eyes twinkling at us through those thick-rimmed glasses of his, we played as if we were possessed. The end of the story was that Zimmermann's eyes did twinkle and I was the richer by a grand-looking certificate and a new viola case.

After having acquitted ourselves so nobly by carrying off the Rube Prize, the idea struck us that it might be well worth while to keep on with the quartet with a view to playing about the country professionally. So far as chamber-music was concerned, the musical world at that time was poorly served and there seemed to be plenty of room for an ensemble which, besides playing the classics, was not above giving the public some of the lighter and more entertaining works.

We now came to the question of a title for the newly-formed quartet. Why not call it the 'Celtic'? The leader a Manxman, the second fiddle a Welshman, the viola half-Welsh, and the 'cellist, who unfortunately happened to be English, could in all probability lay claim to some Celtic strain. So the Celtic Quartet was a *fait accompli*. It had just received its first offer to appear in public, and one very cold wintry morning we were seated in an equally cold, unheated compartment, crawling slowly over the intricate mass of points which infests the approach to Waterloo Station, on our way to entertain an audience in a village somewhere in the wilds of Surrey with a selection from the works of Beethoven, Mendelssohn, Novak and Glazounov.

Most unfortunately, I had just developed one of those streaming colds which, until I reached middle-age, were the bane of my life.

These colds were always accompanied by a terrific appetite and on these unpleasant occasions I felt I wanted to eat everything I could lay my hands on. It was an awful cold and I think it speaks well for the constitution of my colleagues in the Celtic ensemble that they managed to survive the hundreds of sneezes to which I succumbed during that dreadful day. On arrival at our destination my first thought was food and drink. The only hotel turned out to be a modest public-house and here I 'wolfed' ham sandwiches (which I detest) by the dozen and drank beer (which I loathe) by the gallon. Food, in particular, always seemed to dry up my colds, but as this cure was only temporary, and on this occasion I had exhausted the 'public's' supply of ham and bread, I was soon casting about fruitlessly for more sustenance elsewhere.

The hour of the concert drew near and, enquiring of the local postman the whereabouts of the concert hall, we were directed to a little school situated on a common about a mile away from the station. We must have looked a motley four, making our way across the icy common—four figures in black hats, black overcoats and black evening shoes, carrying a queer assortment of cases, and one figure in particular marring the wintry silence with sneezes of a magnitude and a velocity which must have been a cause of wondering comment to the small crowd of villagers who had turned out of their cosy cottages to watch the procession as it passed. It was cold on the common, it was cold in the room at the bottom of the hall, it was cold in the hall, it was cold on the platform, and our instruments were like ice. Nevertheless, there was a packed house; all the inhabitants of the houses from the surrounding countryside seemed to be there. After a good deal of tuning and retuning and an avalanche of sneezes from the viola player, who had failed miserably in his efforts to obtain more nourishment, the quartet threaded its way through the waiting audience to the improvised platform at the other end of the hall. The strange and unexpected happenings which always seemed to accompany us whenever we played together, forced us to the unpleasant conclusion that the Celtic Quartet was doomed to failure from the first.

The platform was reached without incident (about the only thing which went smoothly), the stands were arranged and the music put out. A tense silence pervaded everything. The leader nodded and raised his bow. "Stop! For heaven's sake! I'm going to sneeze!" Nothing could hold it. I sneezed helplessly while the remainder of the quartet waited, bows at the ready. The storm died down, the leader nodded. Another tense silence. Then a scrunching noise like the grinding of teeth from the 'cello. The supporting pin underneath the instrument had disappeared through a hole in the boards and the 'cellist spent an agonised minute retrieving his charge and adjusting the pin to the correct position. We were now becoming nervous and a bit giggly. Once more we were all set and just about to start. This time the interruption came from the second fiddle, in the form of an ear-splitting note caused by the player scraping his chair along the floor to find a more comfortable position. Another avalanche of sneezes from the viola, during which outburst the remaining three giggled so helplessly that they were obliged to resort to the ruse of retuning their instruments as a form of cover. Once again the leader nodded, raised his bow, and was on the point of playing the unaccompanied opening theme when his E string snapped. This was the last straw! Stifling our mirth as best we could and assuming a bold front, we held delirious council over the music-stands. "Have either of you boys got an E string?" Now, viola players never carry E strings, neither do 'cellists; so the only chance lay with the second violin. No, he hadn't one either. And so our leader, rising from his seat, climbed down among the audience and hastily made his way to the room in which we had left our cases, in search of a possible E string. The three remaining members of the Celtic Quartet sat on the platform and waited, in company with the members of the crowded hall, patiently and silently. One minute passed—two—three. It seemed an eternity since we had watched our first violin disappear from sight behind the curtain far away over there. We could bear it no longer and suggested to the second fiddle that he should follow the leader, to see if he could find out what he was doing behind that enveloping curtain. He went, and did not return either. Then the 'cellist decided to go for a tour of inspection. It was becoming like a promenade! The audience had by this time realised that something was radically out of order and began murmuring uneasily among themselves. And there was I, all by myself, sitting on that icy platform among the dejected-looking music-stands and the even more dejected-looking chairs. Yes, I was undoubtedly in for another sneezing bout. I could feel it coming on. Could I get through the audience before the explosion? The curtain seemed a long way off. I would make a dash for it. And gathering up my viola I ran breathlessly down the narrow gangway between the now chattering occupants of the hall and burst into the waiting-room just in time to do my worst over the three truants kneeling on the floor surrounded by hosts of small tin boxes containing bits of rosin, silver strings, gut strings, wire strings, every conceivable kind of string, which they had ransacked from the four instrument cases in their desperate efforts to apprehend that elusive E. What was to follow was little short of fantastic. "What are we going to do?" "I haven't got an E string!" "What on earth made you come along without an extra?" The murmur of voices from the hall rose in insistence and was becoming a clamour. Something had to be done, and done quickly, before the audience took it into their heads to come and see for themselves what was going on behind the scenes. Then a brain-wave. What about that 8.45 train back? Thereupon the mess on the floor was hastily gathered up and crammed into one of the cases, the instruments packed, hats and coats scrambled into, and the budding quartet crept on tip-toe out through the back entrance and were soon running wildly down the frosty moonlit road, one sneezing as he ran and all four laughing hysterically. We laughed ourselves on to the platform, we laughed ourselves into the compartment, we laughed all the way back to London and we were still laughing the next day and wondering whether the audience we had left in the little hall on the moonlit common were still waiting. Thus began and ended the remarkable career of the Celtic Quartet.

*   *   *   *   *

Having recounted the disastrous professional career of the famous Celtic Ensemble, I now come to my own first entrance into the professional orchestral world of the West End. My benefactor was a kindly viola player, Arthur Dyson, who sometimes came along to the Academy to lead the violas when the official leader had something better with which to occupy his time. On the occasions when Dyson took over the violas we had interesting and delightful talks together, when Mackenzie happened to be looking the other way. Besides being a first-rate player, he added to his income by acting in the capacity of secretary to Sidney Jones, the composer, and many were the stories he told me about the fabulously-large cheques which kept on arriving out of royalties from 'The Geisha', 'San Toy', 'My Lady Molly', 'The Greek Slave', etc. Sidney Jones was a composer whom I had always admired; his melodies were spontaneous and his orchestrations first-class. I was to meet him in later years and was struck by his simple charm and complete lack of worldliness. Talking to his brother, Guy Jones, I was remarking on his (Sidney's) seemingly effortless flow of ideas, and was surprised to hear that he frequently became 'stuck'. Guy quoted an instance when his brother was working on one of his operas and simply could *not* get the necessary bar for an effective join-up of a certain passage. He tried again and again but without result. At last Guy came to the rescue with a simple solution to his problem, but would his brother use it? Certainly not, thanks all the same! He could not use any material which he had not come by himself and he continued to struggle with that elusive bar until he was satisfied.

Would I like to take my friend's place at the Vaudeville Theatre to-morrow night? The fee was six shillings and sixpence, provided I wore a white tie, otherwise I should be 'docked' the odd sixpence. I was told not to take any notice of the conductor, because he was really quite all right. What he meant by this I did not find out until later. At first I thought that perhaps the members of the Vaudeville orchestra went their own sweet way on account of their conductor being so inefficient. But on thinking this over it seemed extraordinary and most unlikely that any West End musical director could be as hopeless as that. Edward Jones, usually alluded to as 'Teddy' Jones among the orchestral players, was not a pleasant conductor for a novice to play under. He had a bullet-shaped bald head, piercing black eyes, a vicious-looking black military moustache and a complexion which showed a tendency to high blood-pressure. He had an unpleasant and disconcerting way of 'putting on the spot' any newcomer to his orchestra, by fixing him with those piercing eyes of his and conducting *at* him throughout the entire performance. The only thing that interested me was that he was an old student of the Royal Academy of Music and had been the cause of Edward German Jones adopting as surname his second name of German, to clear up the confusion brought about by there being two Edward Joneses at the Academy at the same time. Teddy Jones certainly did his namesake a good turn by forcing him to drop the 'Jones', and although the Immortal Bard says something about 'What's in a name?', I am sure the taking of the name of Edward German went a long way towards popularising the music of this famous Welsh composer.

I found my way down a dark alley-way and timidly enquired of the stage-door keeper where I should find the band-room. "Down the stairs. Past the lavatory on the left." I do not know whether times have changed, but in those far-away days lavatories and band-rooms seemed to be inseparable. Convenient, no doubt, but as both the former and the latter were nearly always without any ventilation whatsoever, the consequent insanitary conditions which prevailed outweighed any advantage which might otherwise have existed. At any rate, I groped my way down the dirty, evil-smelling staircase, past the evil-smelling lavatory on the left, and found myself at last in the evil-smelling band-room. Here was a motley crowd of musicians; some smoking, some drinking, some playing cards, and all chattering away nineteen to the dozen. One of the men left the rest and came over to me just as I was taking my viola out of its case. "You're here for Dyson, aren't you? Coates, isn't it?" He turned out to be the second viola player, now raised to the dignity of leader through the absence of my friend. I was thankful to have someone to talk to in this badly-lit, smelly dungeon, and he was asking me questions about the Academy when the bell rang, summoning the orchestra into the pit. The orchestra pit, which had to be negotiated by crawling through an undersized door which threatened to knock your brains out if you were incautious in your approach, proved to be just as dirty as the band-room, though being more or less open to the inside of the theatre it was fortunately not quite so unpleasant from the point of view of odour, in fact it was almost salubrious. After I had taken my place on the left of my Hollander friend I was able to look round the theatre. It was packed from floor to ceiling with what looked to me a very magnificent audience. Everyone seemed to be in full evening dress, the men's sober-looking tail-coats making a marked contrast to the colourful dresses worn by their women-folk. White ties and white waistcoats were the order of the day, even the party of young boys and girls in the box facing me at the other end of the orchestra was turned-out perfectly. As I gazed at this array of white ties, shining shirt-fronts and sparkling jewels, I thought of the modest six shillings and sixpence I was earning that evening and was glad that I had had the forethought of possessing myself of a white tie. Suddenly a stir at the entrance to the orchestra. The tuning-up ceased abruptly, a short burst of applause from the upper part of the house, and the man who helped to make Edward German famous was at the conductor's desk, stick in hand. We had not played more than a few bars of the overture before Teddy Jones's keen eyes had sought out the newcomer to the orchestra. I then understood what Dyson had meant when he warned me not to take any notice of him. From that moment I was a marked man. He stared at me, he conducted at me, he waved at me, he glared at me, he did everything except come down from his seat at me. At first I experienced a horrible urge to get out of the orchestra at all costs, but after a little I managed to master this desire and tried, as my friend had said, to "take no notice". But it was not so easy. His attentions became more and more marked, until, unable to stand it any longer and not caring whether I ever set foot inside the theatre again, I looked straight into his eyes, raised my viola on high and played *at* him, at the same time adopting a most extravagant style of delivery with a very much over-done vibrato. It had the desired effect. He went redder than ever and looked hastily away, and from that moment, except for an occasional uneasy glance in my direction, he never bothered me again. The overture finished, the rising of the curtain was the cue for our conductor to retire to the privacy of his own room and the orchestra to the Black Hole of Calcutta near the lavatory, with the exception of a few fresh-air fiends who went upstairs to have a chat with the stage-door keeper or to hang about in the dismal alley which connected Maiden Lane with the Strand. As soon as the curtain rose I decided I would remain in my seat in the orchestra and see the show through. Anyhow, the thought of returning to that disgusting band-room revolted me, and by taking up my position on my neighbour's chair I found I had a front-row-of-the-stalls view of the stage. From that day I made up my mind that if ever I could afford to buy seats for the theatre it would be the front row of the stalls and nothing else, and the front row it has always been and always will be. If ever I have the misfortune to sit some way back from the stage I experience a sensation of isolation which spoils any performance for me.

It was in the dusty orchestra pit at the Vaudeville Theatre in 1907 that I saw my first love. I was in the pit, she was on the stage. We never met. I doubt if she was even aware of the serious-looking, rosy-faced, dark-eyed boy who sat there watching her in silent admiration. She was lovely to look at, fair, fresh, slim, pretty complexion, sang sweetly, danced divinely. She was definitely my ideal. How old? I was not sure. Perhaps even younger than I. I did not care. All I wanted to do was to be allowed to come and deputise here again so that I could spend the time between the orchestral interludes sitting on the leader's seat just watching the fascinating movements of that lovely, adorable creature. I hoped I had not offended the conductor. And then the thought struck me: lucky fellow, he in all probability knew her quite well. But how could she possibly show any interest in anyone as unprepossessing as he? Still, even at that tender age I knew that attractive women sometimes showed marked preference for the most plebean of males. And then I thought to myself . . . But no! A viola player earning six shillings a night with sixpence extra for a white tie, and not even a regular job? It was out of the question. Perhaps if I got out of the orchestra quickly at the end of the performance and rushed up the stairs I might catch a fleeting glimpse of my adored one, or perhaps get a close-up of the fascinating aroma which floated across the footlights and turned the noisome pit below into a paradise of intoxicating sensations. And so I sat and watched and weaved all kinds of youthful romances round the slim little figure flirting so deliciously with Charles Hawtrey. It was Billie Burke, of course.

I climbed the seventy-five stairs to the flat over the haberdashery store in the Kilburn High Road and crept into my bed to dream the night-long through of my newly-found affinity. . . . The next morning at breakfast my aunt proceeded to interrogate me as to the reason for my late arrival home the night before. She was a shrewd old lady and I think she suspected that my first theatre engagement had been something of a very different nature and far removed from such mundane things as orchestra pits. The more I enlarged on my experience with Teddy Jones the more suspicious she became. Dear lady, she was quite within her rights to try to protect the innocent young man from the Midlands, but at the back of her mind I don't think it was my morals she was worrying about; it was the alarming prospect of perhaps having to admit to my parents that, despite her chastening influence, I had been guilty of a major indiscretion while enjoying the hospitality of her virginal home. While we sat and ate a breakfast consisting of Danish bacon and delicate strips of dry toast and butter and marmalade, I felt I was being watched, and when I caught my spurious aunt contemplating me surreptitiously over the cup of China tea which she was sipping out of one of the pieces of her priceless old tea-set, my suspicions were confirmed. To complicate matters I suddenly felt myself changing colour. It was most unfortunate. From that moment I became a suspicious character. If she had only known what had really happened to my heart across the footlights of the Vaudeville Theatre, I firmly believe she would have suggested to my parents the advisability of having me safely tucked away in a place where such things as seductive actresses were unknown. I thought of the bank on the Derby road, and felt slightly sick. If only I could get some sort of a permanent job in a theatre, so that I could launch out by myself and settle myself comfortably in a nice bed-sitting-room where I could live my life in my own way. This being watched was intolerable, and I was sure it would become worse as more engagements came along and made late nights unavoidable. Besides, wouldn't it be pleasant to be near one's work and have no more of those tedious bus journeys! I reckoned I wasted well over twenty hours weekly, watching the top-hatted driver coaxing his tired horses along those interminable streets. And so I laid my plans and waited.

The next R.A.M. rehearsal came along and the official leader of the violas, still employing himself to better advantage elsewhere, had sent my friend Dyson to take over for him. Imagine my relief when I was greeted with: "Well, Coates, you've made a success with

Teddy Jones, and we may stay away as often as we like provided we send you as deputy." The next time the conductor at the Vaudeville Theatre climbed up into his seat he had a smile for the young man from the Academy. As a matter of fact, I seemed to cause a good deal of amusement whenever I appeared in the orchestra, which gave me the uncomfortable feeling that what I had fondly thought was my secret passion had now become common property. Perhaps that was why Teddy Jones smiled.

As I said before, viola players were not plentiful, and through my entrance into the orchestra at the Vaudeville I made a good many useful contacts and soon became known as a reliable deputy. A regular theatre job I never held, although I was offered one on more than one occasion. It suited me better to take odd engagements here and there, partly because I thought I should obtain more varied experience by playing in different kinds of shows and under different conductors, and partly because I did not feel it was wise to have six late nights a week. Every morning, when I could take an hour off from my studies at the R.A.M., I used to wend my way down Gerrard Street to the theatre musicians' 'Mecca', the Orchestral Association, and scan the list hanging up in the hall to see if a viola player was wanted by some 'regular' who needed a deputy, in order for him to avail himself of an opportunity of making a welcome 'one-one' elsewhere. Through the good offices of this advertising medium I found myself one night serenading the lovely Lily Elsie with the viola part of Franz Lehar's delightful music to 'The Merry Widow'. It was the first time I had played in a musical show and I found it a very different matter from straight comedy. It takes a good deal of ingenuity to look at a lovely woman, at the same time watching the conductor, reading at sight a badly-copied manuscript, transposing one number a tone up and another half a tone down, looking out for cuts and turning over for the leader, especially if the conductor and the music are in front of you and the woman is on your right and overhead. But I managed it.

During this period I think I must have played in practically every theatre in London. It was a wonderful experience and one which I would not have missed. There were some first-rate conductors in the theatre at that time, Teddy Jones, Barter Johns and Howard Talbot being the three who were perhaps the most outstanding. Howard Talbot was a character—full of fun, liked a good story and knew how to tell one, wrote delightful music, and was popular with his orchestra. Teddy Jones I have already talked about. Barter Johns I never came into contact with personally, though I played under his bâton many times during the run of 'The Merry

Widow' at Daly's Theatre. The orchestrations were of immense interest to me, many of these being done by I. A. de Orellana, whom I was to meet in later years. Orellana had a remarkable sense of the theatre and, being a sound musician, his arrangements were delicately finished and always in good taste. It was fascinating to get hold of a vocal score of one of the popular musical comedies of the day and run through the music on the piano, and then go and listen in the evening to what Orellana could make it sound like. He never interfered, as do so many of the arrangers of to-day, with a composer's harmonic progressions, being far too much of a musician to take such a liberty, and this attitude earned for him the love and respect of all those writers for the theatre of that day who had not the technique to write for the orchestra and who were grateful for the help and advice of one who never made them feel uncomfortable over their lack of knowledge.

One day not so long ago, as I was about to leave my publishers in Bond Street, I heard a tremendous uproar proceeding from the top of the stairs leading down to the front shop. I enquired of one of the staff what the row was about and was told, with a broad grin, that a famous American composer was in a paddy because he had a tune in his head and could find no one in the place to write it down for him. As it was well after midday on a Saturday, it did not look promising for the famous American, as the doors closed at one. At that moment an excitable little man, wearing a large black hat, a long black coat, with long black hair, pointed patent shoes and blue glasses, rushed down the stairs shouting at the top of his voice: "Vy is der no-ones 'ere to make my music for me?" The temperamental little foreigner, seeing someone whom he thought looked like a musician (I think it must have been the soft felt hat which did it), screamed at me: "It vas terrible! It vas a crime! It vas a tragedy! My peautiful music!" My suggestion that he should try writing down his tunes himself did not impress him. "Dis place is dis-graceful! In America it vas different!" Murmuring that he should have stayed there, I took my hat and departed.

It has frequently struck me how strange it is that there are so many composers to-day who cannot put down a note of music on paper, let alone write for the orchestra. Perhaps it may be that these people prefer being lazy and making easy money to settling down to what looks like a hard job. I feel sorry for them, for they miss a great deal. Hard work it may be, far harder than many people imagine, and I am sure some will be surprised when they hear what a tremendous amount of care and patience has to be exercised in writing an orchestral work, even of the lightest calibre.

When you listen to a Suite, or a Phantasy, or an Overture by a genuine composer of the Light Orchestral School, it all sounds so easy, so spontaneous, but in all probability it has taken hours and hours of concentrated thought on the part of the writer to give you that impression. The sketching out of a work is the least tedious part of the business, though even that may occupy several weeks. A recent Suite of mine in four movements was sketched out in about ten days and the orchestration finished in four months. A laborious and a thankless task, you may think? Laborious, yes, but not thankless. It is one of the most satisfying things I know, after having sat at my desk day in day out, writing, contriving, experimenting, altering, with the work on hand growing slowly under my pen, to be in front of the orchestra, stick in hand, to hear for the first time what I had been listening to in my head for so long. That little passage from the oboe, the divisi string effect here, the woodwind rhythm there, the snappy staccato chords from the brass, the crescendo from the side-drum beginning pianissimo, coming up to a fortissimo and culminating in a terrific climax from the whole orchestra. To know that every sound every instrument was making had been carefully planned and thought out was ample repayment for the weary hours spent over that complicated-looking full-score. Writing within certain instrumental limits, to comply with an orchestra that may not have a complete symphonic personnel, is an intricate problem which you come up against frequently. It is not such a difficult matter to write for an orchestra of limitless proportions (provided you know anything about orchestration at all), for here you have any amount of instruments at your disposal to play with. But it takes a good deal of ingenuity to make an effect with an ensemble which is short, say, of a third trombone, or third and fourth horns, or second wood-wind players, and so on. You will find a composer like Richard Strauss, who usually paints on an enormous orchestral canvas, equally at home when writing for the Chamber Orchestra. This is the acid test, and is the sign of a master.

The decision of the Committee of the Royal Academy of Music to give me a scholarship coincided with a couple of months' engagement as deputy second viola at the revival of the Gilbert and Sullivan Operas at the Savoy Theatre, which meant that I was off my father's hands, and the shadow of the bank on the road to Derby became a thing of the past. There is no doubt that my theatre orchestral life taught me a great deal about the handling of an orchestra, especially with regard to delicacy, rhythm and bright tone-colour, and my engagement at the Savoy Theatre, besides benefiting me financially, provided me with a kind of finishing touch to my education in this respect and at the same time proved a delightful and an interesting experience. I already knew practically every melody out of the Gilbert and Sullivan Operas, for I had become acquainted with them while at Hucknall, going into Nottingham when the d'Oyly Carte Opera Company paid its annual visit to the Theatre Royal. I always felt the performances I heard in Nottingham were a little spoilt by the rather low standard of the orchestral playing; even the extra instrumentalists who travelled with the company did not completely overcome this drawback. It was therefore a joy to me, in this revival of 1907, to hear these lovely operas performed at the Savoy by a first-rate company and a first-rate body of orchestral players. The musical director was François Cellier. He was a heavily built man with a huge double-chin and a tiny beat. Although I never really took to him, Cellier was quite a good sort. He knew the scores of the Gilbert and Sullivan Operas from end to end, but a conductor who sinks into himself and who could stare vacantly at the stage throughout the major part of a show and who was barely conscious of the existence of the orchestra was not the kind of man to inspire respect. Nevertheless, I enjoyed every moment of that delightful season, and as I was still at the Academy and bursting with zeal, I managed to find many passages in the viola parts which I could turn into a kind of technical study and which I practised in the intervals in the band-room, to the disgust of the older members of the orchestra, who looked upon a Sullivan band-part only as a means of making six shillings and sixpence each time they played one through. The viola part to the opening number in 'The Yeomen of the Guard', the effective Spinning Song, was my *pièce de résistance*, even the leader becoming infected with my enthusiasm and joining me in a twosome underneath the stage just before the overture. I do not think Cellier had ever heard this particular viola part played so brilliantly; it was an achievement of the highest order and my partner and I played it as one. The only time I can remember Cellier taking any notice of our side of the orchestra was on the night when, the first viola being away, I had moved up into his seat and Basil Cameron had come in to play next to me. We became so exuberant and so intent on getting every note into the spinning-song number that Cellier was compelled to lean over and ask us to keep down or we should wreck the song.

    During this time at the Savoy I became aware of a weakness and a slight numbness in the third and fourth fingers of the left hand, which was to be the beginning of a trouble that was with me until the end of my viola-playing days and which has remained with me throughout my life. As I said have before, viola players were scarce in those days and this scarcity made me somewhat in demand at the Academy, even before I was given my scholarship; but when this latter event came about I was more or less expected to help out every ensemble which was in need of that necessary instrument, the tenor. My days were sometimes little short of a nightmare, and just as a matter of interest here is a sample of what a really full day was like: leave home 8.30, lesson 9.30 till 10.30, ensemble class 10.30 till 11.30, lesson 11.30 till 12, quartet rehearsal 12 till 1, lunch consisting of coffee and sandwiches at the Academy, orchestral rehearsal 2 till 5, quartet rehearsal 5.30 till 6.30, a hasty dinner, theatre from 8 till 11, home about 12.30 a.m. Practically ten hours playing on an instrument which should have been held between the knees like a 'cello instead of out at arms' length like a violin; and all this with Fortnightly Concerts and Chamber Concerts at Queen's Hall thrown in, sometimes appearing as many as three times at the same concert. No wonder my hand was beginning to show signs of strain. There was nothing I could do about it except try and carry on as usual and make the best of that gnawing ache. I comforted myself with the reflection that perhaps it might be better when the Savoy season was over and I could take a few days off and catch the first train to Nottingham. It would be a relief to be on my bicycle again, wandering along the quiet Nottinghamshire lanes and recapturing the healing spirit of that peaceful countryside.

It was an enjoyable season, notwithstanding the hard work and the late nights. Occasionally when things seemed to be dragging just a little, W. S. Gilbert would appear on the horizon, call a rehearsal, and get the whole of the Savoy Theatre into a state of hysterical nervous tension. Many were the almost free fights between himself and Cellier: Cellier telling W.S.G. that a certain number should go at such-and-such a tempo and W.S.G. replying that he (Cellier) did not know what he was talking about, and anyway *that* was how Sullivan liked it. On these occasions I think we all of us felt a great deal of sympathy for our musical director, for he certainly had to put up with a fearful amount of bullying from the unreasonable author. One day W. S. Gilbert cheered up the proceedings by giving us all a good laugh (which was unintentional), and this was during a rehearsal of the fairies' scene in 'Iolanthe'. Evidently the sprightly ones were not disporting themselves to the liking of the peppery little writer, who began to say his prayers out loud from the back of the stalls. Cellier quietly went on conducting, pretending not to have noticed anything amiss from the rear. Suddenly W.S.G.

rushed down to the orchestra, calling on the Deity to give him patience, and after having shouted at Cellier to stop, ran wildly up through the pass-door at the side of the stalls. Before we knew where we were, the orchestra and the company were being entertained by the little man in a first-rate impersonation of a fairy in full flight.

My engagement at the Savoy over and the term practically at an end, my thoughts turned once more to my parents and to the bedroom at Tenter Hill where the bed was always made up in readiness for me, in case of my putting in an appearance unexpectedly.

Oh, it was nice to be home once more! The journey had been full of anticipation and I could scarcely possess my soul in patience while the little red tank-engine climbed the gradient past the Bottom Pit and pulled up, snorting furiously, into the station. It was good to be greeted by the station master, the porter and the man who, besides acting as booking-clerk, took up his position at the foot of the stairs which mounted to the road overhead, to relieve the arrivals of their tickets. A word to the porter to follow along with my suitcase, and I was soon up the stairs, over the bridge, past the Great Northern station, along Station Road, up the hill by the police station and being received by my family, the cat and the dogs. Yes, it was very nice to be home once more! A fire burning cheerfully in the morning-room (not that the weather was chilly, but coal at twelve and sixpence a ton at the pit-mouth rather asked for it). A magnificent tea was laid out on the snowy-white cloth: fresh eggs, home-cured York ham, lettuces, radishes, home-made cakes, home-made bread with an assortment of pastries and jams to make your mouth water. During tea a ring at the bell—the porter with "our Mr. Eric's" bag. Then up to my bedroom overlooking the fields to the chimney-stacks of the Top Pit in the distance. I unpacked my bag while my mother sat on the bed and talked, and Tim, the black Persian, played with the tassel of my dressing-gown. . . .

* * * * *

Eight days of idleness? Not completely, for I had brought the manuscript of some Shakespearean songs I was working on and I wanted to do some orchestration while enjoying the quiet of my old home. It was a quiet house. After the turmoil of London it seemed a haven of rest. This was how I would like to live, just writing when I felt like it. And then I thought to myself, but surely I wanted to make a name as a viola player, not a composer! What had happened to me? My left hand, of course. From the moment I had felt that sickly ache in my third and fourth fingers I knew that any idea of being a second Lionel Tertis was out of the question. . . .

As I wrote quietly at the table in the dining-room I could hear faint sounds of life going on about the house: a door opening and shutting somewhere upstairs, a ring at the surgery bell, a parcel arriving, murmuring voices beyond the pass-door in the kitchen. Restfulness, restfulness. It was *good* to be home again! And so, to the accompaniment of these friendly household sounds, my score grew rapidly and by the time I had to return to London my 'Four Old English Songs' were ready to show to Corder. It had been a heavenly stay: writing each morning and perhaps spending the rest of the day going over to Southwell to see the Cathedral; or cycling to Hazleford Ferry to watch the tugs still towing their heavy cargoes up-stream to Nottingham; one day going into Nottingham to pay a hurried call on Georg Ellenberger, Fred Warren and Dr. Horner, and just time for a word with my old friend Waterfield; and then to spend a pleasant hour with John Munks in his sitting-room behind the shop in the High Street in Hucknall; then on to the bank to pay my respects to Vine Hall and to 'Mr. Bowler who played the viola', and to finish up the days with long talks with my family late into the night; and then to bed to thank the good God for my being blessed with such a peaceful home.

* * * * *

During our talks I told my parents about my wishing to move nearer to my work and they promised to back me up if I experienced any difficulty in breaking away from the watchful eye of my aunt. It was a delicate business, giving in my notice so to speak, and anyone knows how it is with relations!

So I took the bull by the horns and told my guardian that I had been given the chance of sharing some rooms with another musician. This was perfectly true, but I knew she thought I was prevaricating. At any rate, one chilly, autumn morning I was seated in a four-wheeler, complete with suitcases, music cases and viola case, rattling along a draughty Kilburn High Road on my way to take up residence in that much talked-about form of *ménage*, a bed-sitting-room, usually alluded to in the advertisements as a 'bed-sit'. I had taken leave of my aunt and, although I knew she was hurt at my preferring a room in Park Road, Regent's Park (bed and breakfast), to her perfectly run little home at the top of the seventy-five stairs, she took it very well and said she hoped I would be happy and that if I ever wanted to return there would always be a room waiting for me. . . .

I cannot say I was impressed with my bed-sitting-room. It faced on to the back and the outlook was not what you could call inviting. My friend's room looked out regally on to Park Road itself, but then *he* was paying thirty shillings a week against my modest twenty-five, and in those distant times an extra five shillings had a far larger privilege-buying capacity than it has in these days of topsy-turvy values. Our landlady was a pleasant, ordinary kind of woman, smallish and, if I remember, with slightly greying hair done in a large bun low down on the neck. The thing which exercised our minds was the appearance on the scene of a young and attractive daughter who occasionally brought our breakfasts up to us in our respective bed-sitting-rooms. I don't know why we flattered ourselves to the extent of thinking that the maiden found either of us interesting, apart from the fact that she always seemed pleased for an excuse to come up to our rooms, and when we sometimes found her busily making our beds we were careful to see that the other was near at hand in case of emergency. Now I come to think of it, I reckon we behaved like a couple of numskulls.

* * * * *

I had a free night the day of my arrival in Park Road, and after having unpacked my things I took a bus down Baker Street and went into the Blenheim Restaurant in New Bond Street to enjoy the luxury of a quiet dinner. It seemed strange to be on my own and with no one to question my movements, and so I made the most of my first night out and sat on at my table in the window, watching the lights come up in the street below, until I was the only customer left in the restaurant and there was nothing else to be done but to make my *adieux* to the tired waiter and wend my way back through the softly-lit streets to my humble room. The bed was not so comfortable as the one in my room at Kilburn; I did not like the look of that dreadful wash-basin in the corner; the drawers in the chest did not run smoothly; there was no key to the door (this troubled me considerably); the pillow was as hard as a stone and there was no eiderdown. I wondered whether I had made a mistake in moving nearer in to town, and then I thought of my comfortable bedroom at Tenter Hill and of my mother, probably at that very moment going round the house to see if everything was locked up safely for the night and putting the little black Persian to bed, and I felt homesick. . . .

I was awakened by a knock at the door, heralding the entrance of the attractive brunette carrying a breakfast-tray. This she laid on the table near the window. I decided to have my breakfast in bed, and discreetly waiting until the young woman had made her exit, I reached for the tray, got back into bed, propped myself up as best I could with a hard pillow and even harder bolster and tried to give myself up to the luxury of the moment. It was not a great success and I was glad when the solitary meal was concluded. However, after having greeted my companion of the front bed-sitting-room I felt slightly cheered, and by the time I had shaved and dressed, let myself out of the front door, run down the stone steps to the gate, turned to the right down Park Road and was walking along Baker Street *en route* for the Mecca (the Gerrard Street one) I felt that perhaps life was not so bad after all. With the cool morning air blowing softly on my forehead the discomforts of my new quarters were forgotten.

The first few days at Park Road taught me that, under certain conditions, there was a great deal to be said for living on the spot. It meant, of course, the added expense of having every meal out except breakfast, but the rent was compensated for, in part, by my not having to make use of those lumbering buses any more, thus saving a good many shillings a week, besides giving me the added advantage of getting a little fresh air though being able to walk back after a night at the theatre instead of spending over an hour either sitting inside the 'bus and becoming asphyxiated or else riding on top and being either frozen or drowned. So long as you are in a good state of health this mode of living is to be commended, but woe betide you if you return home late one night and find you are running a temperature in the region of 101°—then it is not so good. Landladies, on these occasions, are hopeless, and landladies' daughters, especially if they happen to be attractive young brunettes, are not the right thing to encourage, so what are you to do? Take thousands of aspirins with hundreds of thousands of soda-mints to counteract (as my father put it) the acid effect of the aspirins. You won't get anything to eat anyhow, so you are spared the strain of trying to solve the food problem (always bad for a high temperature). Drink quarts of cold water, stay in bed, cover yourself up to the neck with as much clothing as you can bear, and hope for the best. I did all these things and became weaker and weaker day by day, soaking my pyjamas with sweat over and over again and running the risk of pneumonia every few hours.

The days dragged on. I was getting to my last tether. I had had enough. It was a dark afternoon in November and as I lay in my damp bed I thought of a cheery fireside, a hot bottle, and someone to bring me some tea and hot buttered toast. I could bear it no longer and was on the point of getting out pencil and paper and scribbling an S.O.S. to my parents far away in the Midlands, when there was a familiar voice on the stairs, a tap on the door, and in walked my mother. If it had been one of the angels of Heaven I could not have been more thankful. In a few minutes my room became like home; there *was* a hot bottle, there *was* tea and hot buttered toast, there *was* a cheery fire in the little Victorian grate, everything I wanted. The transformation in my gloomy bedroom was a major miracle. My mother moving quietly about the room, arranging this, arranging that; it was heavenly to be looked after once more. I closed my eyes contentedly, and the next thing I remember was a man's voice saying something to my mother about could she stay for a day or so? It was the doctor. Not only did she stay for a day or so, she stayed for a week. . . . "Thank you, madam, but dogs don't feed upon dogs"; with these words the doctor dismissed the patient and the request from my mother for his account for medical attendance. What it is to be the wife of a doctor!

* * * * *

The Easter holidays came along with so much deputising that my much-looked-forward-to visit to my home had to be ruled out. It was a great disappointment, but, after all, work had to come first. How I wished my hand would stop reminding me of its existence. Of late it had been becoming a nuisance and I was being forced to the conclusion that sooner or later I should have to consult someone about it. I had spoken of it tentatively to my father and he had suggested a good holiday as the only certain cure, but I do not think he really understood the best way to deal with the trouble.

* * * * *

I had never been in London during holiday-times before, and so this was a new experience for me and one which, on the whole, I rather enjoyed. My theatre dates were not regular, consisting of four or five shows a week, mostly evening, with an occasional matinée. Living in Park Road meant I had plenty of time to myself and I made the most of this and tried to turn my enforced stay in London into a kind of holiday. Being so close to Regent's Park gave me an opportunity, when the morning was fine, of taking out a skiff or a canoe for an hour or so. It was pleasant to skim quietly up alongside one of the little islands and relax for half an hour in the warm sunshine. And then to stroll lazily along Baker Street to have lunch at the Academy Students' Rendezvous in New Bond Street, the Blenheim Restaurant, where I was sure to run into some of my musician friends. After lunch, probably a matinée with Howard Talbot in 'The Belle of Brittany", and then on to dinner at some French or Italian restaurant in Soho, where you could obtain a first-rate Continental meal for the large sum of one shilling and sixpence. Then on to another theatre, going by way of the Musicians' Mecca to see if any more dates had come in since last I was there, and finally walking home quietly up Charing Cross Road, along Oxford Street, down Baker Street and rounding the corner by Clarence Gate into Park Road just as Big Ben, far away in the starlit distance, chimed midnight. And so to bed.

Another lovely day, this time free to do as I would. Where should I go? Regent's Park, Hyde Park, Richmond, Kingston, Hampton Court? And so the Easter holidays passed and the Summer Term came round, bringing with it more lessons, more ensemble classes, more rehearsals, more theatre dates, and what was to become one day an institution almost as important as the Royal Academy itself, the new hall porter, Hallett.

I was interested in Hallett the first moment I met him. He had served in the Boer War, was a cornet player of no mean repute, and could work a Harmony Examination Paper with the best of 'em. I used to sit in his tiny office between lessons and listen to his stories about his experiences in South Africa—Ladysmith, Bloemfontein, Magersfontein, Majuba Hill, Modder River. It made me long to be aboard one of those white Union Castle liners which I had watched rounding the Needles as I stood with my mother on the low cliffs at Milford. The tang of the sea was in my mouth, I could hear the cry of the sea-birds, the whip of the wind, the crash of big seas, the beat of great engines, see the southward-bound ships ploughing their way through oily, tropical waters. How well Rudyard Kipling captured this in those lovely lines, 'You have heard the beat of the offshore wind, the thresh of the deep-sea rain.'

South Africa! Rider Haggard's 'She', 'King Solomon's Mines', 'Allan Quatermain', 'Nada the Lily'; I would love to see the country where the scenes of these stories were laid. To wander with Umslopagaas and the fair Nada across the Mountains of the Moon in search of the Grey Wolf-Pack and his brother warrior and hunter, Galazi. Perhaps to come across Captain Good with his false teeth and his eye-glass, or take a journey along the subterranean river to the great inland sea, to where Allan Quatermain and the Lady Nyleptha are holding court in their kingdom high up in the mountain fastness. South Africa! I walked back from the Academy after that afternoon's rehearsal deep in thought. Baker Street suddenly seemed to have become very small. How could I manage to travel? It was terribly expensive, and I detested journeys unless I could go first-class. South Africa and back—probably £150. Out of the question. One of my best friends at the Academy, a violinist, had spent each of the holidays going to America, Madeira, Scandinavia and the Mediterranean. But then he, dear old thing, had played himself to all these places of romance by joining the ship's band. It certainly was a way of seeing the world. I wondered how one set about applying for a job of that sort? And then I remembered the little band on the paddle-steamer which paddled each day from Bournemouth round the Isle of Wight, and how frightful the musicians looked in their awful uniforms. It was quite possible that the uniforms on the big liners were even worse, they would be sure to be more gaudy. I pictured myself in a tight-fitting kind of bodice, with gold buttons and braid, a peaked cap, tight-fitting trousers with huge Wellingtons (possibly spurred) frantically endeavouring to hold my viola up against a collar so hard and so high that it was all I could do to prevent the thing from slipping down on to my stomach. As it did not seem probable that I should be permitted to be given a preview of the uniform, I decided against it.

At the rate I was going just then it looked as if by the time I was able to book a passage anywhere I should have one foot well in the grave. My hand ached and I felt depressed. It was no good wishing. I put my key in the door, let myself in, climbed the dark stairs, walked into the room and was surprised to find Lionel Tertis waiting for me. Whatever could Lionel Tertis have come for? And then the most amazing thing happened. Would I like to go to South Africa? It could not be true! Would I like to take his place in the Hambourg String Quartet and tour South Africa, starting in June? It would set me up in health and probably cure my neuritis. Would I like to go? Would I like to go! The Hambourgs would like to hear me play. Was I willing to run through a quartet with them to see how I shaped? And so it was arranged that I should be at their house in Clifton Gardens the following morning at 10.30. I arrived to find the Hambourgs waiting for me in the music-room. Jan, the violinist, tall, athletic and talkative; Boris, the 'cellist, smallish, artistic and quiet. The second violin, to my astonishment, was the leader of the embryonic Celtic Quartet (shades of E strings!) and so I felt comforted in the knowledge that one, at least, was not a stranger to me. The Hambourgs had chosen the last movement of the Mozart F Major Quartet as test piece, which started almost at once with a nasty running passage for the solo viola. Fortunately, my sight-reading facility stood me in good stead. At the end of the movement I could scarcely hold my viola because of the ache in my left arm and hand; this, I think, had been aggravated by the nervous strain of playing at an audition which meant so much to me. Thank goodness my hand did not give out *during* the piece. And, luckily for me, the difficult part came at the beginning and again in the middle of the movement; if it had occurred at the end as well, I doubt if I should have got through.

They seemed pleased with me, and we were to start rehearsals at once. Again that ache in my hand. How was I ever going to manage it? I could not possibly do my Academy work and my theatre work and rehearse with the Hambourgs each day. My arm would pack up in no time. Jan and Boris were very sympathetic when I put my troubles before them and suggested holding council with their father.

Professor Hambourg was a well-known teacher of the pianoforte, and it was he who gave his famous son, Mark, his first lessons. He occupied a spacious room looking on to Clifton Gardens, where he lived with his grand piano (as far as I can remember there were pianos in every room in the house). After a good deal of suggestion and counter-suggestion I decided I would act on the Professor's advice and ask Mackenzie if he would release me from my scholarship at the Academy, just keeping on with my studies with Corder, as this would not affect my left arm. The Hambourgs offered to send me to Professor Kreutzberger in Cavendish Square for a course of electrical treatment at their own expense. At first I did not like to take advantage of their kindness, but when they pointed out to me that the treatment was necessary if the quartet was to possess a viola player one hundred per cent efficient, I accepted. The next morning I went into the Academy to see if I could catch the Principal before he became immersed in the day's work. I watched his slightly stooping figure disappear into his room. A few minutes later: "Mr. C., the Principal will see you now", and Green was bowing me into the familiar room at the top of the stairs overlooking Tenterden Street. I broke the news to Sir Alexander about Tertis and the Hambourg Quartet, about the trouble with my arm, the scholarship and Kreutzberger. "Of course we'll release ye from your scholarship. There'll be another glad to have it. And I hope ye'll have a successful trip and come back safely and in better health. Take care of yourself, my boy." The kindly Scotsman then walked with me to the door, patted me on the shoulder, and sent me on my way with a lighter heart. This was Friday morning. I had a rehearsal with the Hambourgs that afternoon and another one on

Monday morning. I should have plenty of time to dash up to Hucknall after the rehearsal to tell my parents the news, and as I should not have to return to London until the Sunday evening it would give me two whole days at home. The afternoon rehearsal at Clifton Gardens went off without incident. My arm was not giving me quite so much trouble at that moment, so I was able to enjoy the couple of hours on the Haydn Quartet. Four o'clock, tea and a cigarette and a talk about the forthcoming tour, the Hambourg family coming in and taking part in the proceedings. They were a united family and the atmosphere in their home was always friendly, both my friend and I soon coming to feel that we were looked upon as one of themselves. Another hour's playing, this time some Mozart and some Dittersdorf, and I was thinking about my train. . . .

It was long after dark as I walked up the hill to my home, and as there did not seem to be a light showing anywhere I concluded that the family must be abed. I did not want to ring the bell and rouse the household, and, remembering that my mother always left the door which gave on to the coachyard unlocked at night, on account of the protection afforded by the army of bulldogs which prowled around, I climbed over the back gate and dropped silently to the ground. Immediately a surge forward from all sides of countless black forms in the darkness. No barking, but growling in plenty, a far more ominous sign. Would the dogs recognise my voice? Before I could speak to them they were all round me, pushing their wet noses into my hand, as if to say: 'We knew you at once, even in the dark. You can't hide that scent from *us*. Glad you're back!' and I was through the kitchen and at the bottom of the stairs, calling softly: "Is there anybody awake?" A stir from my parents' room. I heard my father's voice, and then my mother appeared on the landing with a candle in her hand. "Who's there?" "It's me, Mother. I've come home to tell you I'm going to South Africa." "Are you, dear? I'll be down in a moment." If I had told my mother I was just off to the Vatican to lecture to the Pope on religion she would have said: 'Are you, dear? I'll be down in a minute,' and would probably have added: 'I'm sure you will do it very well!' Everything I did seemed to be quite a matter of course. I think it was partly due to this attitude towards me that my home life was always so happy. I was never made to feel self-conscious. My musical bent was looked upon as quite a normal thing. All the years I knew my father and mother they remained the same. They always spoke of my successes, never of my failures; they were always encouraging, never deprecating, and yet they never flattered me. No, it was just the fact of taking everything I did as a matter of course. My mother would say, after a new work had received a successful first performance: "Well, dear, you deserve it." My father would say nothing, but his smile showed me he was pleased.

"And so you are going to South Africa." My mother had come downstairs, insisted on my having some bread-and-milk, and I was now seated on my father's bed telling them of the exciting happenings of the past few days.

I think we talked practically all the time, right up to the moment of saying goodbye on Sunday evening at the station. It had been a happy forty-eight hours, made yet happier by the rosy complexion which the future had assumed. It might mean I should no longer have to depend on theatre dates—that would be wonderful. The Hambourgs were talking of giving a series of recitals in London after the South African tour. If they paid me three guineas a time, one concert a week would be sufficient to keep the wolf from the door, and I could then give more time to my writing. It would be a relief not to have to play ten hours a day any more.

The journey back to London was spent in making plans for the future, contemplating the complex problem of pounds, shillings and pence, wondering whether Kreutzberger was going to do my arm any good and whether a time would ever come when I should no longer be compelled to play the viola for a living.

As it did not look as though I should be getting a composition published just yet (I had already had some songs turned down by Boosey & Co.), I prayed that Kreutzberger's treatment would enable me to carry on with my viola with a minimum of discomfort, so long as it was necessary for me to have that second string to my bow.

*　*　*　*　*

Then followed an intensive course of quartet rehearsals with the Hambourgs and an equally intensive course of electrical treatments with Kreutzberger. We only had about four weeks in which to get up a repertoire, but at the end of that time we could lay claim to being able to play, almost blindfold, nearly a dozen quartets.

Our ensemble was little short of remarkable. The many hours of playing together developed a kind of sixth sense among us, each member being able to tell intuitively, before it happened, what any of the others might suddenly decide to do. I do not imagine this is altogether an uncommon occurrence where quartet playing, or even orchestral playing, is concerned, but I believe we four had this sense developed to an unusual degree.

The time drew near for our departure, and the Hambourgs had advanced us fifty pounds each to defray the cost of such things as extra suitcases, hold-alls, cabin-trunks, and the clothes necessary for a country with a temperature ranging from tropical to well below freezing.

It was Friday, the day before we sailed, and I was attending one of the Academy rehearsals to hear the Principal run through a couple of baritone songs which I had composed and which were to be performed at the Orchestral Concert at Queen's Hall while I was away. I had completed these songs the previous term, and, the band-parts to the 'Four Old English Songs' not yet being copied, Corder suggested leaving these till next term when I was back from South Africa.

I remember standing at Mackenzie's side while he let me hear what my orchestration sounded like, and I recall his kindness on this, to me, important occasion. Nothing was a trouble; he did everything I asked of him. Too slow?—Just a bit. Fast enough?—Just right.

At the end of the rehearsal he put his arm round my shoulder in front of the orchestra, gave me one of his delightful smiles and said: "We'll take care of your songs for ye. Good luck to ye, my boy.'

The next morning at 12.30 the Hambourg String Quartet was seated in the Pullman attached to the boat-train, speeding towards Southampton.

* * * * *

The ship was the *Kinfauns Castle*. I believe there is a more modern craft of the same name to-day, but in 1908 the original *Kinfauns* was looked upon as being the most luxurious liner in the Union Castle fleet. Her appointments were very elaborate and no expense had been spared to make her a model ship in every respect. Imagine my excitement when I discovered I had been allocated a first-class four-berth deck-cabin all to myself, complete with every convenience, including a basin with running hot and cold sea water. And to know that this was going to be my home for over a fortnight! A floating hotel, indeed. (I was *very* young and *very* inexperienced!)

* * * * *

Then followed seventeen days of romance, so far as I was concerned; the only thing which brought me down to earth and reminded me of the fact that I was one of a party of four on a commercial enterprise was the daily quartet rehearsal in the drawing-room, which usually took place directly after breakfast until about 10.30, before the few elderly ladies who were on board took it into their heads to settle themselves at one of the writing-tables to cope with their correspondence—this routine concluded, the day was mine to do with as I would. These were the days to travel if you wished for quiet; no radio, no daily papers, no anything. The only news you received was by Morse signals from a passing steamer, which only happened once in every four or five days, and any news you could pick up during the few hours spent in the harbour at Funchal, four days out from Southampton.

Seventeen days of new sights, new sensations, new ideas, new contacts, and all so different from anything I had experienced before. Watching the grey seas grow from a gentle swell to towering mountains as we rounded Ushant and ran before the wind into the giant rollers of the Bay (the ship taking on an angle of twenty-five degrees or so when a more than usually heavy sea struck her amidships) and then seeing the grey turn to blue as we ran into the quiet waters at the approach to the lovely island of Madeira and anchored in brilliant sunshine under the gold and brown mountains in the shelter of Funchal harbour, to be entertained for the next hour or so by Portuguese boys diving for sixpences and generally making nuisances of themselves, performing all sorts of tricks for the edification of the 'Eenglishman'. And after Madeira, the long, cool, summer days turning slowly warmer as the ship nosed her way towards the Tropical Zone, the sun taking on a shorter angle day by day until one twelve o'clock noon you find you make no shadow as you walk, and then you know you're on the Line.

It was good to be alive in a world so full of beauty and my arm was already beginning to feel better. Only an hour and a half's rehearsal a day and one concert which we gave for the ship's company, as compared with those dreadful days in London. How long ago all that seemed now, it was like another life. And to-morrow we should arrive at Cape Town. I thought about packing.

* * * * *

I awoke with a sense of something having happened; at first I could not make out what it was; and then it dawned on me—it was the throb of the engines which I missed. There was a silence which you could almost hear. I looked at my watch—five o'clock. I got out of bed, put on my dressing-gown, drew back the curtains and stepped out on to the deck. There did not seem to be anyone about; the deck was deserted. I leant over the rail; it was a marvellous morning, not a breath of wind to spoil the reflection of the semi-Moorish houses with their white walls and flat roofs, reflections which danced and curled in the deep waters as the ship turned slowly and silently into the picturesque harbour. There seemed to be a magic spell over the world at that moment: the unreal movement of the ship; the sense of desertion all around; the silent seagulls; the occasional splash of water from the exhaust falling into the sea from somewhere underneath my feet; the sound of a windlass on shore turning rustily; some empty boats going by; a small tug, a paddle-steamer, a launch, two or three sailing ships; all empty. How long shall we drift on like this? And then out of the early morning mist comes Table Mountain, dwarfing everything by its beauty. Table Mountain must be seen to be believed—no description, least of all one of mine, could do it justice. I leant over the rail and marvelled; everything Hallett had told me looked like coming true; he certainly had not exaggerated his description of his first impressions on arriving at Cape Town. I stepped back into my cabin, drew the curtains and began to dress.

* * * * *

We drew alongside about seven, and after having disbursed major and minor tips and made our *adieux* to the captain, the officers, the engineer, the ship's doctor and purser, we clambered down the gangway to be met at the bottom by the agent who was going to look after us on our twenty-five hundred mile trip round the country. . . .

* * * * *

We spent four days in Cape Town, giving a couple of recitals here and paying a flying visit to Stellenbosch, where we entertained the girls at the school.

Boris, I remember, made such a conquest with a particularly pretty little girl in the front row that one of the mistresses removed her to a more out-of-the-way position at the back of the hall. I noticed that after the dismissal of his inspiration our 'cellist's playing deteriorated.

Earlier in the day the second fiddle and I had made an unsuccessful attempt to climb to the top of Stellenbosch Mountain. It was much too much to do in a day and we were both about done up. On the way back I remember our calling, in the hope of having a rest, at a Dutch farmstead on the banks of a swiftly-flowing river which we had just crossed by means of a rickety rope bridge, and we were both feeling a bit shaky when we knocked at the forbidding-looking back door. We knocked several times and were eventually answered by a cackling and a grunting from within. We thereupon opened the door and, looking inside, were astonished to see the place covered with an assortment of animals and birds. They were all over the floor, the table and the chairs, and the smell was indescribable: goats, pigs, fowls, ducks, pigeons; but not a sign of a human being anywhere. We closed the door, went out of the yard and were just about to take a narrow path which looked as if it might be a short-cut back to the hotel where we were staying the night, when we saw a suspicious-looking animal disappearing into the long grass at the side of the path. It was a Cape lion. As we were not sure whether the thing might bite us, we decided, discretion being the better part of valour, that it would be wiser to keep to the road. We arrived back at the hotel slightly scared and far too exhausted to give a good account of ourselves in the evening. From that day we reserved excursions for 'days off'.

I cannot say which of all the towns we visited I liked the most. Johannesburg: where I was taken up on to the heights outside the town by a Dutch friend and shown a view so lovely that it would be impossible to describe it in writing, except to say that it reminded me of a story I used to read when I was a child, entitled 'Beyond the Blue Mountains', for there were my Blue Mountains far away across the veldt. It was here that the second fiddle and I decided to take a walk one morning out on to the veldt, to an inviting-looking kopje we had had an eye on for some time; and on being asked by the hotel porter where we were thinking of making for and our pointing out to him our intended destination, he held up his hands and exclaimed: "Good heavens, gentlemen, that's a good fifty-mile walk!"

Pretoria: where we spent hours exploring the deserted blockhouses on the edge of the town (unpleasant memories of the Boer War and the death of Queen Victoria and the dreadful mourning celebrations). Harrismith; Kroonstadt; Pietermaritzburg; Ladysmith; Bloemfontein; Durban: which reminds me of the afternoon recital in the course of which one of those sudden tropical storms broke, and we had to stop in the middle of a quartet until the hurricane abated once more. Durban: where the pavements were a couple of feet higher than the road to allow for the rise of the water after one of these downpours; where you take your walks abroad in rickshaws drawn by Kaffirs; where you could go almost anywhere for a 'ticky' (a threepenny bit); where the Zulu policemen wore leggings tied on with string over bare feet and have been known to carry and use umbrellas; where it says 'Beware of sharks' on the inviting seashore; where little Kaffir boys of fourteen years old can lift your cabin-trunk as easily as a grown English porter; where it is hot in the winter and baking hot in the summer; and where they know how to make a perfect Indian curry. Perhaps Durban was my favourite;

Kimberley was unfortunate, for we came unprepared for the weather; and yet Cape Town was lovely; and that view of the Blue Mountains from Johannesburg I shall never forget; I enjoyed my stay in Bloemfontein; Harrismith I found very pleasant to be in; Pietermaritzburg, too. It is impossible to have preference where South Africa is concerned, for everyone there makes you feel so happy and so at home that it is always the last place you stay in which seems to have been the best of all. Therefore I have no favourites.

It had been a wonderful experience.

I arrived at Waterloo with a silken shawl from Madeira for my mother, a pipe from Basutoland for my father, a sjambok from Pretoria for my brother to keep the dogs in order, a cheetah skin from Johannesburg to adorn my room in Park Road and a knobkerrie from Natal to accompany me on my walks.

* * * * *

It had proved a successful tour, at any rate from an artistic standpoint; the financial side had not been so satisfactory. We had followed too close on the heels of the Hambourgs' eldest brother, Mark, who had been out some months previously, and also the Cherniawsky Trio, who had anticipated our appearance in the various towns by a couple of weeks, and in some cases by only a few days. Still, it had been a splendid experience and had had the result of making a name for the Quartet in readiness for the series of recitals announced to take place at the Aeolian Hall in the autumn and winter.

On returning to London I was delighted to hear that my two baritone songs had been well received at the Royal Academy of Music Students' Concert at Queen's Hall, and also to find a letter from Messrs. Boosey & Co. awaiting me, with an invitation to call and see them with regard to the songs' publication. And so, one morning early, armed with my manuscript, I presented myself at No. 295 Regent Street and craved audience of Mr. Daniel Hatch, the writer of the letter. Hatch turned out to be one of the kindest of men and I shall never forget how encouraging he was to the young composer as he sat at the grand-piano in the salon at the far end of the building, playing over the pianoforte arrangements of his new songs. Five pounds down and a threepenny royalty after one hundred copies had been sold—my first earnings as a composer. It was a red-letter day for me—the world was being very kind at that moment. No more deputising dates from now on, on account of Quartet engagements; five unexpected pounds in my pocket; and my neuritis, which had benefited greatly through the electrical treatment

I had received, was now, since my return from the Cape, hardly noticeable. I seized my knobkerrie and hurried off to the Academy, where I was due for a lesson with Corder.

If only I could find some really good modern words to set to music. I could not go on setting Shakespeare for ever; the poems I had chosen for my song-cycle, 'Four Old English Songs', already had famous musical settings. Schubert was responsible for one, 'Who is Sylvia?', and Edward German for two, 'Orpheus with his lute' and 'It was a lover and his lass'. 'Under the greenwood tree' did not appear to possess anything approaching a modern setting, so I did not feel I was treading on delicate ground here. I certainly had had the temerity to write to John Galsworthy to ask him if he would allow me to set to music a poem of his which had appeared in an issue of *Punch*. He had written two delightful letters to the young, unknown composer, in the first giving his permission to use his verses and in the second saying how sorry he was not to be able to be present at the first performance at the Academy Concert at Queen's Hall. Then I thought of the famous lyric-writer, Fred E. Weatherly. Should I go straight to the point and write direct to him? On second thoughts, perhaps, I had better wait until the two new songs had been launched and my 'Four Old English Songs' had received their first hearing.

By the end of my ruminations I had arrived at the Academy. Here I spent a few minutes in the little office, looking over Hallett's shoulder as he laboriously made notes on a piece of paper in his efforts to solve a more than usually difficult problem in the Harmony Examination Paper spread out before him. Hallett, with his twinkling blue eyes behind his gold-rimmed spectacles, his cheery smile, his tight-fitting uniform and shining top-hat. Hallett, to whom many a little girl in the Academy went with her secret troubles; what should she do when such-and-such a professor said so-and-so to her? should she go out to tea with a certain male student? what did Hallett think about so-and-so's behaviour, should she go to the lady superintendent about it or should she just ignore it? Hallett the Counsellor we christened him at first, but after he had brought about several matrimonial events among the students, acting as mediator and arranging unexpected meetings so as to bring matters to a head more quickly, he came to earn the title of Hallett the Matchmaker. How frequently have I sat with him in his office and seen him tip the wink to some young blood in search of an amorous adventure, or protect some innocent Juliet by informing an unwanted Romeo that on leaving the Academy she had gone in the direction of Hanover Square when she was in reality half-way down New Bond Street. I think we all of us made use of the Matchmaker at one time or another, for besides being a shrewd judge of character he was reliable and, like the elephant, the possessor of a long memory. His manner was sometimes disarming, and he could keep you at arm's length while thinking out what he was going to say in reply to some question you had put to him, appearing to be deeply engrossed meanwhile in one of his examination paper problems: "Well, sir! This question about the correct resolution of the six-four chord has got me beat. I've already had two shots at it and neither answer seems correct." And then, under his breath and with a far-away look in his eyes, still studying the paper: "Let me *see!* Lesson with Mr. King at five-thirty. So if you wait outside just before six-thirty you *should* catch her!" He knew the movements of every professor and student who came in and out of the old building, and woe betide you if you had the misfortune to possess some idiosyncrasy or mannerism, for Hallett would mimic it to perfection, very often notifying you of the presence of some professor in the building by a characteristic shrug of the shoulders, a tilt of the gold-rimmed spectacles, a twist of the moustache or a lift of the hat.

To be in Hallett's good books was to count yourself as being among the blessed, for then you could go your way in peace—I was fortunately one of these, for Hallett was my friend. Hallett it was who secreted those loving little notes and delivered them so tactfully; Hallett it was who passed on those delicately-worded messages by word of mouth, with just that slight variation in the repetition which worked such wonders on the feelings of the recipient; Hallett it was who forgot to remind the two in Room 14, at the top of that long winding staircase, that everybody had left the building and he was about to lock up for the night (which reminds me that, in his autobiography *Farewell my Youth*, the room Arnold Bax writes about as being the ideal place for an assignation was No. 27. I wonder whether we are thinking of the same room and our memories have played us false, or can it be that, at that time, Arnold was one up on me? Not that I had anything to complain about over the advantages of No. 14, for to my young mind they were manifold).

Corder seemed pleased with my 'Four Old English Songs' and even went so far as to praise the orchestration, which was a great deal from one whose appreciation was more easily expressed by way of a smile. What a splendid teacher he was; never interfering with your ideas and always encouraging and trying to bring out the best in you by making you feel free to write exactly as you liked;

possibly making a suggestion now and again but never with the intention of forcing his ideas upon your own; always leading, and even then, gently.

* * * * *

She was in her late teens, had a delightful soprano voice, flexible and pretty in quality, and, besides singing intelligently, looked charming and was the fortunate possessor of an engaging platform manner. She and I had gone through the songs together over and over again before the orchestral rehearsal, for I knew how important it was for her to make a good impression with Mackenzie at the first hearing, especially as it depended on the Principal's decision as to whether the songs should go into the Orchestral Concert at Queen's Hall at the end of term. I remember how horribly nervous we both were on that Tuesday afternoon, waiting at the side of the platform for Green to call out our names. It was a crowded rehearsal, everybody seemed to be curious to hear the new singer and the new songs. I remember standing at Mackenzie's side, shaking inwardly with my heart pounding like a bicycle pump; but on glancing at my little friend I was alarmed to see that she was shaking outwardly, so what her heart could have been doing at that moment I did not like to think. Fortunately Mackenzie decided to run through the orchestral accompaniments alone, and this gave her an opportunity to calm down.

We need not have worried—she sang like an angel, the Principal beamed the whole way through, the orchestra excelled itself and the audience was enthusiastic. Dear Mackenzie, why was it he was so kind to me when to so many of the others he was awkwardness itself? My friend Arnold Bax evidently had no use for him and I expect the feeling was reciprocated, for it is not natural to be popular with anyone whom you dislike. Mackenzie loathed anything approaching the modern idiom, and Arnold, considered modern even to-day, must in 1906 have seemed to the Principal like some composer come up from the Lower Regions especially to irritate his sense of orthodoxy. Now, I have always written melodies, I simply cannot help it, and I think it must have been my tunes which made me popular with Mackenzie, but do not imagine that because I got on well with him I shared with him his dislike of Arnold Bax's music. Arnold Bax's command of the orchestra, allied with a vivid imagination, has been the means of the orchestral library being enriched by a large variety of lovely works. Besides being blessed with a *facile* pen he has the quality of knowing his own mind, by which I mean that when he has once composed a work, he produces it and leaves it at that. In the old days I always seemed to be playing orchestral works by composers who appeared never to know exactly what they wanted to say. I could cite several instances of new works by supposed composers of repute coming up for a second performance, sometimes altered almost beyond recognition. One composer, at the period about which I am writing, never seemed able to leave a work alone and *would* keep on retouching and adding, but, being one of our 'serious' composers, he was permitted by the 'powers that be' to produce, with much waving of flags and beating of drums, a Second Edition (called by the viola section a 'second attempt'), which would never have been sanctioned in the case of a composer of the 'light' school. Fortunately the composer of Light Orchestral Music usually knows his own mind, and his second performance is due not to the necessity of having another try-out but to the very good reason that the public wishes to hear the work all over again, just as it was in the beginning.

And now I would like to take my reader back once again to the autumn of 1908 and to the garden at the back of the Hambourgs' house in Clifton Gardens. It was a gloomy afternoon, not at all suitable for the taking of photographs, but it was this very matter which had brought the Hambourg String Quartet out of its nicely warmed studio to watch four well-known composers and a budding fifth giving their best smiles while being abjured by the photographer to "hold it". The four well-known ones were Hamilton Harty (later to become Sir Hamilton Harty), Frank Bridge, York Bowen, and J. D. Davis; there is no need to inform you of the identity of the budding fifth. The occasion was the completion of a String Quartet written round the famous 'Londonderry Air' which had been commissioned by the Hambourgs, each composer contributing one movement. It may sound as if the result of five movements built round the same theme would have proved monotonous, but such was not the case, and as a matter of fact it was surprising what a great variety each composer had contrived to work into his own individual piece. I cannot remember offhand how the movements were divided or which composer wrote which. My own small contribution took the form of a minuet (which had to be repeated at the first performance at the Aeolian Hall) but the movement which stands out in my mind as being the best of the five was by Frank Bridge. This was a beautiful piece of quartet-writing with a very effective viola solo at the opening, which gave me a thrill whenever I played it. It was my first meeting with Harty, Bridge and Davis; York Bowen I had met several times while at the Academy, where I used to curse the day which possessed him to write a Sonata in

C minor for Viola and Pianoforte. I never could tackle the last movement of this and was afraid that Tertis might put me down for a Fortnightly Concert with it—fortunately he never did. Hamilton Harty I came to know well and saw much of him in later years when conducting my works at the various Festivals about the country—he was a great musician and a loss to us both as a composer and a conductor. Frank Bridge (another viola player, by the way, and a very fine one) became a great friend of mine and in later years gave me a useful 'tip' regarding orchestration which I have never forgotten. To the uninitiated it will mean nothing: "Eric, don't double more than you can help." What a nice fellow he was, sympathetic, kind, helpful, understanding, an artist to his finger-tips and generous in his praise of others.

* * * * *

My student days at the Royal Academy of Music drew to a close and I said farewell to Park Road, Regent's Park. The Hambourgs were anxious that I should live nearer them so that we could put in more time rehearsing for the recitals and engagements which had to be fulfilled about the country. I was not sorry to say goodbye to Park Road in some ways, although I had had some happy times during my stay there, but in the boarding-house close by the Hambourgs' house I thought I might be able to get more home comforts than in my bed-sitting-room looking out on to those uninteresting chimney-pots. More home comforts there certainly were, and many other things too. It was one of the most astonishing places I had ever lived in, this house standing back from the road in Clifton Gardens. A large house with a spacious dining-room and drawing-room, a host of bedrooms and a huge ballroom which was let out every Saturday night for dancing. The first morning at breakfast I met my fellow-boarders, among them being a barrister, an Australian baritone, a 'cellist, a Scottish violinist, a young pianiste and pupil of Professor Hambourg, a pretty chorus-girl from the 'Chocolate Soldier' Company, and one or two Indian students. Miss Hamilton, who ran the establishment and who was dubbed by the Scotsman 'the Hamilton', was middle-aged, peroxided her hair and wore very long ear-rings. She reminded me of the traditional old 'pro' and, being good-natured, kindness personified and completely unreliable, confirmed my belief that at one time or other she must have had something to do with either the music-hall or the stage. Her affections were divided between her guests and a marmoset; the latter, being unused to the vagaries of the English climate and suffering from a weak chest in consequence, spent the major part of the day nestling in the Hamilton's bosom, and during meals our hostess was fully occupied, ministering to the wants of her large family and at the same time attending to the shivering and gasping little creature bobbing about under the protection of her silken blouse. I cannot remember ever seeing the marmoset in full, for it never actually came out into the open; all I can recall is the vision of a face of a tiny old man popping up every now and then and having a look round at the assembled company and then popping down again into that inviting warm patch below. This was during its better moments. At other times it would be very still and we sometimes wondered whether it had suffocated in the generous folds of the Hamilton's flesh. But at one memorable breakfast the wretched little creature appeared to be more than usually lively and bounced up and down to such an extent that we were afraid it might fall into the Hamilton's porridge. We were pleased to see the little thing in such an apparently good state of health and were wondering whether it would emerge entirely from its nest at last and come down on to the table (horrid thought!) when, all of a sudden, it gave a squeak and disappeared. A hasty downward glance from the Hamilton was followed by a scream of "Oh! it's dead!" She rose and hurried from the room, taking the corpse with her, and left the company to see what it could make of breakfast after having witnessed this heart-rending scene.

It was a strange house, made the stranger by the presence of the Indian students, who brought a faint Eastern atmosphere into the place. They were so quiet in their movements, their comings and goings being barely noticeable, and at night, when one passed them on the stairs, they were not even visible. At first I thought the *ménage* was a little unusual, but when one night, coming out of my room at the top of the house to investigate a queer noise, I stepped on to a couple in a somewhat compromising attitude, I was forced to the conclusion that the establishment was more than unusual, it was definitely odd. It appeared they were a couple of 'liers-out' from the Saturday night dance downstairs in the ballroom, and with a polite request that they would in future confine their attentions to the floor below I retired once more to my bed, but not to sleep.

In some ways it had its advantages being near to the Hambourgs, for it meant I only had to go downstairs, out of the front door, round the corner and up a few more stairs, to be hard at work at a new quartet, and all within the space of a few minutes; but when it came to Jan and Boris sending their youngest sister to haul me out of bed one morning for a specially early rehearsal, I wondered whether it might not have been wiser if I had settled in a more remote district. She was a bright-eyed, rosy-cheeked little girl, a little too determined for my liking, and had evidently been given her orders to get me round to the house at all costs, for my protests ended in every stitch of clothing being dragged ruthlessly off the bed, and I firmly believe that if I had argued any more she would have had my pyjamas off as well. At any rate, the gleam in her eye was sufficient to make me swear to her that if she would leave me alone I would be round as soon as I could get dressed.

* * * * *

After I had been at Clifton Gardens for some weeks the food began to deteriorate, and the violinist, with whom I had struck up a friendship, suggested our going along to have a second breakfast at Reggiori's, in Edgware Road, this after we had breakfasted on an underdone egg and some toast and were beginning to feel 'fed up' as well as empty. We arrived at the restaurant ravenous. What a meal it was: porridge, fish, bacon and eggs, toast and marmalade and pots of steaming coffee! My Scottish friend and I had not eaten such a breakfast for months, nay, it seemed like years. From that date it became an understood thing that twice a week Mac and I should make a journey to Edgware Road for the purpose of fortifying ourselves. The food at the Hamilton's becoming daily worse, we decided that we simply could not live on two breakfasts a week, and one morning early the two of us, seated in a hansom with instrument cases and suitcases, headed across Maida Vale to settle ourselves into a couple of pleasant bedrooms in Loudoun Road, where we were told the service was good and the food excellent.

Then came a letter from Mrs. Henry Wood telling me that it was her intention to give the first performance of my 'Four Old English Songs' at one of the Promenade Concerts in the forthcoming season at Queen's Hall. Would I go to her house and run through the songs with her? And so I went one day and spent a happy afternoon with the Woods at their home in Elsworthy Road, playing the songs to her on her piano and going through the full-score with him on the table. It was all so exciting that I could scarcely believe it. How wonderful to be going to hear my songs sung by this fine singer and to have them played on such a famous orchestra, and with Henry Wood conducting! A great deal seemed to be happening just then. I had screwed up my courage and written to Fred E. Weatherly to ask him if he would entertain the idea of giving one of his lyrics to an unknown composer. He answered by return of post with an invitation for me to call and see him at his house in Woburn Place.

I was shown up to the study by an elderly house-keeper, and as we mounted the broad staircase of the old house in Bloomsbury I was endeavouring to picture what this famous barrister-poet would be like. To tell the truth, I was beginning to feel a little nervous at being given an interview by a man who had a string of popular songs to his credit and who, besides being a shrewd lawyer, was forty years my senior. I walked bashfully into the pleasant study, and there, with his back to the light, in the window overlooking Woburn Place, sitting in a swivel-chair, was the famous author. He was one of the smallest men I had met and, for such a remarkably gifted man, strangely enough, was the possessor of a small head. He rose from his seat with the agility of a boy, shook me by the hand, offered me a cigarette and made me feel at home in a few seconds. I noticed on his desk two piles of papers, the one on his right looked like lyrics and the one on his left had the appearance of legal documents. I was right in both cases, for during the conversation which followed he told me he wrote poems while working out difficult problems of law. As I sat by his side listening to him read his latest verses, I felt as if I might have been writing music for years, for he did not ask me what I had done but merely enquired as to what kind of lyric I wanted. It appeared that he always composed his poems to a tune or rhythm of his own, and when reading his verses to you he would adopt a listening attitude and croon his lines in the most extraordinary manner. If the words were particularly moving he would frequently break down with emotion and have to wait until he could compose himself sufficiently to continue. His knack of painting pictures with his poems ("word-pictures", he called them) was uncanny, for with a few delightfully chosen words he could conjure up a scene which it would have taken anyone else a whole page to describe.

We sat in his study and talked, he playing about with a little brass ornament on his desk and I pulling at a cigarette. At last he turned sideways towards me, crossed his legs, lifted his hands, pressed his finger-tips together and said: "How do you feel about a West Country song?" Now I had always wanted to write something in the heavy three-four rhythm of the West Country, and when he pushed 'Stonecracker John' into my hands I knew instinctively that this was what I had been looking for.

On the top of the horse-bus jolting me north-west along Maida Vale, with the words to 'Stonecracker John' lying in my pocket, a tune came into my head which I managed to scribble down, between bumps, on to the back of an envelope. A couple of days later I was in the room at the back of the building in Regent Street, playing the song over to Arthur Boosey (the owner of the firm), Harry Dearth (the famous bass), Mudie, Hatch and Harold Samuel (the reason for Harold Samuel's inclusion in the gathering at Messrs. Boosey & Co. being that he was at that time the official reader to the firm). Harry Dearth was for singing it at the next Ballad Concert at the Albert Hall; Arthur Boosey was dead against publishing it at all, on account of its rhythm being different from anything they had hitherto published; Mudie and Hatch were neutral; and Harold Samuel, true to type, was for trying it out right away. I came away with another five pounds in my pocket and received the proofs in due course. The song was put away on the shelf, where it remained for the best part of a year. Eventually, thanks to repeated requests on Harry Dearth's part, it was at last brought out, dusted, and sung by this magnificent artist at the Albert Hall. It was an instantaneous success—sold thousands of copies and started a vogue in this type of song.

For many years Fred E. Weatherly kept me posted about his latest poems, and between us we turned out quite a number of successful songs. I used to stay with him and his wife in their house on the hills overlooking Bath on the one hand, and away to the famous White Horse on the other. Here we three would sit and hatch and plot, and I would play tunes and he would write verses and she would listen and approve. In later years a fourth joined the party, in the shape of my wife, and then the two males would discuss music and poetry while the two females discussed *them*.

I never think of those days without recalling the delightful way Weatherly had of sometimes communicating with me through the medium of little poems—it may have been in a letter or even on a card dropped into the letter-box if he had called at the flat and I had happened to be out. Here are two which I think are worth quoting—both of them, as you will sense, being a kind of prod at me for what he considered was lack of method on my part, added to a desire to live a life of ease. The first is in a letter, dated December 29th, 1920. . . .

10, Edward Street, Bath.

MY DEAR ERIC,

My new book contains a song you said you were going to set. . . .

'Have you forgotten, voice of my heart,
Which was the song you chose?

Or has the melody fallen apart,
Just like a broken rose?
Or is it only the same old tale
That on my memory floats,
What do the poor old words avail
When set and forgotten by Coates?'

> Love to you both,
> Ever yours,
> F.E.W.

The following was slipped into the letter-box and had evidently been composed on the door-mat as a result of receiving no answer to his ring. There is no date. . . .

I knocked last Monday at your door,
My faithful promise keeping,
The only answer was a snore!
  I said,
    ' 'Tis Eric *sleeping!*'

Next week if work and fate be kind,
A trip to Town I'm taking,
And then I trust that I shall find
My little songbird *waking!*
  F.E.W.

*　*　*　*　*

My stay at Loudoun Road was very satisfactory. Mac did not seem to know what it was to lose his temper, he never let anything ruffle him and was the most genial of men to live with. We got on well together and our ways seemed to lead us strangely along the same paths. We played together for weeks in the octet directed by Stanley Hawley for the Lena Ashwell Season at the Kingsway Theatre, we were together in the first orchestra formed by Sir Thomas Beecham and later in the Queen's Hall Orchestra with Sir Henry Wood. It was while playing at the Kingsway Theatre that I met Lena Ashwell; after she had asked Stanley Hawley who was the bright-faced young man in the orchestra who was always smiling.

Edward Knoblock, who spent a good deal of time in the theatre reading plays for Lena Ashwell (this was before his Royalty Theatre successes, 'Milestones' and 'My Lady's Dress'), used to come down into the band-room to see our musical director, Stanley Hawley, and it was during one of these visits that I made his acquaintance. At that time, if my memory does not play me false, Knoblock lived in some delightful rooms in Wigmore Street, where I was so intrigued by the canary which flew round his sitting-room at will and during meal-times settled on his shoulder and pecked food from out of his mouth. Knoblock had also taught his little feathered friend the art of kissing, which it did with marked effect by tweaking his cheek with its beak. He and I used to sit and talk for hours on end, and then he would say: "I want to show you the most lovely sight in London," and we would wander out along Wigmore Street as the day was drawing to a close and turn into New Bond Street, where the golden light of the evening sky seemed to have turned the fashionable thoroughfare into a thing of beauty. What a charm there was about New Bond Street in those far-away days and how different it all seems to-day! He would gaze at the scene for some time in silence and then would turn and invite me back to his rooms for a final drink and a smoke, before putting the canary to bed and settling down to do some writing. I used to run into my friend in unexpected places; the most unexpected of all was during Sir Herbert Tree's production of 'Le Bourgeois Gentilhomme', which included Richard Strauss's music to the ballet, 'Ariadne auf Naxos', at His Majesty's Theatre. The orchestra had been specially selected, all the players being soloists, and Beecham was the conductor.

In one of the acts, Tree, dressed up in a fantastic costume, had to take his seat at the side of the stage in company with a crowd of friends in equally fantastic clothes, to watch a *corps de ballet* dance to the strains of Strauss's music. One night during the ballet I chanced to glance up over the footlights from my seat in the orchestra, to see Tree deep in conversation with a little man in an outrageously extravagant dress, seated on the floor on his left. Now Tree should have been giving the whole of his attention to the entertainment taking place on the stage. As I watched, something about the small figure on the ground seemed to me to be vaguely familiar. I kept looking up from the music and across the stage at the two so deep in conversation, when all of a sudden the little figure turned its head, looked straight down at me and with an enigmatical wink put its first finger down the side of its nose, as if to say, 'Mum's the word!' It was Knoblock, taking advantage of Tree's only free time to discuss the details of a forthcoming production at His Majesty's Theatre. To me this was the one bright spot of the season. I did not care for Tree's production of Molière's masterpiece and, 'Ariadne auf Naxos' being the one work by Richard Strauss which I find dull, I was not sorry when the season came to an end; but it was worth the drudgery to have seen Knoblock's first appearance as a mummer.

I was not associated with the Beecham Orchestra for more than a few months, but the time I spent with this fine ensemble under its inspiring and enthusiastic conductor was full of interesting and amusing experiences. I doubt if there has ever been heard in this country or elsewhere a more electrical-sounding body of players than that which went to make up the personnel of the orchestra which came to be known among orchestral players as 'Beecham's Pill-harmonic'. The orchestra was electrical and the conductor was electrical and, as Beecham had acquired practically every well-known principal string, wood-wind and brass instrumentalist he could lay his hands on, the renderings were electrical too. In the viola section alone there were eight at-one-time-or-another principals, and as the leader was Lionel Tertis himself it goes without saying that the eleven players behind him were on their mettle. Never before or since have I heard an orchestra play with greater brilliance than the Beecham Symphony Orchestra of forty odd years ago.

Beecham had an amazing way of getting the best out of his players by making some irrelevant remark in a high-pitched voice, just as he was about to raise his stick for the opening piece. "Now then, gentlemen, do your *worst!*" seemed to bring out the 'devil' in the orchestra, and the performance which followed after this misleading exhortation was never anything but terrific. I have seen audiences raised to a pitch of enthusiasm after a performance such as this which makes the plaudits of a Promenade gathering on a Saturday night appear lukewarm. There is no doubt that the Beecham 'Pill-harmonic', under its high-tension conductor, was a thing which had to be heard to be believed, but I do not think I should have cared to have ended my days playing under this temperamental musician, for I am sure my nerves would have suffered in consequence. Calling rehearsals at ten o'clock in the morning and keeping the orchestra waiting until eleven-thirty, and then running straight on without a break till three and four in the afternoon, is enough to try the temper of an angel. This is what happened frequently during the rehearsals for the first performance of 'Elektra' at Covent Garden, and it brought the orchestra nearly to the point of breakdown. Lionel Tertis gave in after the first night, I took over the job of principal viola and gave in after a couple of nights, Siegfried Wertheim (the principal viola of the Queen's Hall Orchestra) took over and finished the season. It was a gruelling business: Beecham coolly continuing to rehearse from hour to hour, with the orchestra becoming more and more exhausted; Richard Strauss standing in the front row of the stalls (with that enormous head of his and arms which reached down nearly to his knees), directing, suggesting, interrupting; the artists in a state of bewilderment, not knowing which was most important, the voice parts or the orchestral part; Beecham, just before the curtain rose on the first night of 'Elektra', shouting at the orchestra: "The singers think they're going to be heard and I'm going to make jolly well certain that they are *not!*" Whether the singers managed to make themselves heard above the din of this much-over-orchestrated score I could not tell, but, judging from what I *could* hear from my submerged position in the orchestra, I hoped they weren't.

How clearly I remember the time when the versatile Camille Saint-Saëns came over and gave a series of recitals with the Beecham Orchestra at Queen's Hall, and how the diminutive Frenchman cursed our conductor in voluble French at one of the concerts. It was during the playing of a passage about which the soloist and the conductor each had their own ideas, and Beecham, vaguely waving his stick, looked down at the first desk of violas, pulled his beard and then gazed heavenwards with an expressive smirk as if to say, 'What *does* it matter?'

I do not know whether it was anything to do with the members of the Celtic Quartet being among the personnel of the orchestra, but wherever the Beecham Philharmonic went it was dogged by amusing and sometimes disconcerting interruptions. At Exeter, for instance, Debussy's 'L'après-midi d'un faune' had to be started all over again because of the barking and splashing of performing seals which had been left behind in their tank at the back of the stage from the show on the previous night, and the stream of water caused by their riotous behaviour, trickling across the stage and dripping on to the floor below, caused a minor diversion among the occupants of the front row of the stalls. At Southampton, 'Mr.' Jolly and 'Mr.' Merry, the two percussion players, fell off their perch at the back of the orchestra and carried the bass-drum with them, and the ovation which greeted their reappearance, complete with drum, was the signal for everything we played that night to make a sensation. At Hanley, the first clarinet player fell asleep during the performance (after many sleepless nights in trains) and dropped his instrument in a silent bar, and as it rolled its clumsy way down to the footlights, clicking its keys as it went, the silent bar turned out to be the noisiest bar in the piece. The *pièce de résistance*, however, came by the way of Elgar's First Symphony, which was played nightly on tour, and its performance gradually diminished in length as Beecham became more and more impatient with the daily repetition of the work. At first he instituted carefully thought-out 'cuts', but, as time went on, these became more and more drastic until, one night just before the performance, he announced that there were going to be 'cuts' of the most ruthless nature, from here-to-there in each movement, and he ended up defiantly with the words: "I don't know how it sounds and I don't *care!*" Now, as it takes a great deal of music to play fifteen minutes you can imagine what Elgar's First Symphony in A flat, taking normally about fifty minutes to perform, sounded like with the playing time cut down to thirty-five minutes. I can remember what it sounded like the first time we played the work *in full* on account of nearing the 'Elgar' Country—we had become so used to the cuts that it was like playing the symphony at first sight and the result was little short of catastrophic—it sounded awful. Then came the arming of the orchestra with crackers which were thrown out of carriage windows as the train was leaving a station. One enormous one (of the cannon variety) with a time-fuse, deposited by the principal 'cellist under a luggage trolley on Birmingham station, exploded just as the train was entering the tunnel outside the station, and we were stopped and backed into the platform, where the station-master threatened to arrest every member of the orchestra, Beecham included. And in contrast to this, there was the delight with which the porters on the railway in Ireland received the volleys of jumping-crackers which we hurled at them as our special train slowed down to pass through some wayside station; which makes me think of Birmingham and the Black-Gloved Watch Committee which insisted on the great Pavlova wearing stockings before she was considered fit to be seen by the innocent youth of the city—no wonder they objected to our crackers! Towards the end of the tour we had an Italian tenor with us, towards whom Beecham conceived a hatred. This singer had a prodigious capacity for holding a long note and delighted in showing off this accomplishment (most inartistically) in the last note but one of Wagner's famous 'Lohengrin's Farewell'. At each performance this note increased in length until Beecham one night, unable to stand the strain of it any longer (the whole orchestra, in company with Beecham, felt they had to hold their breath during the time it took to sing this note, with unfortunate consequences to the wind instrument players when they re-entered), took out his watch, turned deliberately on the singer and *timed* him. The consequent 'drying-up' of the poor man, and the label attached to his overcoat, announcing to a crowded railway station the next morning, 'I AM A TENOR', sent the orchestra on its way without a singer. I shall never forget the noise caused at the Adelphi Hotel, Liverpool, due to our irresponsible conductor, in a fit of exuberance, throwing dozens of electric light bulbs down the elevator shaft for the fun of hearing them go off at the bottom; nor the major riot in the hotel the morning Beecham changed the shoes outside the bedroom doors, a few hours before the departure of the American boat. These and a hundred and one things were the daily fare of the members of the Beecham Symphony Orchestra, and I do not think it is to be wondered at that this fine ensemble had such a short life.

My arm began to pain me a good deal about this time; no doubt long hours of playing, long journeys (many of them at night), lack of proper meals, lack of sleep, all contributed to accentuate the trouble. The Hambourg String Quartet had been disbanded some time earlier on account of Jan going off to Paris and Boris taking up a post in Canada, which alleviated the playing problem for a time. But as I was invited by Philip Cathie to take his brother's place as viola player in his quartet, I was soon back again where I started. My association with the Cathie String Quartet lasted a good many months and in some ways was a pleasant experience. During this time I was frequently reminded of the ill-fated Celtic Quartet, partly because the leader of the Celtic was the second fiddle of the Cathie and partly on account of the funny things which kept happening at unexpected moments. One night, when we were playing at an important musical gathering, the leader turned over two pages by mistake, and the momentary silence which followed this manœuvre was prolonged by the second fiddle and the 'cello 'drying up' from sheer nerves, during which time the viola crawled along unheeding, all by himself. The re-entrance of the 'cello, followed by the second fiddle, followed by the first, gave the impression of a fugue, which was loudly applauded by an unsuspecting audience. Another time we were commissioned to give the first performance of a new string quartet by one of the professors of the Royal College of Music, and the lead up to the climax in the last movement was so like the 'March of the Men of Harlech' that we were never able to rehearse the finish of the quartet as written, but went into a spirited rendering of this famous march-tune, rising from our seats at the same time to mark the effect. I remember the nervous state to which we were reduced when it came to the actual performance in the Bechstein Hall and the agony of apprehension we were in, as to whether we should be able to take that inviting corner without succumbing to the temptation of rising from our seats and giving away to the audience the true derivation of the theme of the last movement. Funniest of all, though, was the night when we were all reduced to a state of mild hysteria through our leader, who had a peculiar habit of holding his bow very lightly between his thumb and the tips of his four fingers, playing with such nonchalance that he threw his bow into the second row of the stalls. A mild-looking little man with blue glasses gallantly got up from his seat and handed it back to its owner and was thanked with a charming inclination of the head.

All these experiences were tempered by the nightmare of the ache in my left arm, which occasionally, especially after a difficult passage, became so acute that I was forced to drop my arm down by my side in order to let the blood run down into my hand to remedy the numbness which had set in. Before a recital, and even during the programme, I would try to find a cold tap to put my hand under, as this always seemed to impart strength to my fingers which would carry me through at any rate a couple of pages. I remember the anxiety I used to feel when playing the opening viola solo in Smetana's 'Aus meinen leben' Quartet, if it happened to be a hot summer night with no cold tap handy; a cold douche on my wrist and hand would always see me through this solo (what happened after that did not matter). If there were a tap to be found anywhere in the building I used to wait until the very last moment before going on to the platform, so as to give my muscles the extra impetus needed to carry me through that first vital page. Practising was quite out of the question, it being all I could do to cope with the rehearsals and the concerts without breaking down altogether. All the same, my viola-playing days had their bright moments, and I think the most entertaining of them all was when I was asked to play second principal in a specially-chosen orchestra for two concerts devoted to the works of one of our moderns. The composer, in the first place, was a poor conductor, and in the second place had an unusual appearance. If only his music had been as acceptable as himself (for he was a charming, unassuming man) all would have been well. It struck me as extraordinary that a man with such a mild personality should have felt the urge to express himself in such crude musical terms, although in all probability in the modern age in which we live to-day I should not have noticed anything out of the ordinary. The worst of it is that queer sounds issuing from an orchestra always give me an insane desire to laugh, and as the sounds which greeted my ears at the rehearsal, besides being queer, were comical in the extreme, not only did I laugh, I cried. The rehearsal, with the conductor's eye on me, was a nightmare; the more I tried to control myself the more hysterical I became, and by the time announced for the concert I was really in no fit state to appear. I took my seat beside Waldo-Warner (at that time a member of the London String

Quartet), who was playing principal, and prayed silently that I should be able to keep myself in hand. Just before the composer came on to the platform I asked Waldo-Warner if he would let me know when we got to letter H in the new work we were playing, as it would save me having to count about one hundred and seventy bars before I made my entry. Now, Waldo-Warner had not a single bar's rest in the whole work, so I knew it was quite safe leaving it to him to give me the cue when to come in. It was the one hundred and seventy silent bars which bothered me, and the composer being an inferior conductor and the time-signature changing every few bars from six-eight to seven-sixteen, from eight-two to seven-four and so on, the chances of losing my place were considerable.

It was a full house, everyone seemed to be there. I spotted Mackenzie, Beecham, Corder, Landon Ronald, Stanford, Parry, Henry Wood, and music critics by the score dotted here and there about the stalls. The composer mounted to the rostrum, looking very artistic, clad in velvet coat with sleeves several inches too long. The music started. I prayed hard. After a few bars the desire to giggle overcame me. I lifted my viola before my face and laughed outright and felt a little better. The noise in the orchestra grew. It was becoming funnier and funnier. I glanced down into the audience. Mackenzie was shaking and dissolved in tears, Corder was grinning, Beecham was looking heavenwards, Parry was smiling, Wood was hiding behind his beard, Stanford looked bored and Landon Ronald was weeping in concert with Mackenzie. The music seemed to have been going on for a long time and there was no sign from Waldo-Warner. I glanced towards him through a mist of tears and there he was, playing away for dear life and looking frightened to death. I hid behind my viola for a space and laughed some more, and then peeped over the top of the instrument to see Mackenzie's stooping figure making its way down to the bottom of the hall, followed by Landon Ronald with Corder bringing up the rear. Beecham was now laughing openly, Wood was making notes, Parry was dozing and Stanford was looking hostile. I bobbed down again behind my viola and cried helplessly. Suddenly I became aware that the principal viola was trying to attract my attention. My cue at last! I raised my eyebrows, but was answered with a shake of the head; then, still playing wildly and with his eyes starting out of his head, he managed to gasp at me over his shoulder: "Where are we?" Then the idea of his being lost and still playing struck me as so fantastically funny that, throwing all reserve to the winds, I raised my viola, the tears pouring down my cheeks, across the belly of the instrument and into the enormous F holes, and played the last bar of the work over and over again, and not once did it fit into the scheme of things. I was still playing the same bar when the conductor drew my attention to the fact that the work was over. I was not invited to attend the next concert.

* * * * *

I remember how delighted I was one day to receive a pre-paid telegram from Dan Godfrey, asking what were my terms for a performance of Elgar's 'Gerontius' at the Winter Gardens, Bournemouth. At last, I thought to myself, I had the opportunity to demand a decent fee—no more of your paltry 'one-ones' and 'two-twos'. It should be at least ten guineas. And then the unwelcome truth dawned on me and I hastily put the telegram into an envelope and sent it off to John Coates. How my namesake laughed when I told him this pathetic story one day, during lunch at the musicians' table at Pagani's. Poor old Pagani's, knocked about so badly in company with our beloved Queen's Hall by a Nazi bomb-aimer trying to put an end to our broadcasting system. At this table at Pagani's each day, and especially on Symphony Concert days at Queen's Hall, would foregather every musician of note in London at that time. Sometimes you would see world-famous artists sitting at other tables about the restaurant, if they were desirous of talking over some private business or other, the musicians' table not being the place where you could talk in an undertone. The pride of the table was David Devant, of the famous Maskelyne and Devant, Illusionists, of St. George's Hall. His arrival at luncheon was the signal for you to see that your watch was safely tucked away in your pocket and keys under careful guard, for his presence would be sure to coincide with the disappearance of sundry spoons and forks, watches, golden sovereigns; even rings were known to appear at the bottom of some empty coffee cup. Next to Devant in importance, but certainly not in popularity, was Harry Dearth, who for some time answered to the name of 'The Stonecracker' on account of his association with my first song success, 'Stonecracker John'. His name brings back to me memories of hilarious evenings spent with him at the Sketch Club, where I used to sit by his side at dinner in a bewildered state, trying to arrest the plates, knives, spoons and forks as they were hurled at me from the head of the table—the *habitués* of the club were, of course, dexterous at catching these utensils in full flight, but it was not so easy for the guests. This famous bass was tremendously popular and it was fortunate for me that my songs suited his style, for he sang them wherever he went. Many a time have I known the curtain to be rung down on him at such places as the Palladium on a Sunday night, after he had sung 'Stonecracker John' twice, followed by 'A Dinder Courtship' twice, with an enthusiastic audience still clamouring for more.

Among other visitors to the musicians' table were such artists as John McCormack, Moiseiwitsch, Kreisler, Mark Hambourg, Cyril Scott, Percy Grainger, Norman O'Neill, Roger Quilter, Herman Finck, Edward German, Mengelberg, Ysaye, Nikisch, Raoul Pugno, Moriz Rosenthal, Mischa Elman, Jacques Thibaud, Alfred Cortot, Pau Casals, Delius, Solomon, Pachmann, Rachmaninoff, Ben Davies, Peter Dawson, Plunket Greene, Santley, Gervase Elwes; names without number. There was not another place like it in the whole of London—and over this great and fluctuating family presided Maschini, the proprietor and most perfect of hosts, who went from table to table followed closely by his little bulldog.

Stanley Hawley, the Director of Music for Lena Ashwell at the Kingsway Theatre and Secretary to the Royal Philharmonic Society, lived just round the corner from Pagani's in Oxford Circus Mansions, and sometimes I used to wander in with him after lunch and listen to his stories about musical London as it was in the days before I knew it. They were fascinating talks; sometimes about a new Chopin Edition he was working on; or of the time when he and Lena Ashwell were students together at the Royal Academy of Music; of Mengelberg, when he came over to this country to conduct, refusing to be paid in anything but golden sovereigns; of Edward German shooting cats from his bedroom window in his lodgings in Maida Vale; and the lovely story of the time when he (Hawley) was a student at the Academy and was sent to meet Edvard Grieg at Waterloo Station when this great musician came over to England to play his concerto at a Royal Philharmonic Society Concert at Queen's Hall. Grieg had promised to come to the Academy in Tenterden Street, where he had signified his intention of hearing Stanley Hawley play his concerto with Mackenzie and the Academy Orchestra. Could Hawley get Grieg across Waterloo Bridge? He refused to budge, standing there in his tweed cape, mushroom hat and leggings, fascinated by the shipping down towards Tower Bridge; talking, gesticulating, pointing, anything rather than bother about such trivial things as pianoforte concertos in A minor. After a good deal of persuasion, Grieg consented to continue the walk to the Academy, and, judging by the way Hawley said he stopped and looked at everything *en route*, it must have taken literally hours. At any rate, Tenterden Street was reached at last and the concerto, as played by Stanley Hawley, made such a deep impression on the composer that he said it was quite absurd for him to be playing the work himself at the Queen's Hall the next day. As Hawley played it so much better than he—Stanley Hawley must certainly take his place; he insisted on it and would not hear another word. However, when it was pointed out to him that he was under contract to the Royal Philharmonic Society and also how disappointed the audience would be at having to hear an Academy student instead of the great maestro himself, the enthusiastic little Norwegian smiled and saw reason.

It was Stanley Hawley who suggested my sending my 'Four Old English Songs' to Agnes Nicholls (a famous soprano of that time and wife of Sir Hamilton Harty). I blush when I think of the parcel which arrived at the prima donna's house and on which she had to pay postage, through my having forgotten to attach the necessary stamps, and I shudder when I bring to mind my apologetic letter which followed the realisation of the omission, which also went into the pillar-box minus this most important appendage. No wonder she never sang my songs.

Stanley Hawley in those far-away days, besides being famous as an accompanist and a composer of some repute, was quite a power in the musical world. He was one of those men about whom you knew practically nothing, and yet he seemed to know when anything important was afoot and used to help us young musicians tremendously by telling us when he heard that an orchestra or a quartet was needing extra players. He was in some ways a strange man and to all intents and purposes a lonely one, too, living as he did in his bachelor chambers off Oxford Circus, with no other company than his grand-piano and an extensive and valuable collection of first editions. Sometimes we used to walk back together from the Kingsway Theatre of a night and I would go in with him for half an hour and have a smoke, and talk over the doings of the theatre and the new show which Lena Ashwell was thinking of putting on. Then I would say good-night and carry on my way, leaving him sitting in a cloud of smoke, about to get down to finishing the corrections of the final proofs of the Chopin Edition on which he had been working for so long.

* * * * *

The house in Loudoun Road was a 'writey' kind of place, being nicely back from the road and with a good elevation, which gave you a feeling of height and caught all the afternoon sun. To write, it is essential that I am high up, away from the ground. I cannot work on a ground floor, so if my abode is in a house I must have a room upstairs to work in. I should like to live either in a balloon suspended a thousand feet above Regent's Park, or in my own private lighthouse on a rock two hundred feet above a semi-tropical sea, or, failing this, on the summit of a mountain in a house with a tower from which I could see three hundred miles each way. As it is, I have had to be contented with living one hundred feet up on the top floor of a block of flats. This diversion is merely to point out what elevation means to me, and to explain why I was so happy in my room in Loudoun Road. Here I did a good deal of writing and pocketed a number of cheques for five pounds, royalties on several new songs which had been accepted by Messrs. Boosey & Co., besides substantial and welcome cheques from the sale of 'Stonecracker John', which had already reached its tens-of-thousands.

It was during this time that I invested in my first fur coat (extraordinary what ideas present themselves to a man of twenty-three). The weather was becoming cold and I had one or two night journeys before me, so I travelled one morning to Great Portland Street and paid a visit to a furrier's in whose windows an inviting-looking coat, lined with musquash and with a fine beaver collar, had lain for some days, positively crying out to be bought. It fitted me perfectly, and the price, being well within my means, presented no obstacle. I walked away down Great Portland Street, conscious of a feeling of well-being which only a fur coat can impart and with the knowledge, a most gratifying knowledge, that I was being regarded by the passers-by as one of the idle rich out for a morning constitutional. But before I had travelled many yards I became aware that hansoms, and even four-wheelers, kept on hailing me as a prospective customer. The position was embarrassing. How was I going to board a bus in this imposing-looking article of clothing? If I had to spend the rest of the winter and the royalties from my songs in being obliged to take a cab wherever I went, because of the affluence emanating from my newly-acquired purchase, it would not be long before I found my way into the bankruptcy court. So I denied myself the luxury of a cab, scorned the cheaper method of the horse bus, and walked. The sun came out and warmed the autumn morning air, and still I walked, and as I walked I sweated. I remembered one day having seen Beecham hail a hansom, throw his fur coat into it and request the cabby to follow him down Regent Street with it. Now it was out of the question for me to do anything as daring as this, but on the other hand it was equally impossible for me to continue my walk hampered by this colossal impedimentum. So I removed my coat and staggered along Wigmore Street with it over my arm. "Keb, sir!" I shook my head feebly. "Take your coat for you, sir!" This was really too much. I sank into the cushioned seat with a sigh of relief and wondered whether it would not be wise to dispose of the fur coat at the earliest opportunity. The knowing look the cabby gave me when I paid the fare at Loudoun Road seemed to say: 'The sooner the better!' and led to the fur coat, like the Celtic String Quartet, enjoying a short life.

I do not know whether the inordinate sweating brought about by my coat was the cause of a nasty attack of influenza which followed on my pilgrimage to Great Portland Street. Suffice it to say that for the next week or ten days I was laid by the heels, my 'ministering angel' being Mrs. Henry J. Wood. She herself was convalescing after an illness and, on hearing that I was ill, insisted on sending her nurse round to look after me for an hour or so each day. She had already sung my songs, and sung them beautifully, at the previous Promenade Concerts, and since then I had been to the house in Elsworthy Road several times to play her my latest efforts in the song line and sometimes to have tea with her and Henry Wood. One afternoon, I remember being taken for a motor-car run somewhere north of London, seated with her at the back while he sat in front with the chauffeur and played with what, at that time, was the latest novelty in motor-car hooters, a four-note bugle-call. I felt that Mrs. Wood was faintly shocked at the maestro's show of boyish enthusiasm for his latest toy and the exuberance with which he 'sounded the alarm' at the least possible provocation. My friendship with Mrs. Henry Wood was brought to an end by her death, following on her illness, in 1909. With her passing went one who had done much to help me on my way and to whom I shall always feel a sense of gratitude for singing my first songs for me and for being such an encouragement to me in the early days of my writing.

My 'Four Old English Songs' made me many friends in the singing world, thanks to the publicity they received through Mrs. Wood giving them their send-off at a Promenade Concert. It was these songs which were the means of my starting a life-long friendship with Ada Forrest, the South African soprano, later to become the wife of Cherry Kearton, the hunter of big game with the camera.

Gervase Elwes was another singer whom I associate with these early songs of mine. How beautifully he used to sing them, especially the two slower ones: 'Who is Sylvia?' and 'Orpheus with his lute'. He was a great artist and, like all true artists, would not sing a song until he had first of all heard the composer's intention; and as for altering a note or even a mark of expression, the idea never entered his head. And then there was Melba, the friend I made through the medium of these songs but whom it was my misfortune never to meet. I heard that she remarked to a friend when she was coming over to this country soon after my songs were published: "The first thing I want to do when I reach England is to meet the composer who wrote, 'Who is Sylvia?'" Unfortunately we never seemed able to be in the same place at the same time and so it was my sorrow never to know the singer who took my 'Who is Sylvia?' with her round the world and honoured me by calling it her favourite song.

Then Mac went off and got married and I went back to Maida Vale to a boarding-house run by another Scotswoman, this time in Portsdown Road. It was a well-run house and the food, watched over by a young Frenchwoman, was excellent. My room on the top floor (I was lucky in this) faced on to the front, and here I lived in company with a bed, a table and chair and my small upright piano, going downstairs to the dining-room for my meals. There was a flight of stone steps leading down from the french windows in the drawing-room to a delightful garden which was shared by the residents of the houses which surrounded it on each side. On making a voyage of discovery soon after my arrival, I found that the drawing-room of 'the Hamilton's' house gave on to the same garden. To the casual observer this fact does not appear to be of much import, but as one of my 'specials', one whom I had not seen for some time, still happened to be domiciled under 'the Hamilton's' roof, the importance to me of this convenient approach could not be over-estimated, neither could it be ignored. I had often felt the urge to call and pay my respects to my friend on the top floor, but as I was not on the best of terms with 'the Hamilton' after having 'jilted' her for the landlady in Loudoun Road (added to the fact that she frequently opened the front door in answer to the bell, and I should in all probability have been refused admission), the entrance by way of the drawing-room at the time when 'the Hamilton' was taking her afternoon nap was as tempting an invitation to an assignation as you could hope to find. Picture a sunny room overlooking a pleasant garden, a kettle just about to boil, tea in the pot, some cakes from the little confectioner's over the way, a box of cigarettes, plenty of time to waste and someone very charming to waste it with. Heaven be praised that 'the Hamilton' was a heavy sleeper!

My fellow-boarders at No. 39, Portsdown Road, were again a mixed lot. The barrister from Clifton Gardens was there (he had evidently jilted 'the Hamilton' for the same reason as I), there was a delightful American with an equally delightful daughter, a supposed-to-be-wealthy young Frenchman and member of the

French aristocracy, a Scandinavian, and, above all, Marie Novello, the Welsh pianiste. On the nights of a recital she would turn the somewhat drab and tired-looking company into a veritable *Arabian Nights* orgy of colour and scent by gracing the dinner-table resplendent in full evening-dress, filling the evening air with intoxicating perfumes of the East and causing a riot among the men-folk. Marie, besides being a first-rate pianiste, was an attractive creature, and as it is seldom you get a combination of the two, you can guess that she was a success with the public. She and I became great friends and many were the conversations that took place far into the night when we had met by chance on the front steps, she returning from an evening recital and I from some orchestral concert or other. It was through her that I made the acquaintance of Alfred Kalisch, an important figure in London musical life at that time and a well-known music critic on the *Daily News*; and one day she produced, very proudly, her half-brother, Ivor Novello, then in his teens. Ivor Novello, for whose versatility I always had a great admiration, was a mere boy when first we met and I was several years his senior. Our ways took us down very different paths after those distant days, but whenever we met, up to his death in 1951, it was just as if we were back once again at Portsdown Road, and Marie was saying: "Eric, this is my brother ,Ivor."

The Beecham Symphony Orchestra being a thing of the past and my theatre orchestral days now over, I found myself one day a member of the Queen's Hall Orchestra. I had asked Henry Wood if he would think of me if a vacancy ever occurred among the violas, and in 1910 I was engaged as outside player at the second desk, sitting behind the leader, Siegfried Wertheim, and another Hollander. I received a guinea for a Symphony Concert and rehearsal; ten shillings and sixpence for a concert without a rehearsal; and for the Promenade Concerts, consisting of six concerts a week with three rehearsals, the vast sum of two pounds ten shillings a week. What the orchestral player receives to-day is none of my business, but I warrant it is a sum greatly superior to that of 1910. You may say that over forty years ago the cost of living was nothing approaching what it is to-day, but I can vouch for it that two pounds ten shillings a week did not go very far, even then.

Henry Wood was at the peak of his energy and spared no effort to keep the standard of the performances at its very highest. He had a fine set of men under him, including such well-known musicians as Jacques Verbruggen, principal first violin (later Maurice Sons and Arthur Catterall); Hugo Hundt, principal second violin; Siegfried Wertheim, principal viola; Jacques Renard, principal 'cello; Adolf

Lotter, principal double-bass; Alfred Fransella, principal flute (later Robert Murchie); de Buscher, oboe (later Léon Goossens); Haydn Draper, clarinet; the James brothers, bassoons; Oskar Borsdorf, Alfred Brain and Aubrey Brain, horns; Gutteridge, bass-trombone; Alfred Kastner, harp; and among the strings, during the period of my membership, were such names as Basil Cameron, John Barbirolli, Nandor Szolt, Eugène Goossens, Cedric Sharpe, Herbert Lodge, Ambrose Gauntlett, Raymond Jeremy, James B. Lockyer, Philip Sainton, Claude Hobday, Arthur Blakemore and Victor Watson. Far be it from me to belittle the English orchestral player in any way, for there is not a finer in the world, but I cannot help thinking that a sprinkling of foreign blood in an orchestra is a good thing. I remember the remarkably high standard of playing of the orchestra of the Statsradiofonien in Copenhagen, which I first had the honour to conduct just before the outbreak of World War II. On my remarking to Erik Tuxen, the Director of Music, that it would be a long time before I came across another orchestra which was so responsive and which played with such abandon, he interested me greatly by telling me that he had collected his players from all over the Continent. "My orchestra," he said, "is composed of musicians of every nationality, all chosen specially by myself. That is the way to make a fine symphony orchestra," and judging from what I heard that day I should think that what he said was undoubtedly true. Later on, Henry Wood was to say exactly the same thing to me about orchestras, and he attributed the excellence of the original Queen's Hall Orchestra to there being so many *étrangers* among its personnel. I expect if you enquired into the make-up of an orchestra such as the famous Philadelphia Symphony or the New York Symphony you would find many nationalities in its ranks.

* * * * *

Spring was here, and homesickness for my Nottinghamshire lanes made me think of my bicycle. Knowing that it would be some little time before I could get up to Hucknall to satisfy my *wanderlust*, I thought to myself: 'Why not do some wandering about London and use my bicycle as a means of getting up and down from Portsdown Road to Queen's Hall?' And so I wrote to my mother and asked her if she would get someone to put my bicycle on the first train for St. Pancras.

London in 1910 was little more than a large village and it was a pleasure to cycle through the semi-deserted streets of a spring morning, *en route* for the ten-o'clock rehearsal at Queen's Hall:

along St. John's Wood Road, Park Road, into Regent's Park and down the imposing Portland Place. On nice days, when there was not a great deal afoot, I used to get my machine out and tour the London streets. Can you imagine taking a bicycle out to-day and riding about London for pleasure? And yet, in those days, there was nothing more delightful than an hour's leisurely run along Edgware Road, through Hyde Park, across Hyde Park Corner, through St. James's Park to Westminster, along the Embankment and home by way of Regent Street, Oxford Circus, Portland Place and Regent's Park, and if you had brought your lunch along, with the intention of sitting down in the middle of Oxford Circus to enjoy it, no one would have taken any notice.

* * * * *

The rehearsals with Henry Wood were, on the whole, interesting, especially when any of the works by the great Richard Strauss were put out on the music-stands.

He was a fiend for rehearsing and the more difficult the work the more he seemed to thrive on it. At 9.55 a.m. sharp he would be on the platform, his tuning-fork in hand, almost tumbling over the music-stands in his eagerness to hear the A of every member of the orchestra and still be able to start rehearsing on the first stroke of ten. Only once have I known him to be late and that was through being held up in the fog when travelling up in the morning train from Brighton. This unheard-of event was celebrated by the members of the orchestra, punctual as usual, who spent a glorious half-hour changing instruments with one another and entertaining the empty Queen's Hall with a much-pulled-about version of the 'Blue Danube', in the middle of which the absentee entered. The noise subsided, seats were quickly recovered, instruments returned, and without a smile the conductor raised his bâton and the rehearsal commenced. I wonder what Beecham would have done under the same circumstances?

The rehearsals were from ten o'clock till one, with a break of ten minutes at midday, timed perfectly for those members who wished to run round to the 'Glue-Pot' in Great Portland Street to 'have one', or for the more abstemious-minded to enjoy a cup of coffee and a bun in the genteeler surroundings of the A.B.C. across the road in Regent Street. I can hardly ever remember a rehearsal finishing before one o'clock, even when there was nothing of importance on hand. We were engaged for a three-hour rehearsal and a three-hour rehearsal it had to be. One hot August morning we had been rehearsing Bach's 'St. Matthew Passion' for a couple of hours and

Eric Coates conducting

Six leading composers and musicians at the 1910 Bournemouth Centenary Festival. Back row, left to right: Edward German, Hubert Parry. Front row: Edward Elgar, Dan

The Hambourg String Quartet, when it visited Capetown in 1908. Eric Coates is on the right.

William Boosey

Fred Weatherly

Basil Cameron

Alick Maclean

Henry Wood

The Dominion Theatre, Tottenham Court Road, London, in 1935: Coates appeared in this role on three occasions, drawing large audiences to see him and his orchestra.

A signed photograph — 'To Eric Coates with many thanks' — from Jack Hylton and his orchestra.

Phyllis Black at the time she was a successful West End actress.

Phyllis with the young Austin Coates.

The Coates cottage at Selsey

Eric and Phyllis Coates (right) in 1932, with cellist Madame Suggia and Ernest Goss, musical director to Torquay Corporation.

Eric and Phyllis Coates (right) in 1947 with Leslie Boosey (left) and Zoltan Kodaly.

Eric Coates (right) in 1954 with Sir Adrian Boult (centre) and Herbert Lodge, then retiring as conductor of the Worthing Municipal Orchestra.

Eric Coates (left) with Sir John Barbirolli (centre) and Herman Lindars, at Sheffield in 1950.

Stanford Robinson

Eric Coates as he was in 1932.

Eric Coates, aged about 20, at Hacknall.

Eric Coates conducting the Scots Guards Band in Trafalgar Square at the opening of the 'Salute the Soldier' war savings campaign.

Eric Coates in 1957, a few months before his death.

after the ten-minute break went back to it again. There were no singers, and by the time 12.45 came round we were all sick and tired of playing nothing but 'recitatives' and long, slow bowings. I was just wondering how much longer we were going to be subjected to this endless wading-through of that interminable mass of semibreves, when there came a touch on my shoulder and a voice from the desk behind said: "Eric, if you've got any time to waste, give it to 'Timber'." Do you wonder I introduced the B System into the viola section of the Queen's Hall Orchestra? And speaking of systems, later on, when I was to become principal viola, I inaugurated a method (which did not go further than the first desk) by which the most intricate and impossible passage became as child's play. The system was to divide each bar into two parts, the outside player taking over the first half and the inside player being responsible for the second: thus, the notes which occurred at the beginning of the two respective halves of the bar were doubled, giving an added accent to the rhythm and imparting brilliance to a passage which, if attempted by one player in full, usually ended in a scramble. The result of this system was that in pieces like the 'Ride of the Valkyries' the first desk remained cool and collected, while giving a performance of remarkable clarity, whereas the remaining players were 'sweating blood' in their efforts to prevent what they were playing sounding like a dog-fight. I'm afraid my colleague and I carried our 'divisi' pastime to the lengths of being responsible, on one occasion, for a performance of *one half* of the 'St. Matthew Passion' each. There were two works by the great John Sebastian Bach which I would gladly have paid a deputy double to play for me, and these were the 'B Minor Mass' and the 'St. Matthew Passion'. I was amused to hear that Hellmesberger, the famous violinist, was overheard saying to a colleague after a performance of the latter work: "Well, it may be St. Matthew's Passion, but it's not *mine!*"

After having played with Beecham, who did not seem to understand the first meaning of time from the point of view of keeping an appointment or turning up for rehearsal at the appointed hour, it was a relief to have as conductor a man who, besides being a fine musician, was business-like and to all appearances orthodox in his ways. It was an object lesson to hear Wood take a rehearsal and to watch him tackling some difficult passage and going over it again and again until it was note-perfect. His score-reading was remarkable and when rehearsing a new work, no matter how intricate it might be, you could see that he was familiar with every bar before getting up on to the rostrum, and you could imagine the hours of thought which he must have given to it in the quiet of his study beforehand. Many were the invaluable tips I picked up from him while watching the way in which he got his various effects; tips which were to be useful to me in later years when conducting my own works. His beat was clear and easy to follow and you were never in doubt as to the meaning he wished to convey, and if he conducted a work in a certain manner at the rehearsal you could be sure that the rendering at the actual performance would be exactly the same. I found Wood very helpful and understanding on the occasions when I was feeling off-colour and had to play some difficult and exacting solo. The first time I came up against the solo part in Richard Strauss's 'Don Quixote' I fancy he knew I was anxious, and at Sancho Panza's entrance, instead of looking towards me and thus automatically directing the attention of the audience to the principal viola, he pointed with his stick towards the horns, seated at the other side of the orchestra, and by the time I had played the first few bars unnoticed, my 'nerves' had left me. After having seen the lack of self-control displayed at a rehearsal by Arturo Toscanini, I congratulate myself that my viola-playing days were over long before this excitable Italian appeared for the B.B.C. in London, and I feel grateful for the fates which decreed that it was to be Henry Wood, and not Toscanini, under whose bâton I played for over eight years, for I am sure that in the latter case it would not have been with affection that I looked back upon my time as principal viola.

* * * * *

Siegfried Wertheim, who was the principal viola at the time when I joined the Queen's Hall Orchestra and with whom I shared the first desk after the first year of my membership, was Cervantes's 'Sancho Panza' come to life. He was short, thick-set, had a roundish head, was practically bald and the possessor of jet-black, piercing eyes. To hear him play the viola solo in 'Don Quixote' was to receive a vivid impression of the faithful little servant of the chivalrous old knight. Wertheim was a first-rate violist and as a leader second to none. I should not say he was particularly artistic, and his renderings of anything other than the macabre were not always pleasant to listen to. He was a kindly man who somewhat belied his antagonistic appearance. I got on well with him, though I believe he was not popular with certain members of the orchestra, with whom he occasionally had bitter quarrels, strangely enough the most frequent being with those of his own nationality. The Dutch element in the orchestra was the one responsible for most of these *fracas*. I have known a fiddle smashed in pieces by an incensed

Hollander just before a concert, so that, without his instrument, it would be impossible for him to sit next to the object of his fury during the performance.

I have heard many performances of 'Don Quixote', but none to equal those in which the solo 'cello was played by Warwick Evans, who followed Jacques Renard as principal 'cello in the Queen's Hall Orchestra, and the viola solo by Siegfried Wertheim. Warwick Evans seemed to catch the spirit of the gallant knight to perfection, and invested Strauss's lovely music with a warmth of feeling which I have never heard equalled by another artist; and the comical figure of the little squire, blundering after his mad master astride his tubby pony, was so in keeping with the figure of the principal viola himself that it does not strain the imagination to picture the effect.

It was a great enough ordeal for me, when my time came as principal, to show what I could do with a solo which had been so perfectly rendered by my predecessor, but still worse was the occasion when I had the misfortune to play 'Sancho Panza' to Pau Casals's 'Don Quixote'. In the first place, I feel sure that Casals's interpretation of the solo part was not in the character of the old Spaniard, and, in the second place, in the intervals when he was not playing he would persist in conducting *at* me with his bow over the top of the intervening grand-piano, not only during the rehearsal but at the performance as well, to my discomfort at the former and to my annoyance at the latter. The only excuse I can offer for him is that he must already have been feeling the urge to blossom out as a conductor. The only other time when I felt like getting up from my seat and leaving the orchestra was when Pachmann was entertaining a packed house with a performance of a Chopin Concerto and I happened to be facing him through the opened lid of the same grand piano. I had heard alarming stories of his requests to occupants in the stalls to leave the hall, as they interfered with his train of musical thought, and it occurred to me how ghastly it would be if he 'fixed' me with those fishy eyes of his and said he could not continue playing so long as I sat opposite him on the other side of that opened piano-lid, although of course the prospect of being dispatched to the band-room for a half-hour's rest might have been worth it. I spent a miserable forty minutes getting down as low into my seat as I could, to get out of his line of vision without seeming to appear peculiar, but it evidently happened to be one of his 'off' days, for beyond drawing the attention of the audience to a few 'dicky-birds' on the key-board, he did nothing.

This grand-piano played an important part in my life at Queen's Hall, for through and across its lid I had a close-up of all the artists who appeared at the Promenade Concerts, the Symphony Concerts and the Sunday Afternoon Concerts; a full-face view of the pianists *through* the lid and a side view of the singers, violinists, 'cellists and others *across* it. Many were the minor and sometimes major crises I witnessed through the opened lid of this familiar grand-piano. There were pianists with ecstatic expressions which changed to looks of horror on the realisation of having played a bar too many in a cadenza, while the conductor vainly cast about for a cue on which to bring in the orchestra; pianists whose features became more and more distorted as the technical difficulties of that last movement taxed their powers of endurance; pianists with radiant expressions; pianists with no expression at all, either in their faces or in their playing; pianists who drooped; pianists who smiled; pianists who glared; pianists with inspiration; pianists without inspiration; pianists with abandon; pianists aggressive, mild, determined, gentle, anxious, confident, timid, erratic, hostile; and *one* pianist who went so far as to snort.

The crises relating to the artists *across* the piano-lid were not so obvious, on account of the viewpoint being at an angle, but I expect they were quite as dramatic as those seen *through* the lid, judging by the noticeable reactions of the close-up Promenaders and the occupants of the first few rows of the stalls at Symphony Concerts and Sunday Concerts. Among the through-the-lid artists, those who stand out in my mind are the great Rachmaninoff with the immovable expression and the fur coat, fur gloves and hot-water bottle (even in midsummer); the virtuoso Moiseiwitsch; the brilliant Moriz Rosenthal; the imperturbable Mark Hambourg; Pugno of the great girth and the small podgy hands; the genial de Greef; the explosive Sapellnikoff; the enigmatical Busoni; the charming Myra Hess; Fanny Davies (who reminded me so much of my religious aunt); the young prodigy Solomon; the steel-fingered Percy Grainger; the equally steel-fingered Cortot; the beautiful and bewitching Harriet Cohen; and, last but not least, the terrifying Pachmann. Those of the across-the-lid are the lovable and inimitable Kreisler; the picturesque Suggia; the debonair Thibaud; Maurice Sons of the rich tone and the turned-in toes; the huge Ysaye; the attractive Beatrice and May Harrison; the stooping Catterall; the swaggering Elman; the lion-maned Kubelik; and the heavily-lidded Casals. Then there was a host of singers: Tetrazzini, Caruso, Santley, Plunket Greene, Gerhardt, Kirkby Lunn, Calvé, Henschel, Maggie Teyte, de Alvarez, Ackté, Louise Dale, Carrie Tubb, Clara Butt, Ben Davies, Peter Dawson—to mention only a few.

I shall never forget one of the opening Saturday nights of the

Proms, when some practical joker in the orchestra got on to the platform a few minutes before the programme commenced and unscrewed Warwick Evans's 'cello bow and screwed it up again after having threaded the hair through the 'cello strings. Warwick's face when he picked up his instrument, added to the look on Wood's face as he watched our principal 'cello feverishly trying to unravel the mess, while an impatient audience waited to hear him play the opening bars of the 'William Tell' Overture, was a comedy. Then there was the night when someone locked the first horn player into the lavatory and the conductor's attention became divided between keeping the orchestra together and looking up anxiously at the vacant seat. The subsequent appearance of the missing man at the door at the top of the platform, hair all over the place and minus collar and tie, having escaped by climbing out of the window and down the drain-pipe, just in time to play his solo, set the audience in a flutter.

One night we were enjoying an unusually long interval in the band-room when, to our discomfort, we heard the opening brass-chords of Suppé's 'Poet and Peasant' Overture coming down to us from the platform overhead. In those days the strings inhabited the subterranean room, while certain of the wood-wind and brass were in a room near the artists' entrance in Riding House Street. Either Wood had forgotten to ring the bell which summoned the inhabitants of the lower regions to action, or else we were making too much noise to have heard anything, I do not know (I have a shrewd suspicion he forgot us on purpose). At any rate, it was some minutes before the 'Poet and Peasant' Overture took shape, and the picture of sundry musicians creeping stealthily into their places one by one, and the famous 'cello solo being played to the accompaniment of two violas, pizzicato, in lieu of a harpist who had not yet made his appearance, must have gladdened the hearts of the humorists in the Promenade.

Besides the grand-piano, another instrument, this time *in* the orchestra, holds many memories for me. How often have I blessed the thought which prompted Wood to place the harp on his right hand just in front of the violas, for behind its sheltering bulk Wertheim and I dozed many an hour away during long rehearsals on hot mornings. Only once did our conductor fish us out from behind the strings of Mackenzie's *bête noire*. It was in the Small Queen's Hall. The rehearsal had been dragging on. The drone of the music lulled us like the hum of bees on a hot summer afternoon in a shady garden. We were fast asleep, utterly unconscious of what was going on around us. And then Wertheim's bow slipped from his nerveless fingers and fell to the ground, hitting one of the harp pedals as it went. A long silence, broken by Wood's voice: "Will Mr. Wertheim and Mr. Coates come out from behind the harp? I want to see what they are doing!" Mr. Wertheim and Mr. Coates came out and after a "That's better", followed by, "Now, come along, gentlemen!" the rehearsal continued.

Sleepiness, next to neuritis, was the thing which troubled me most during the Summer Season, especially at certain Promenade rehearsals, at *all* Symphony Concerts and rehearsals, and Sunday Afternoon Concerts. Three o'clock in the afternoon, just as that desire comes over you to indulge in a pleasant 'forty winks', is not, in my opinion, the time to listen to music, let alone play it; and those Saturday three-o'clocks and the Sunday three-thirties (an even worse time, because you should be 'well away' by then) were the most awful sleep-inducers I have ever known. This is not meant to be a reflection on the concerts, for they were of the best. It is a nasty experience to fall asleep while playing the viola and, incredible as this may seem, I have many times 'forgotten myself' while wading through a slow movement in a Beethoven or a Mozart Symphony. Have you ever felt that overpowering desire to sleep while driving a motor-car on a long journey? You close your eyes for a couple of seconds and open them to find yourself heading straight for a telegraph pole at the side of the road, and you realise with a shock that you have just escaped a catastrophe. This is exactly how you feel when you fall asleep while playing the viola at a concert. I remember the morning we arrived at St. Pancras at 8.30 a.m., after travelling all night without a wink of sleep, and went on to Queen's Hall for a rehearsal from ten till one, followed by a Symphony Concert at three. The only person who appeared to be as fresh as a daisy was our indefatigable conductor. He was on the top of his form. At the rehearsal we thought of the luxurious first-class 'sleeper' in which he had spent the night, and as he let off the energy stored up during the hours he had lain unconscious we became more and more exhausted. At the concert we were practically dead and, judging by the 'dominoes' (to the uninitiated this is an orchestral expression for a note played by accident in a silent bar) which came from all parts of the orchestra, telegraph poles must have been appearing by the dozen. Fortunately, to my knowledge, I have only been guilty of one domino—it was an unpleasant experience and made me nervous for the rest of the evening. One puny viola playing a four-note chord fortissimo, while the remainder of the orchestra was silent. I felt ashamed, and in the interval I hurried round to the maestro's room to apologise and was greeted with:

"Never mind, Coates, it was a *good* one!" As Nikisch said to his principal first violin, on chiding him over making a mistake in a solo passage: "It is not permissible for *you* to play a false note but for *me* it is different, for when *I* make a mistake I do it *with conviction!*" There is nothing worse than a domino strangled at birth, for it gives the show away, and I hope my bloomer on this occasion was good enough to give the audience the impression that it was an effect intended by the composer, for it was certainly played 'with conviction'.

The subject of sleep brings me to a story which was going the rounds in Amsterdam when I visited Holland a few months before the last war to conduct a concert of my music at Hilversum. Willem Mengelberg, the conductor, while on the platform at the railway station one wintry morning waiting for the train to take him and the Concertgebouw Orchestra to fulfil an engagement, spotted one of his musicians swaggering in a luxurious fur coat. Now, Mengelberg considered that, fitting his position as Kapellmeister, he himself was the only person who could possibly array himself in anything so magnificent as a fur coat, and besides, hang it all, the man inhabited the back desk of the second violins! It was ridiculous. So he strolled down the platform and accosted the culprit (why, would you believe it, the fellow's coat was more magnificent than his own!): "How do you manage to possess yourself of such a fine coat? You cannot possibly do it on what I pay you!" "Well, sir, you see, I do not depend solely on my engagements with you." "But what else do you do?" "I play at a restaurant on the afternoons and evenings when there is no concert, I teach on the mornings when there is no rehearsal, I play at a night club after the restaurant closes and after the night club I go on to the AVRO to do some early-morning broadcasting. So you see, it is easy!" "But when do you *sleep?*" "Ah, that is during your rehearsals."

* * * * *

It was during the first few months in the orchestra that I met Basil Cameron. This was in the days when he played the violin and sat opposite me on the other side of the platform, somewhere behind Maurice Sons. He was determined to leave the orchestra as soon as possible and become a conductor, and many were the long talks we used to have together about our ambitions. Basil was altogether after my own heart, for here at last I had found someone who appreciated the monotony of endless rehearsing; even the knowledge that he adored Beethoven did not mar our friendship. At times we went completely crazy together and did the wildest things to 'let off steam' after having sat for hours rehearsing a work that bored us. I wonder if he remembers one fantastic afternoon when we hired a hansom during a stay in Norwich, where we were playing in the Festival, and between rehearsal and concert went for a wild ride into the country. We both leaned out over the doors of the cab and made faces at every person who hove in sight, and every now and then Basil would emit an ear-splitting screech which caused the cabby to open the trap-door overhead to enquire if we were feeling all right. This mad behaviour on our part sounds idiotic but it did us a great deal of good, having been pent up for hours rehearsing the 'St. Matthew Passion'. How vividly I can recall the occasion when we went to have our palms read, while staying in rooms together in Norwich, and the little fortune-teller telling Basil that he was going to be a 'leader of men', and me, that I was always going to be in 'the public eye'. I know we both thought he was daft.

Basil told me that when he was the conductor of the Seattle Symphony Orchestra his arrival on to the platform at a rehearsal was the signal for the oboe, the clarinet and the bassoon to break into a pianissimo rendering of the opening motif of my phantasy, 'The Three Bears', which two bars came to be known as Basil's Private Signature Tune. "And you know, Eric," he added triumphantly, "*I* conduct 'The Three Bears' much better than *you!*"

Another member of the first violins, also sitting somewhere behind Maurice Sons, but after Basil had left to take up the post of conductor of the Torquay Municipal Orchestra, was Eugène Goossens, whose name I often think of in connection with Basil's Private Signature Tune.

This was some years after Eugène and I had given up orchestral playing, he for his conducting and I for my writing. I was showing him my newly-finished manuscript full-score of 'The Three Bears' and pointed out to him a little private joke between the bassoon player and myself, in the form of the first few bars of the famous intermezzo from Mascagni's 'Cavalleria Rusticana', which I had introduced into the score for this instrument. Eugène was very intrigued with the idea of this unobtrusive jest and felt it was far too good a one to pass unnoticed. He suggested my adding it in the trombones the second time it occurred, and in the trombones and the trumpets, fortissimo, the third and last time. I acted on his suggestion, but I might just as well have let the bassoon have his little joke all to himself, for the remarkable thing is that no one has ever noticed the allusion, not even the orchestral players themselves.

I do not know whether Mascagni would have been annoyed if

he had known I had taken his lovely melody in vain, but I do know he was furious when an organ-grinder appeared outside his hotel and serenaded him with a funereal-like rendering of his immortal masterpiece. So angry was he that he rushed out into the street, went up to the man shouting *"This* is how it should go!", seized the handle and rattled off the piece 'con spirito', to the delight of the organ-grinder and a crowd of visitors on the hotel terrace. His wrath changed to smiles when, the next day, the same street musician appeared outside the hotel with the organ bearing a large placard: 'PUPIL OF MASCAGNI'.

* * * * *

My 'star turn' was the solo movement in Charpentier's 'Impressions d'Italie'. I always loved playing this, partly because of performing it behind the curtains at the side of the stage and thus being out of sight of the audience, but chiefly on account of its being so beautifully written for the viola. I remember how struck I was the first time I heard this, on the occasion many years ago when Gabrielle Pierné came over with the Colonne Orchestra and gave such a magnificent performance of this Suite.

Richard Strauss's 'Don Quixote', although an exacting piece of writing for the viola, never worried me unduly after I had recovered from the 'nerves' I experienced the first time I played it. I was to find that there were many solos far more nerve-racking: solos in which there was not time to establish yourself, such as the showy few bars in the A Minor Roumanian Rhapsody by Georges Enesco; nasty little bits in some of Richard Strauss's works; and the solo in Saint-Saëns's 'Algerian Suite' which, if taken by the conductor at a certain tempo, becomes awkwardness itself. The only solo I enjoyed playing, next to the one in Charpentier's 'Impressions d'Italie', was in the rhythmic 'En Saga' by Jean Sibelius, and even this had its drawbacks if the C string happened to go out of tune during the performance. I do not think an audience has the remotest idea of the strain to which orchestral musicians are at time subjected, just as it does not realise the immense amount of time and thought which a composer puts into a work before it is ready for performance.

There is no doubt that to play any instrument well one has to be physically strong, and I think that all the great executants have been blessed with good health, otherwise they would never have been able to have made and kept their names. Practising, getting up new and difficult concertos, keeping *au fait* with the already established ones, long journeys to fulfil engagements and the ever-present anxiety of atmospheric conditions which can do so much to spoil a good performance. Was it not Kreisler who, being told how lucky he was that his fiddle gave him the opportunity of seeing the beauty spots of the world, replied sadly that his knowledge in this connection was confined to concert halls, hotels and railway stations? Of course, when solo artists and conductors travel they are usually able to do so in comparative comfort, but my recollections of going from place to place, in the days when I played in orchestras, are of waiting for hours on draughty stations in the early hours of the morning for some belated connection; arriving at provincial towns to find hotel accommodation limited; rehearsing without decent meals in icy-cold concert halls and, in my own particular case, haunted all the time by the spectre of neuritis. I recall Harold Samuel, who also suffered from my complaint, telling me in later years of the agony he went through on the concert platform in his efforts to conceal from the audience the fight which was going on between himself and his aching fingers, and did I know of a cure?

How frequently, during the latter part of the eight years I spent in the Queen's Hall Orchestra, had I prayed for the time to come when I could put my viola away in its case for good, and devote my time to writing and conducting my music! Occasionally during this period I experienced for a few fleeting hours what this happy state of affairs would be like, for I was invited by my friend Basil Cameron to write a new work for performance at Torquay, where I spent a carefree holiday forgetting all about such humdrum things as Promenade Concerts in the excitement of producing my new piece. I had also made one or two appearances with the London Symphony Orchestra at the Sunday League Concerts in London, and Henry Wood had already launched my 'Miniature Suite' at the Proms, so I felt that the day when I should be free to live my life in my own way was perhaps not so far distant after all. At the same time, I could see it was not going to be an easy thing for me to give up the steady income which my instrument earned for me each year; and, alas, one did not write a 'Stonecracker John' every day, and it seemed there was nothing to be made out of orchestral works, bar a few pounds from the sales of the pianoforte arrangements. Still, I was lucky to hold the position I had in the orchestra. Had it not been for my health, the life I led would have been, if not always pleasant, at least interesting. It was interesting from two points of view: the first was the experience I gained by playing all the well-known masterpieces, as well as a good many of the modern works; and the second, coming in contact with the interesting personalities of the composers, who either came to the rehearsals to hear their new works played under Wood's direction, or sometimes took over the conducting themselves. Added to this there were the guest conductors. After playing under most of the composers it was a relief to return once more to the clear-cut beat and sure touch of the reliable 'Timber'. I think the most uncertain of all the composers I played under was Sir Edward Elgar (whom I was to meet in later years and for whom I have always felt an affection), for his highly-strung nature, added to a habit he sometimes had of starting to conduct a work before the orchestra was ready, was unnerving. How well I remember the night at Queen's Hall when he was conducting a performance of his overture, 'In the South'; he raised the stick without warning and executed a terrific down-beat, which was responded to by the first desk of the violas only (that being myself and my colleague), the remainder of the orchestra joining in on the second bar! Elgar's restlessness seemed reflected in his part-writing and I always found his music, lovely as a great deal of it is, extremely tiring to play. You never seemed to be in the same position for more than a few seconds, and were kept dodging up and down all over the strings, *sans cesse*. He was a great writer, even if you did not like everything he wrote, and he at least knew his own mind well enough never to have to resort to the expedient of a 'second edition'.

Sir Edward German (whom I was also to meet in later years and for whom I also shall always have a special affection) was another composer who did not inspire you with confidence when taking his stand on the rostrum. Here was a man who, besides being highly strung, was over-particular about the rendering of his music and often carried his love of detail to the point of pernicketiness, in this way tending to destroy the outline of a work as a whole. Here again was a composer who knew his own mind; the only occasion when I remember his suffering from indecision was the time he was commissioned to write a work for a special concert at the Queen's Hall during the First World War. There were two rehearsals on consecutive days. On the first morning he arrived at the hall while the rehearsal was in full swing, with his full-score under one arm and a pile of MS. band-parts under the other. Five minutes were taken while the parts were being put out, during which the players took advantage of the diversion to make a great song and dance. Music-stands were pushed over, music dropped on to the floor, feet were scraped on the ground; in fact, all the orchestral musicians' tricks were given full play. The band parts put out at last, silence was restored. During the play-through of the work German did not seem happy. He was sitting in the stalls fidgeting about. He walked up to the conductor. Might he trouble the gentlemen of the orchestra to let him have the parts back, to make some slight additions for to-morrow's rehearsal? This was a signal for more scrambling, more horse-play and more shuffling of feet. The parts collected, German quitted the hall, his full-score under one arm and the pile of band-parts under the other. The following morning he arrived on the scene with the rehearsal again in full swing. Renewed demonstrations on the part of the personnel of the orchestra, more noisy if anything than those of the previous morning, while the band-parts were being put out. The second play-through started. German sat in the stalls fidgeting more than ever, and at last got up and walked about the hall like a man possessed of many devils. At last he could bear it no longer and, going up to the platform, he craved the indulgence of the conductor and the players and asked them if they would kindly take no notice, after all, of the blue-pencil markings which he had taken such pains to write in overnight. So much for second editions.

Although we played a great deal of Frederick Delius's music, I can only recall playing under this composer on one occasion and even then the memory of it is not of the clearest. He seemed to me to possess a remote kind of personality, not unlike his music, and as a conductor did not make an impression. Much of his music is undoubtedly lovely, but I never experienced pleasure when playing it in the orchestra, on account of its lack of finish. His writing always seemed to me to be that of a man who got his ideas down on paper by a fluke. To play a work of his in the orchestra was to realise that his knowledge of instrumentation was in some respects amateurish, and a good deal of 'doctoring' had to be done in the various parts before anything approaching a finished performance could be obtained. Of phrasing he seemed to know practically nothing, particularly when writing for the strings.

Gustav Holst was another composer who did not inspire you with confidence when taking charge of the orchestra. He gave me the feeling that at any moment he might apologise to us for his presence on the platform, and his entrance at a rehearsal was usually the signal for some 'wag' or other to be heard saying in a slightly clerical-sounding voice: "I hope you don't *mind*, but I'm here!" Holst had the appearance of being completely without feeling, though I am sure he must have been sensitive or he could not have written as he did. A curious man he seemed to me, one day acknowledging you and the next day passing you by as if you did not exist. How clearly I can see him, standing up there, stick in hand, peering at us through his spectacles as if he were contemplating a lot of performing seals. His music was always interesting to play, and one thing which went a long way with me was that he wrote grateful viola parts.

A frequent visitor was the gentle Sir Walford Davies, who nearly stopped the proceedings on the first occasion he appeared on the rostrum by addressing the orchestra as if it were a mixed chorus, alluding to the various string sections as sopranos, altos, tenors and basses. When it came to the wood-wind and the brass we were all full of anticipation as to how he would tackle them, but luckily he remembered the names of the instruments and, so far as they were concerned, all was well. But it was not so well when he mixed us up so badly with his activities at the Inner Temple that we ended up by becoming the 'choir' (pronounced 'quaar'). He wrote delightful music which reflected his geniality. I shall always remember the first time I heard him play the piano in his 'Conversations' for solo piano and orchestra, and the charming atmosphere created by his refined artistry and his sweet music; and, again, how moved my wife and I were when we listened, many years ago at the Aeolian Hall, to the first performance of his imaginative 'Peter Pan' Quartet, with its reiterating notes on the rhythm of the name 'Peter'.

No wonder Walford Davies came to be loved in later years by a great listening public, for besides possessing a personality which radiated kindness, he had a way with him which was irresistible. He was a little academic in his outlook at times, perhaps, which takes me back to a meeting I had with him in the artists' room at Eastbourne many years ago when we were both appearing at the Festival there, he as composer and solo pianist in his 'Conversations' and I as composer and conductor of 'The Three Bears'. He had evidently been listening to my phantasy through the open door of the artists' room, for when I came off the platform he greeted me with: "A very creditable work, my dear Coates, a very creditable work. Now I should suggest your writing a dozen works every year and out of that dozen you will probably find just such another good one!" I do not think it had occurred to him what a great deal of time and thought it had taken me before 'The Three Bears' became a *fait accompli*, but I realised it was his way of paying me a compliment. I often recall our first meeting, and the times I used to hear him play the recording of my 'Three Bears' Phantasy to demonstrate some point in his delightful and inimitable talks on the radio. My memories of him are of the happiest.

Then there was the kindly Sir Granville Bantock, taking us through some of his lovely Eastern music, looking more like a country squire in his sweet-smelling Harris tweeds than a man who could conjure up the East in the space of a few bars, his music bringing added beauty to the already lovely 'Omar Khayyam'; and Sir Frederic Cowen, who always conducted without a score and who knew the position of every indication number without having to refer to the printed part. He, again, wrote some charming melodies, but they do not seem to have stood the test of time.

The great master, Richard Strauss, came along once or twice. I did not care for him as a conductor; he did not inspire you and left his music to express itself. In later years I remember going to the Queen's Hall to hear him conduct the Dresden Opera Orchestra in a concert of his works, and received an impression of a fine body of musicians apparently playing by themselves. To this day I feel certain they would have given just as good an account of themselves if they had been without any conductor, for all the help Strauss gave them. He did not appear to indicate a single lead anywhere and pointed nothing. You do expect a conductor to do *something* when eight horns enter 'fortissimo' unexpectedly, as in the tremendous passage in 'Don Juan'. Richard Strauss just stood there and beat time, but that was all. But what wonderful music to listen to and to play! Not a note too many or too few. One of those rare composers who writes for an immense orchestra and knows how to use it. This was very evident at one of the Promenade Concerts at the Albert Hall during the last war, when we were subjected to a programme of music by composers who, to cover up their discrepancies in thematic material, had employed an orchestra of gigantic proportions.

I remember thinking, at the time, that one ought to take into consideration the fact that we had been hearing works which had been composed by comparatively young men. But then my thoughts turned to Richard Strauss and to the great works he had written when still in his twenties, and in which he used an orchestra of equally great dimensions with incredible skill and clarity of purpose to exploit thematic material of the most melodious order. 'No,' I said to myself, 'we shall not hear these young men after a year or so.' Time will show.

* * * * *

It was at one of the Symphony Concerts at Queen's Hall that I had the experience of playing under Claude Debussy, and an unforgettable experience it proved to be. For a composer, Debussy, so far as I can remember, was a good conductor; at any rate, he knew what he wanted and got his effects. We were giving a performance of his famous 'Nocturnes for Orchestra' and had played through the first two movements without incident, but in the final movement,

'Fêtes', he fell foul of the rapid changes in the time-signature, which, as any musician knows, in this particular movement alternates at high speed between three beats and five beats in a bar. All was progressing well until he began beating three in a bar when it should have been five. Try as he could, he failed to pick up the rhythm again, and with a despairing look at the orchestra he stopped conducting, dropped his arms helplessly to his sides, with tears pouring down his cheeks, while we carried on to the end without him. It was a furore. The audience had seen what had happened and cheered him to the echo, the orchestra joining in to add to the ovation. Debussy held his arms out to the orchestra, too overcome to acknowledge the applause coming from behind, and encouraged by shouts from the musicians of "Encore!", "Play it again!", he shrugged his shoulders, smiled through his tears and took up the stick.

It was thrilling to be playing under the genius who had given us that most exquisite of all tone-poems, 'L'après-midi d'un faune', the lovely String Quartet, the Orchestral Suites, the pianoforte music, the songs, the opera 'Pelléas et Mélisande', and I enjoyed to the full every moment of that memorable afternoon. Some years later I was to hear from Madame Messager how Debussy came to compose his famous opera. For a long time André Messager, the Director of the Paris Opéra, had been urging the master to write an opera and had suggested his using Maeterlinck's 'Pelléas et Mélisande' as his theme. Could he get him to do it? No! Debussy was in lazy mood and writing an opera was far too lengthy an affair to be considered seriously. But one day when Debussy was visiting the Messagers and was about to take up his hat to wish his host and hostess good-night he found the front door locked and bolted. "Oh, no, my friend! You do not leave my house until you have written your opera!" said Messager. There was nothing for Debussy to say. What could he say? So he stayed.

And speaking of 'Pelléas et Mélisande' takes me back to the evening when I played in a special orchestra at the Theatre Royal, Nottingham, when I was a boy, when Sarah Bernhardt and Mrs. Patrick Campbell paid a flying visit to give a performance of the play to the accompaniment of Gabriel Fauré's music, and I remember how disappointed I was with 'the Divine Sarah' and how I 'fell' for Mrs. 'Pat'. In my youthful ignorance, I thought how much better she spoke French than her colleague; the reason being, no doubt, that I could understand her more easily on account of her English accent.

* * * * *

It is a queer sensation playing in an orchestra when the bâton is in the hands of a woman, and my feelings were mixed the first time we welcomed Dame Ethel Smyth to the rostrum at Queen's Hall. (I had previously come in contact with her music through her opera, 'The Wreckers', which had been produced at His Majesty's Theatre, and I had never forgotten the final rehearsal, with Ethel Smyth sitting on the floor of the stage beating one tempo and Beecham in the orchestra pit beating another). The effect produced at Queen's Hall by her stick, coming out from somewhere underneath the folds of her Doctor's robes, and carrying the cape with it as it waved, gave an impression of a monstrous vulture about to swoop down on its prey. At first it was not an easy matter to take her seriously, but after we had had a sample of her grasp of the orchestra, and had been treated to one or two humorous sallies, we took her to our hearts and gave her of our best. Besides being a fine musician she proved to be an excellent conductor, knew every inch of her score and kept rehearsing until she had made all the points she wanted. I met her many years after in the artists' room at one of the Eastbourne Festivals. It was during the interval at a rehearsal, and she was sitting on a settee deep in conversation with Willy Reed, then the principal violin of the London Symphony Orchestra. As I entered the room Willy Reed looked up: "You know Dame Ethel Smyth, of course?" On my replying that I had never had the pleasure, but that I had had the honour of playing under her many years previously, we were formally introduced. The introduction over, she turned once more to Reed and continued the interrupted conversation—my name had meant nothing to her. Suddenly she stopped in the middle of a sentence as if a thought had struck her, and in that brusque voice which we all knew so well:

"You are the man who writes tunes?"

I bowed my acknowledgments.

She then fired off at me: "Come and sit down beside me and tell me how you manage to make your effects!"

We talked for a long time about orchestrations, about whether it were possible to make two horns sound like four, the pros and cons of single, double and triple wood-wind, about muted brass and dance-band combinations, everything from opera to jazz. The following day I saw her on the promenade, where I found her scanning the London papers.

On seeing me approach her eyes lighted up:

"Do you know," she said, "you've got better notices than any of us for your new work last night! The papers are full of it! I'm *so* glad!" ('What!' you will say, 'one composer to talk to another

LENTO—ANDANTE—ALLEGRO

like that? I don't believe it!' Then you can never have known Ethel Smyth.)

* * * * *

I never had the good fortune of playing under the great Alexandre Glazounov, though when I was a scholar at the Royal Academy of Music I remember his coming into the Concert Hall in Tenterden Street to hear Mackenzie take one of the students through his lovely Violin Concerto, and many years afterwards I ran across him in Eastbourne, where he was due to conduct one of his Symphonies and his Piano Concerto. He was sprawling over a writing-desk in the lounge of the hotel where we were both staying, scribbling on a piece of paper, the while puffing furiously at a huge cigar. His bulky frame obtruded through the framework of the arm-chair in which he was sitting, which looked as if it might collapse at any moment, and as he wrote he grunted and snorted like a grampus. I did not disturb him, lest he might not 'recapture the first wild careless rapture' of the phrase which had just come into his mind. So I remained in my chair by the fireside and watched and listened to the great man in the first agonies of delivering an embryo masterpiece.

I have to thank Glazounov for giving me as much pleasure with his music as I have received from any other composer. His Symphonies, his Ballets, his glorious Violin Concerto, his Piano Concerto and his String Quartets are a never-ending source of delight to me. I think it is a pity that we hardly ever hear any of his chamber music over the radio, for the String Quartets which I loved to play in the old days would, I am sure, delight music lovers to-day. I remember how beautifully he wrote for the viola and how I always looked forward to a programme which gave me the opportunity of playing the lovely 'Orientale' movement in his 'Noveletten' for String Quartet. To me he was one of the few composers who could write a slow movement without becoming dull—he excelled in them. Listen to the exquisite second movement in his Violin Concerto, to see what I mean. Was it not he who said he wrote his best slow movements when under the influence of English gin? Which makes me feel we owe a debt of gratitude to the Burnetts and the Booths and the Gordons of this country for helping to make the world the richer by a great deal of lovely, colourful music.

Among other composer-conductors who came along from time to time were the energetic Hamilton Harty; the somewhat dour Sir Charles Stanford; the smiling, rosy-cheeked Sir Hubert Parry; the witty Sir Frederick Bridge, who, when I was a boy, performed the ceremony of opening the new organ at Hucknall Parish Church and

F

whom I considered at the time to be vastly inferior to our local organist. (When I had had a taste of his conducting, I decided he was even worse at the latter than at the former.) Then there were the silvery-voiced Coleridge-Taylor; Landon Ronald, he of the mighty nose, who used to tell a story against himself about the occasion when he was in a hurry to catch the night train for the north and could not attract the attention of the booking-clerk, and on pushing his nose through the window in a last desperate attempt to get his ticket before the train left being greeted with: "All right, guv'nor! take your elbow out of the way and I'll see what I can do for you!"; the kindly Frank Bridge, who was just as expert on the viola as he was at writing music; Arnold Schönberg, who caused a riot among the horns by making them emit noises anything but in accordance with the tradition of this ancient instrument; the sensitive John Ireland; the serious Vaughan-Williams; the charming Norman O'Neill; and lastly, Sir Alexander Mackenzie and Sir George Henschel, who deputised once or twice for Wood on the rare occasions when some Festival or other which he was due to conduct clashed with the Promenade Concerts.

* * * * *

It was a disappointment to me that Maurice Ravel never took over the orchestra himself for some of his fascinating music, for I should like to have heard him rendering his own works. I had always had a deep admiration for this remarkable musician, and when I was invited to meet him many years later, I accepted with alacrity. We lunched at the Ritz. He was quite different from anything I had expected from such an unusually characteristic composer, and I confess I found him a little unprepossessing. This was understandable when you take into consideration that my French is abominable and his English was negligible, which meant that our conversation had to be carried on mostly by signs and musical expressions. Still, I am glad I had the opportunity of meeting at close quarters this astonishing Frenchman, and whenever I hear his ravishing orchestral work it reminds me of that summer day at the Ritz and the lengths to which we went to make ourselves understood.

The two conductors who stand out the most vividly in my mind are Willem Mengelberg and Arthur Nikisch. Mengelberg, with the appearance of a prize-fighter about to take on the whole orchestra in single combat, was a mixture of good-humour and aggressiveness, the latter predominating. His appearance at Queen's Hall aroused a good deal of interest, for it was his first visit to this country. He was undoubtedly a fine conductor with immense driving-force, but his pugilistic attitude could be irritating at times. He gave me the feeling that he had a good opinion of himself, a feeling which, I imagine, was shared by some of his countrymen, judging by the stories about him which were in circulation when I visited Amsterdam before the war. I do not think it would be possible to name two conductors more opposite in character than Mengelberg and Nikisch. The one bombastic in his manner, and the other quiet and reserved and apparently without any sense of his own importance. I think Nikisch, under that calm and dignified manner, had a will which could make itself felt when it was necessary, and I have heard tales about what, to us, would be called his callousness when enforcing discipline in his own orchestra.

It was an evening at Queen's Hall: as the great maestro walked quietly up to the rostrum and took the stick, there was a hush in the orchestra which made you feel the power under his outward calm. We began with Mendelssohn's Overture, 'Fingal's Cave'. From the outset we were all completely under his spell. The way in which he conjured up the picture of a calm sea drowsily lapping against the sides of the great cave was extraordinary, and the working up to the stormy climax was as exciting a musical adventure as I have experienced; in fact the whole rendering, from the quiet opening to the tempestuous violence which presages the sudden calm at the close, was an inspiration never to be forgotten. I have yet to hear a performance of this picturesque overture which could equal the one that Nikisch gave that night—he invested Mendelssohn's music with a new life.

As I look back upon this galaxy of great musicians I cannot help but feel a pang of regret, when I think of the number of them who have 'passed on'. I wonder if the next forty years will prove to be a period as fruitful as the four decades that are behind me as I write?

THIRD MOVEMENT

ROMANZA IN MODO VARIAZIONE

THIRD MOVEMENT

ROMANZA IN MODO VARIAZIONE

I MUST now go back to the evening of March 4th, 1911, and to a table in the window on the first floor of the Blenheim Restaurant in New Bond Street, where I was dining with an old Academy student friend of mine, a violinist. He and I had run into one another earlier in the evening and he had suggested our going in to the Fortnightly Concert at the Academy, at the same time stressing the importance of having a decent meal beforehand, in case the concert proved too much for us. Over dinner we talked, he about his experiences on board some of the liners in which he had signed on as musician in order to see something of the world, I about my trip with the Hambourgs to South Africa, and both about our old student days at the Academy. Dinner concluded, we made our way across the road to the old building in Tenterden Street. Here we found a crowd of students, professors, past students and parents, some pressing through the downstairs door into the Concert Hall and others swarming up the stone staircase to the more advantageous position of the balcony, whence they could observe the stage, the occupants of the stalls below and their own balconyites at one and the same time.

Over the scene of suppressed excitement presided the familiar figures of Green, the general factotum of the Academy, and Hallett, the hall porter. The balcony being full, we took our seats in the body of the hall, now filled to overflowing with a chattering public, and perused the programme. Our eyes lighted together on the word 'Recitation' and we knew we were in for a good laugh. Who was the reciter? A new student by the name of Phyllis Black. This meant nothing to us. What was she going to recite? Coleridge's 'Kubla Khan' and Tennyson's 'The Mermaid'. This meant even less.

The entrance of the Principal accompanied by Lady Mackenzie, with Corder following at a respectful distance, quelled the hubbub, which broke out afresh after they had settled themselves in the centre of the front row of the stalls. We cast our minds back to the fearful ordeal of coming on to the platform for the first time and seeing Sir Alexander's be-pince-nezed eyes fixed on one with the glazed stare of a man who had dined well and who had been dragged away from a comfortable arm-chair and a cigar, in order to be bored by a lot of unfinished young hopefuls displaying their talents in front of a crowd of critical professors, hypercritical students and adoring parents. We both shuddered involuntarily. Of course reciters were a different thing, because, in the first place, they were always funny and, in the second, they never seemed to be nervous; in fact they usually gave the impression of being pleased to have an opportunity of getting into the limelight. It was the wretched violinists and 'cellists with their recalcitrant strings for whom we had sympathy. We knew what it was for one's instrument to go out of tune in the middle of a piece and one's hands to be too sweaty with nerves to be able to get any sort of grasp on the slippery pegs, to bring the rotten thing back to pitch again—and we were both devoutly thankful that our student days were over.

A signal from the Principal and the concert commenced. We were both far too impatient for the 'comic' turn to come on to take much interest in the first few performers, and we spent the time making guesses as to what the lady would look like when she took the boards. We made up our minds she was going to be awful and that we should spend a glorious five minutes of delirious mirth. "Pity she isn't doing something like 'Bergliot' with the piano," said my friend, "this 'Mermaid' thing sounds a bit too anæmic for my taste." I silenced him with the comforting remark that on that account alone it ought to be entertaining, and at that moment on to the stage walked a charming little girl, arrayed in the loveliest of white dresses and with two fair plaits which fell below her waist. She could not have been more than sixteen, at the most. "Phew!" said my friend. I could not take my eyes off her, and, for that matter, neither could he. So we both sat and paid homage to one of the most fascinating little girls we had ever seen. At first I was far too impressed with her looks to take in what she was reciting, and then I became aware of an unusually attractive voice giving a rendering of Tennyson's 'Mermaid', and I remember thinking what a lovely poem to which to put music.

" I would be a mermaid fair.
I would sing to myself the whole of the day;"

(the music of her voice charmed my senses)

"With a comb of pearl I would comb my hair;
And still as I combed I would sing and say:
'Who is it loves me? Who loves not me?'"

What lovely words to set to music! And I thought to myself: 'Who could not help loving her!'—for she looked exactly like an illustration of a little Princess out of a treasured book of fairy-stories, to whom I had lost my heart many years ago when I was a child. "Who is it loves me? Who loves not me?" The lovely lines and the pretty voice carried on their gentle way. And then, the spell under which I had fallen was rudely interrupted by a burst of applause and by the time I had collected myself the vision had vanished. I could scarcely control my impatience during the remainder of the concert. If only I could find her and speak to her! Probably at that very moment she was surrounded by a crowd of admirers, or else she was being spirited away in her fairy coach to some magic castle where it would be impossible for me to reach her. So I sat on with my friend and fumed at the rule which decreed it to be bad form to go out in the middle of a performance.

* * * * *

The concert over, I made my way to the entrance hall and eagerly scanned the crowd in the hope of finding the little girl who had captured my heart so completely. I could not see her anywhere. To whom could I turn for help? Then I saw my friend Hallett standing near the door. Did he know anything about Phyllis Black, the girl who had recited that night? I must have shown what I was feeling more clearly than I was aware, for Hallett looked at me in that enigmatical way of his and smiled one of his most provocative smiles as if to say: 'My word! You've got it bad!' Instead of which: "All the young gentlemen are asking me about her," he whispered. "Come in on Monday morning and I'll see what I can find out for you about the young lady." I had a feeling that he knew all about her already but at that moment he happened to be without one of his Harmony Examination Papers over which to impart the information I so urgently needed, and I knew him well enough to realise that argument was useless. So I joined my friend, whom I found waiting for me with a broad grin on his face, and we left the building and wended our way slowly along Oxford Street. Did I say 'wended'? It may have been 'wended' in his case, but in my own it would have been nearer the mark to have said 'floated'!

A sleepless night, followed by an exasperating Sunday with an intolerably dull concert at Queen's Hall in the afternoon, and an evening spent in restless speculation as to whether I should ever see my Princess of the fairy-book again, followed by yet another sleepless night, brought to a close one of the most unhappy weekends I had ever experienced. To know that somewhere or other someone whom I did not even know, but with whom I had fallen in love at first sight, was going about her daily tasks just as if nothing had happened nearly drove me crazy. Hallett was right, I had 'got it bad'!

Monday morning saw me on the steps of the old Academy almost before the doors were opened. I peered into Hallett's little office and, heaven be praised, he was studying an examination paper. Over a problem of the correct resolution of Hallett's *bête noire*, the six-four chord, I gleaned that she was studying elocution with Annie Child; an augmented fourth produced the information that she was with Cuthbert Whitemore for the piano; and her Harmony Professor, Dr. Greenish, emerged out of the tangle of two consecutive fifths and a glaring 'false relation'. To say I wasted hours in the Academy after having learned the foregoing illuminating details is to put it mildly, for unfortunately Hallett did not know the times when the object of my adoration graced the doors of this ancient Institution. There was nothing for it but to hang around on the days when Whitemore, Greenish and Child came in to teach their respective trades, and as the three of them seemed to have legions of pupils, my vigil became a full-time job. I had to possess my soul in patience for a couple of days, and then one morning, while I was in Hallett's 'holy of holies', she walked in, came over to where we were poring over a Harmony Paper (he with his eyes on the paper and I with my eyes on the door) and, in that attractive voice which had haunted me every moment since the first time I saw her, asked for the key of a practice-room.

The blood rushed to my head at her approach and instead of boldly speaking to her and congratulating her on the lovely performance of the previous Saturday, I turned away like a clown, just in time to catch Hallett giving her one of his most special smiles. I took courage and glanced at her through the little window. Hallett's advances had been ignored. It was as if she had treated the office like a penny-in-the-slot machine, had inserted her penny and expected a key in return, nothing more. She looked as lovely as ever, with her two fair plaits falling over her pretty shoulders. Then she turned, and with a cool 'Thank you' walked like a Princess across the hall and vanished for the second time. Hallett twirled his moustache, raised his eyebrows and looked over his glasses. Besides examination papers he evidently had a weakness for a pretty face and an attractive figure.

"There she goes!" he said. "Isn't she lovely!" and for the first time since I had known him I had a desire to box his ears. During the morning I hung about the bottom of the stairs leading to the rooms to which students could retire, to practise if they were conscientious or to carry on clandestine conversations if they were not. I waited for a long time and then, realising there was another way down, across the concert platform, and that in all probability the key was once more in Hallett's possession, I retraced my steps to the inner hall and found her chatting to a group of students, among whom was an old friend of mine, a charming young soprano from the West Country. From that moment I shadowed my friend until I managed to find her alone.

"My dear boy, of course I'll introduce you. She's perfectly sweet. You'll love her!"

"I love her already," I assured her, "and I cannot rest until I meet her."

So she set about the task of arranging a meeting, but it was not so easy. My Princess, it appeared, absolutely refused to have anything to do with me. Another young Academy puppy trying to find someone to waste time with! No, she was adamant. I was becoming desperate.

"Tell her I want to write some music for her to the poem she recited."

It worked!

"Why on earth didn't you tell me in the first place? That is quite a different matter. Of course I'll meet him!"

I accompanied my friend to where the slim little figure was standing in the hall, waiting for us.

"This is Eric Coates. He wants to talk to you about writing some music for you."

She then discreetly left us alone.

Our hands met, and as we looked into one another's eyes it was just as if we had found one another once again after having been separated for a long, long time.

* * * * *

We climbed the rickety old wooden staircase together and settled ourselves in the room to which Arnold Bax refers as being No. 27, but which, with all due respect to him, I can still swear to being No. 14. I sat at the piano and played to her while she sat by my side with her feet on the rung of the chair and her hands clasped round her knees. I gave her an idea of the kind of music I had thought of writing for her recitation, and each time I turned to explain a detail she smiled her approval. Then we talked. What about? Oh, of the sunset; of the sadness of the changing seasons; of dusty roads after rain and the sound of running streams; the scent of damp woods and the gull's cry; and we both knew that our thoughts were as one. Then we spoke of music, of poetry, of art, and our tastes were the same as they were over the things of nature. We talked and talked until dusk fell and the chimney-pots outside the window looked to me like little dwarfs leaning forward to try to hear what it was all about. And then, down the rickety old staircase, a minute to wait for her in the hall while she went upstairs to fetch her coat and then out through the door, round the corner into New Bond Street and upstairs in the Blenheim Restaurant for some tea and to talk some more. The wicked look Hallett gave me, as we made our way through the hall together, was a masterpiece of facial manipulation.

Over tea, which we took at a table in the window at the far corner of the room, so as to be undisturbed by such mundane things as Academy students, we talked and talked. We talked of the present and of the future, of ambitions, of my being in the Queen's Hall Orchestra and of hoping one day to be given the post of principal viola, of the music I was going to write for her and of the orchestral work which I was thinking of showing to Henry Wood.

Oh, yes! She went to many of the Promenade Concerts, and I found that she liked the works which I liked and was bored by the ones which bored me. And she played the piano—"very badly", she assured me. Her mother wanted her to take up the piano professionally, but her heart was set on going on the stage, though I gathered that her parents would not permit this. Then I told her of my Thinking Place on the Nottinghamshire hills, and she told me of *her* Thinking Place on her hills around Elstree. (I could see the little train far away in the hazy distance winding its way noiselessly through the sunlit fields). Then we talked of our homes and our families. My father a doctor, her father an artist and Principal of an Art School—her mother living most of the time in France (with her youngest daughter and a delicate son), where they had a cottage to which her father went during the holidays in order to paint. It appeared she had two sisters and two brothers, and their home was in North London. Lastly we talked of our ages. I was twenty-five and she was sixteen, but she would be seventeen to-morrow. She looked at me across the table and smiled one of her adorable smiles.

How we wished it could have gone on for ever, but it was getting late, the evening had set in and it was time for home. We went together down the stairs as if in a dream and walked along the dark, cold streets hand-in-hand, and as we walked we still talked of the things we knew and loved. The waiting horse-bus outside Appenrodt's

Restaurant in Regent Street was about to start. A quick 'goodbye', a shout from the conductor, a 'Gee-up!' from the be-rugged figure away up in the driver's seat, and for the third time my Princess of the fairy-book vanished. I stood on the pavement until the lumbering bus had turned the corner into Mortimer Street and, deeply disturbed, found my way to the flower-shop in Harewood Place where they had the loveliest of red roses, ideal for a lovesick swain to send his lady.

"I want something very special," I said. The flower girl smiled. She understood. Then back to Portsdown Road to dinner and to bed, to dream of princesses, horse-buses which took on the appearance of fairy coaches, and of a little girl who smiled with her eyes —and they were grey, and in one of them was a brown spot.

* * * * *

I leaned out of the carriage window to see old Dobbs standing by the side of the station-master, his mushroom hat sheltering his ears from the cold nor'-wester which had sprung up and which was blowing little flakes of snow along the platform as the train came slowly to a standstill. It was Monday afternoon, and I was fulfilling a long-standing invitation to the old Vicarage at Churcham, one which, in my heart, I would gladly have cancelled if I had only known what the previous Friday was to have held in store for me.

"How do'ye do, surr! I be mighty pleased to see you! There'll be a warm fire and a hot dinner waiting for you up yonder and the master'll be glad to welcome you to the old place again."

A cheery nod from the station-master and we were soon making our way along the path across the fields, now white with snow, to the house nestling under the protection of the giant trees up on the hill. I was met at the door by my friend Harding and Bob the fox-terrier and was soon unpacking my bag in the pleasant bedroom overlooking the orchard and the distant line of the Welsh mountains, dimly discernible through the gathering dusk. The view was as lovely under its garment of white as it was when the summer turned the countryside into a riot of colour, but to-day the beauty of this Gloucestershire had lost its appeal for me and I would fain have been back once again in the streets of the great city which sheltered my beloved.

* * * * *

There was a faint scent of burning peat about the house as I descended the staircase into the drawing-room. Dobbs was right. There was a log fire blazing cheerfully in the hearth and my friend had put out his best sherry to prepare me for the good things to follow. We talked about my father and mother, of our mutual friends in Hucknall, of the doings in his far-flung parish, of the latest musical events in Gloucester (where Herbert Brewer was still fighting the acoustics of the old Cathedral by playing the organ half a beat ahead of his choir), of my activities with the Queen's Hall Orchestra, of the new orchestral work which I was writing, while Bob the foxterrier sat staring into the fire with one ear cocked in anticipation of the silvery tinkle of a little bell to summon the three of us into the dining-room.

I awoke the next morning to find a world covered in white. The wind had dropped during the night and snow hung thickly on the branches of the great trees. Away in the distance I could just glimpse the line of snow-clad mountains. I opened my window to try to see them more clearly and, as I did so, I heard, coming to me over the still, wintry air, the familiar cry of a pheasant calling to its mate. I thought of a house in North London and of someone probably at that very moment looking out of her window at the house-tops covered in the same soft snow and wondering to herself whether her fur coat and her pretty little fur cap and muff were going to keep her warm enough to give a good account of herself at her pianoforte lesson with Whitemore. Had she given me a thought? I sighed, closed the window and was brought down to earth by another faint scent, this time proceeding from the old flagged kitchen at the foot of the three worn stone steps—and it was of rashers.

The papers not arriving at the Vicarage until the morning was well on meant that breakfast was another signal for prolonged conversation. Ten o'clock, or thereabouts, saw my host preparing himself to set out on his visits, and his tall figure, clad in greatcoat and goloshes and complete with umbrella to protect his clerical hat, crunched down the drive and out through the gate into the little lane which led down to the Gloucester–Ross road. This meant that I had a couple of hours to get out my manuscript, sit at the study table and sketch out the ideas which had been simmering in my head, so that I should have something to show my Princess of the fairy-book when I returned to London on Friday.

* * * * *

I will not dwell longer on my stay in Gloucestershire, save to say that I felt ashamed to think that the last time I visited my friend it was only with the greatest difficulty that I had managed to tear myself from under his hospitable roof—but now everything was changed. The countryside which I loved so well had taken on a new colour (and it was not the snow); I longed to get away from the stillness of the old Vicarage and to be in the hubbub of London once again; the quiet twisting lanes had lost their charm to noisy streets; the sleepy 'burr' of Dobbs's old voice was not the music to my ears that it would have been ten days before; the sound of the pheasant calling to its mate in the woods across the fields had a different note. The distant rumble of the train pulling up into Oakle Street station might have reminded me once upon a time of the little train in Nottinghamshire, but now I only saw the grimy roof of the Great Western terminus in London, and it almost seemed like a thing of beauty to my tortured mind. Even poor little Bob's doggy attentions were tiresome and I fear he felt my preoccupation keenly. I do not think my host noticed anything strange about me, except that once or twice he remarked that I was quieter than usual and looked tired and could I not stay a little longer and get a few more nights' decent sleep? I'm afraid I was an unwilling guest. I was in love.

* * * * *

It was over tea that I heard about the storm in North London. It was Friday. I had caught the early morning train from Oakle Street, and in the afternoon, after having fetched my Princess from her lesson at the Academy, we repaired to the corner table upstairs in the Academy Students' Rendezvous and tried to make up in sixty minutes for the one hundred and sixty-eight hours we had been separated (I had counted them). In a way it was a major tragedy of a Gilbertian order, for her mother, it appeared, had come over from France specially to attend the Fortnightly Concert at which she had recited, partly because she wanted to be present at her little daughter's début, but primarily for the very good reason that she felt it was an occasion when a chaperone was of the utmost necessity. But she had overlooked the possibility of a young musician of twenty-five upsetting her carefully-laid plans, and the arrival at the house of a huge armful of red roses on the eve of her little one's birthday brought her to the realisation that she had come up against a crisis of the first magnitude. She had been out to tea with a man? (Her journey all the way from France for nothing!) Who was he? What was he? An old Academy student? A composer? Worse and worse! More questions were asked. Her father was called in, and still more questions.

Uncles and aunts were consulted. One member of the family on her mother's side, an amateur musician, gave his opinion that if the fellow under discussion were a professional and thought he was going to make a success as a composer, then God help Phyllis! This made matters worse, for he had the reputation of knowing a good deal about musicians and in consequence his words carried weight. In the face of overwhelming odds my Princess stood her ground. Fortunately she was able to inform her inquisitors that her composer already had one song to his credit which had sold nearly five hundred thousand copies and that he had been invited by Henry Wood to write a new work for the next Promenade Season. This unexpected *coup de grace* was followed by a general sobering down of the family and an invitation, or rather a summons, to tea on my return from Gloucestershire.

Saturday afternoon at three o'clock; I arrayed myself in my 'best bib and tucker', by which I merely mean a clean collar and shirt, and as my Harris tweed jacket and grey flannel trousers and I were inseparable and worn on all occasions except the ones when a concert called for morning or evening dress, I flouted the conventions and boarded a bus for the Northern Heights.

* * * * *

I returned to my room on the top floor in Portsdown Road with the uneasy sensation that my suggestion that we should be married at once had failed to make an impression. This was confirmed when my Princess met me for tea on the following Monday and told me that the family had decided we were not to see each other again.

"Why?" I asked.

"I'm too young!" she replied, and we laughed and made up our minds to see one another every day.

* * * * *

Weeks of clandestine meetings followed, sometimes lunch or tea at the Blenheim, until we discovered a tea-shop with tables conveniently screened from the public gaze and a waitress who was the soul of discretion. At other times Room No. 14 played an important part in deciding the fate of the young lovers. And always there was the bus journey at the end of the day and the walk down the side road to her home, as long as the evenings were dark. Our difficulties increased with the lengthening days, and people began to talk. At that time it never occurred to us that there was anything unusual about a man of twenty-five being seen continually with a girl of seventeen and gradually the composer and the little girl with the long fair plaits became an object of speculation wherever they went. The arrival at the Academy of flowers on Tuesdays and Fridays and of letters every day of the week was commented on by the Lady Superintendent and enquiries were made as to the identity of the sender. I fear the reputation of being impressionable, which I had earned for myself during my student days at the Academy, had not been entirely forgotten, and the recipient was taken aside and tactfully warned. From what I heard about this encounter afterwards it would seem that the Guardian of the Female Element at the Academy was told, quite nicely but *very* firmly, that it had nothing whatever to do with her, and that she should mind her own business. Then her professors became suspicious. And all this, added to the knowing looks of the students and the almost impudent expression with which I was greeted when I met my friend Hallett, made us more than ever determined to get married without delay and so put an end to all this nonsense once and for all. But what could we do? It was not even known at my Princess's home that we had disobeyed their orders and were seeing each other every day. And then, an invitation from one of the relations asking us jointly to tea happened to coincide with the unexpected appearance of her father and ended in our both being marched back to her house and severely catechised by two extremely angry parents.

We could not understand what it was all about. We only wanted to be married. It was perfectly clear. After all, we had known each other for quite a few weeks and it was the most natural thing in the world that we should want to spend the rest of our lives together. Marriage, we were given to understand, was quite out of the question. It was no use talking about prospects, no man had ever managed to keep a wife on those. Then could we be engaged? More opposition. Perhaps when she was twenty-one, but they would see. But that would not be for another four years, it was unreasonable for them to expect us to wait as long as that. We then put forward every argument we could think of in favour of our being married *at once*, and at last, as a great concession, we were told that if we would wait until she was nineteen they might agree to our being engaged. They would allow us to see each other occasionally, only very occasionally, but we were not to meet out anywhere, and I was invited to lunch with them on Sunday. Not to meet each other except at home! It was like trying to stop the stars in their course, and we saw one another more than ever.

They were an original family, as I was to discover when I made my second journey to North London. Her father, who had spent most of his early life in France, and was to all intents more French than English, possessed a temper and a keen sense of humour not unlike that of my father, had an abundance of amusing stories which he told with an irresistible twinkle, and when he was angry he was terrible to behold.

Her mother was lovely, with the fairest of fair hair and the fairest of fair complexions, and, like the rest of the family, possessed of great personal charm. Fortunately I had something in common with her from the first, for she, like myself, had studied at the Academy and had been a student with my beloved Corder.

"That," she told me, with a charming smile, "was in the days when Sir George Macfarren was Principal." The rest of the family, with the exception of her eldest brother, either painted or played the piano. I suspect I was the subject of much amusement when the family gathered together for the next meal; I say the next meal, because after lunch each one of them retired to their respective rooms and I gathered from my Princess that nothing would be seen of them again until the next gong sounded. This conservative behaviour on their part had its advantages where we were concerned and we made the most of the drawing-room until the clock told me it was time to make a move towards Queen's Hall and the horrors of an afternoon concert.

My recollections of the ensuing months were of trying to divide my attention between rehearsals and concerts, composing at my little upright piano in my room on the top floor in Portsdown Road and turning up at all sorts of places at all times of the day to spend stolen hours with my Princess. It was an unnatural kind of existence and for the two young lovers unsatisfactory. As time passed we became more and more discontented with our lot and conceived all kinds of plans as to how we could contrive to force her parents' hand into our being at least engaged, so that we could go about together without being compelled to resort to the unpleasant but necessary expedient of inventing imaginary lessons at the Academy, to satisfy the overwhelming desire to be in one another's company.

The firm of Whitemore, Greenish and Child was literally worked to death, but as it was not aware of the inordinate amount of lessons inflicted on it; it was we who felt the strain, not it. At long last, after we had fought many parental battles, early in 1912 the long fair plaits were taken up and neatly arranged around my Princess's head, a joint visit to Regent Street in search of a diamond ring, and we were engaged to be married. After this, life proved to be slightly easier, although the parental war continued unabated, and one cold January morning in 1913 found me on board the cross-Channel steamer *en route* for Boulogne and a cottage among the pinewoods of Trépied, près d'Étaples, *le Quartier Latin du Pas de Calais*, where my Princess had been unwillingly taken by her parents in a final attempt to get her away from the persistent advances of her young composer.

* * * * *

It was the first time I had been to France and I remember how impressed I was with the theatrical display on the quayside at Boulogne as the steamer drifted into the harbour. After the dignity of the English porter who had carried my suitcase on board at Folkestone, the fellow who took charge of me through the *Douane* had the appearance of a pirate out of Robert Louis Stevenson's *Treasure Island*. I was secretly rather in awe of the whole proceedings, from the warlike demonstration by beswarded and becarbined gendarmes, swarming round the ship's gangway, to the compartment, in the train, where I had to suffer the Frenchman's aversion to a *courant d'air*, being nearly asphyxiated with filthy pipes and even filthier tobacco. I was met at Étaples by my Princess, looking lovelier than ever with her cheeks flushed by the cold sea air, and we walked the pine-scented couple of miles to Trépied, my bag being carried for me by a young ragamuffin who was pressed into service after much bargaining and gesticulating.

* * * * *

As I think I said some time previously, I loathe the cold, and evidently my aversion to anything appertaining to the winter had been marked, learned and inwardly digested by the family, who had made a bet among themselves that my first words on arrival would be: 'Isn't it cold!' My entrance into the cosy cottage from the biting wind outside being greeted with uproarious laughter proves that I came up to scratch.

As soon as I had unpacked my bag the battle commenced afresh. The prospects already alluded to as being thin material on which to build a home, having now materialised in the form of a contract as principal viola in the Queen's Hall Orchestra, gave us a good argument in favour of our being married. We pointed out that I now had an assured income from my viola, added to which more songs of mine were coming on to the market. In fact the future held all kinds of possibilities for me. Her mother seemed to waver for a moment, but only for a moment, and then the battle broke out afresh. It swayed backwards and forwards. At last my Princess delivered her ultimatum:

"You know, Mother, if you do not let us be married now, *one day you will go up to my room to find that my bed has not been slept in!*"

A long pause followed, during which I wondered what on earth was going to happen. I pictured myself being told to say goodbye to my Princess for good and ordered to take the first boat back to England. And then, to my utter astonishment:

"Very well, children."

My Princess's timely threat had brought about complete capitulation. Letters were despatched immediately to Paris for her trousseau and we were despatched back to London to search for a flat. There is one thing to be said for the Coates and the Black families: when they act, they act quickly. The flat was decided upon, and the landlord made a special concession over the rent on account of the young couple being so *very* young, though I believe the real reason for this gallant gesture was that he fell so completely under the spell of my charming future mother-in-law that his business capabilities temporarily failed him.

Now I look back at the time intervening between our first meeting and our marriage, I wonder how we managed to put up with the hundreds of obstacles which were put in our path by my Princess's parents in their endeavour to sicken us of one another. Even when we were engaged, all kinds of restrictions were imposed, including a ten o'clock curfew, the latter somewhat cramping our style where theatres were concerned. It is not amusing to be forced to leave a show before the last act has started, but we became quite accustomed to supplying our own conclusion to several of the plays which were on in the West End at that time. Many were the times when we were tempted to take the law into our own hands and run away together, but we had the good sense to realise that as she was only seventeen the Law might not have regarded our action in a favourable light. So we stayed the course. I am sure, if I had a little daughter of seventeen to-day, I should be just as worried as my Princess's parents were, though I think I have learned by personal experience that opposition, instead of delaying matters, usually ends in precipitating them.

And so, on February 3rd, 1913, just under two years since I first saw her on the platform in the Concert Hall at the old Royal Academy of Music in Tenterden Street, Phyl and I were married, and besides being accepted as one of the family, I was allowed the unusual and entirely unorthodox privilege of lunching with them before the ceremony.

*   *   *   *   *

Then followed nine happy, carefree years of blissful married life together. By this I do not wish to give the impression that our happiness was limited to this specified period but merely to stress that it was not until the beginning of the tenth year that either of us had the vaguest notion of the meaning of the word 'responsibility'. It was just one long glorious adventure. Months passed before we were able to appreciate to the full the unbelievable fact that nothing could ever separate us again, after having re-found one another on that afternoon in the inner hall of the Academy. How we managed to deal with the problems of running a flat and attending to all the irritating but necessary details connected thereto, such as rent, rates, gas, coal, electricity, telephone, house-keeping expenses and income tax forms (ninepence in the pound and rumours of a threepenny rise!), is a thing which I have never understood, for I doubt if you could have found a couple more irresponsibly wrapped up in each other than the one which arrived promptly at two-thirty in the afternoon at the flat on the top floor where Abbey Road takes a bend at Quex Road. Phyl, confident in her powers as a married woman of eighteen years old, had scorned her mother's offer to prepare the flat in readiness to receive the bridal pair and had made arrangements herself for the firm of Messrs. Shoolbred of Tottenham Court Road to move in the furniture at three o'clock on the same day that we returned from our honeymoon, thus leaving us thirty minutes in which to prepare ourselves to cope with the onslaught. It happened promptly on the stroke of three and while it lasted was hardly what you could have called a pleasant experience. Everyone was there, not only the removers but the servants of the various public services as well, and by the time the furniture was in, the china unpacked (some of it), the carpets unrolled and the electric light and the gas and the water and the telephone connected by the experts of those various companies, we had made up our minds that if ever we married again we should not mind who put our house in order so long as it was not we. How well I remember the magic hour for tea arriving. The wedding presents not being unpacked yet, no teapot was forthcoming (sometimes I think the happiness of one's life revolves round this most essential of domestic utensils), and how clearly I can recall the telephone message to Shoolbred's, half an hour after they had closed, which brought post-haste a large van, complete with three men and one small teapot, to the succour of the anxiously waiting pair and the already boiling kettle. Can you wonder that this grand old firm went out of commission when it was so easily moved to compassion by the misfortune of a newly-married couple who had neglected to include a teapot on the list?

*   *   *   *   *

To say that we lived in each other's pockets would scarcely be an exaggeration, the only times we were separated being those when my duties as principal viola called me to Queen's Hall or later on when her stage activities took her into the Provinces prior to coming to the West End, and even then we were connected by a sense of telepathy which to this day is present when an emergency of extreme urgency calls for other than ordinary means of communication. The first time we became aware of this phenomenon was during a Sunday Afternoon Concert at Queen's Hall in the spring of 1914, about a year after our marriage. I had arranged with Phyl that she should meet me immediately after the concert in the entrance hall at the front of the house, where she was well known to the attendants. I had previously warned her that she was on no account to wait about near the artists' entrance in Riding House Street as it was a lonely thoroughfare and often frequented by undesirable characters.

The concert was nearing its close when suddenly I had a sensation that all was not well. The last five minutes of the programme seemed like a century and I could scarcely restrain myself from putting down my viola and making a dash for it. Before the final note had ended and even before the applause had started, my instrument was on my colleague's lap with instructions to put it away for me as I had to get away in a hurry. I remember the startled look on my friend's face as I made this unusual request, for I had never been known to trust my viola to anyone before.

I rushed off the platform, across the still deserted band-room, up the stairs and out into the quiet street at the side of the hall, and it was not until I found her talking agitatedly to one of the attendants that I realised my sensations had not been imaginary. A man, a foreigner, had spoken to her in Riding House Street and it was only through her being extremely active that she managed to elude the hand that had been laid on her shoulder in preparation to bundling her into the waiting motor-car standing so quietly at the side of the kerb.

Several times in our life together have we experienced this telepathy; it comes quite suddenly and without seeking, but when it comes there is no doubt about it. It is just as if some tremendous vibration takes hold of you and fills your mind with a sensation of acute uneasiness. I have even been awakened at one o'clock in the morning and walked a couple of miles to a public call-office in order to put through a long-distance call to satisfy myself that all was well (that was in the days when long-distance telephony was not as simple as it is to-day), and the little voice, three hundred miles away, which assured me that nothing was wrong (to put my mind at rest) told a very different tale when next we met.

Although we loved our flat on the top floor we did not spend a great deal of time in it. The view across London proved too much for us and made us feel the call to be continually running up to the West End. It has always been like this with us, and wherever we have lived (and the number of the districts in and around London in which we have made our home at one time or another is legion) we have never missed an opportunity of making an excuse to get once again into the heart of things. In Phyl's case it was purely her love of life, but in my own I sometimes think it was to try to blot out of my mind the urge to see my beloved Nottinghamshire lanes as I used to do so frequently before I was married. It was some years before I managed to break myself of the homesickness I felt for my native county and it was not until we moved into the West End and had lived there for some considerable time that I began to look upon London as my home; and although the country always held a fascination for me, I always knew that it was in the heart of the Metropolis that my musical ideas usually came into being.

To live in a beautiful home in lovely grounds, surrounded by flowers and rare birds, did not seem ideal for the composing of music. I found the things of beauty, especially of nature, too distracting to permit of my getting down to work seriously—it was like endeavouring to compete with the Infinite and had the same effect on me as when I listened to the poor impression made by music when played out of doors. A flat on a top floor in the heart of London with a writing-room looking across the city far away to the Surrey hills and the sounds of traffic coming up to me from way down below and my fellow-creatures giving the appearance of pygmies going about their daily tasks; add to this a pile of music-paper (twenty-five to thirty staves) and a well-sharpened pencil—this was my recipe for composing. I have tried both ways of living and, even to-day, I feel that the country is for dreaming and the town for work.

* * * * *

When I gave up my viola-playing in 1919 I remember thinking to myself that at last I was free to live where I liked. I conjured up visions of a villa in the South of France where I could bask in the sunshine all the day and compose music under what seemed to me would be ideal conditions. But I was soon to find that London called me far too strongly to contemplate such a mode of living, even for the winter months, let alone permanently, and I was to realise how important it was, and still is, to be near the scenes of one's activities and never too far away to attend to a personal telephone call.

A lovely, long summer holiday together in Devonshire in 1913 preceded my first Promenade Season as principal viola and we returned one hot summer day early in August in time for the three rehearsals prior to the opening concert on the Saturday night. I had bought a season ticket for Phyl in the first row of the Grand Circle, just over that side of the platform which led into the artists' room, and there she used to sit, night after night, sometimes visible through the opened lid of the grand piano when a pianist happened to be the soloist, but most frequently across it, when either a string instrumentalist or a singer was appearing, or more often when there was no soloist at all. In the seat directly behind her sat Lady Wood, usually making notes throughout the concerts, and I have a shrewd suspicion that she made up her accounts when some artist or some work which we were playing bored her!

I remember the opening night gave me my first viola solo—it was in the few bars' introduction to Max Bruch's 'Ave Maria' for soprano and orchestra, and I can still recall the anxiety I experienced at making this, my début, at Queen's Hall; I can also remember how grateful I was to my dear old friend, Wilfred Smith, who sat at the desk immediately behind me, when he remarked in a stage-whisper to his colleague at the close of my short cadenza: "He pulls a good tone!" But the worst ordeal of all was the morning when the much-dreaded 'Don Quixote' appeared on the music-stands. Under conditions of strain or intense anxiety such as this, my heart used to beat at such a rate that it temporarily blinded me, deafened me and suffocated me at one and the same time. It was not of the least use trying to stop it by assuring myself that there was really nothing to worry about, for this mode of approach usually ended in making matters worse. Fortunately this alarming condition was not noticeable to the casual observer, in fact my companion of the first desk remarked to me one evening that he wished he could manage to keep as cool as I appeared to be when I had something difficult to tackle.

What happened during the first few bars of the tricky viola solo in Richard Strauss's work I cannot remember, except that Wood disappeared from view, the orchestra faded out completely, the hall suddenly became devoid of any kind of ventilation and my heart accelerated up to one hundred and thirty beats a minute. But the strange thing was that, when Wood reappeared, the orchestra had once again come to life, the hall re-ventilated itself and my heart had returned to normal, no one appeared to have noticed anything peculiar about either me or my viola. Even to-day I experience the same unpleasant sensations, especially when someone else is producing a new work of mine: just about five minutes before the performance my heart starts to hurry, and by the time the conductor is up on the rostrum it is 'well away'.

The worst of it is that the reaction following these internal demonstrations of nerves is one of exhaustion and sometimes it takes me several days to recuperate. I go through the same emotions when conducting a new work myself, but it usually wears off after a few moments and is never such a nerve-racking experience as playing the viola. There is something so disturbing about producing any sort of musical noise by your own efforts, and then again, there is the ever-present fear of that horrible 'domino' about which I wrote some time previously. One thing about conducting, if you *do* make a 'domino' with the stick, no one but the orchestra players will notice it, unless you are misguided enough to employ an unnecessarily long bâton which makes a 'swish' as it comes down in that silent bar. Personally, this is the reason I prefer a short stick, though I do not imagine that it is the reason for the famous Leopold Stokowski using no stick at all!

*   *   *   *   *

The Promenade Season went its way, the Winter and Spring Concerts were over and once again the summer came round, bringing with it the promise of another lovely holiday. Having stayed for one noisy night at Penmaenmawr (trains and slate-quarrying are not ideal rest-inducers), followed by a day in Llandudno, the prospect of spending five weeks there in company with ten thousand lads and lasses from Lancashire forced us into taking the first train down the coast in search of peace and quiet. The following weeks found us enjoying a pleasant but somewhat wet holiday at Barmouth in the same rooms and with the same landlady with whom my father and mother and I stayed after my father's illness in 1899.

Our stay at 'Craig-y-don', despite all we could do to try to forget about it, was marred by rumours of war. We walked on the hills behind the town and looked across the peaceful bay, we visited Arthog (which, by the way, was infested with wasps—horrible insects!) climbed the walls of Harlech Castle, lunched at Dolgelley, explored the little old church at Llanaber, took a boat out on the Mawddach, motored in an old 'Tin Lizzy' (which shed a tyre every few miles) to Ffestiniog, Lake Bala, Cader Idris, and bathed when the inclement weather permitted. How could there be such a thing as war? But the trains passed through Barmouth every few hours laden with troops, and the town became more deserted day by day, which seemed to point to the inevitable. On that fateful fourth of August, 1914 (still fresh in my mind through the tragedy of the complete destruction of Phyl's best hat, which was sat upon by our landlady in her horror at the turn events had taken), a hasty and uncomfortable journey back to London brought us up against the unpleasant realisation that the Promenade Concerts and all my future dates had been cancelled. What was to be done?

We talked late into the night. We could not possibly continue living on at our flat with no engagements in view. Phyl was a tower of strength. There was nothing for it but to let the flat furnished and go into rooms—"We shall be quite all right," she said, "and there is nothing to worry about." How often since those far-away days has she proved herself to be the soul of practicality and how often has she stood by me when things have not looked too promising. So we let our flat and went into rooms in Hampstead.

Our accommodation consisted of a large bed-sitting-room in which we slept and took our meals, and in which, with the aid of a little upright piano, I managed to do some composing. It is astonishing how comfortable you can be, living under circumstances such as these, and, putting aside the anxiety we experienced over the fall of the Promenade Concerts, we were as happy as a couple of lovebirds. Then came word that Sir Edgar Speyer, the Patron of the Queen's Hall Orchestra, intended to re-start his musical activities, and after a break of a few weeks the Proms were once again in full swing. There was an outcry from a certain section of the music public when Richard Strauss's name figured prominently in the programmes, but Edgar Speyer's Teutonic leanings played a trump card—if he paid the piper, then the piper must play to his tune. And so Richard Strauss remained. We all expected that there would be a demonstration the first night we played one of the master's works, but fortunately for the world of music we were disappointed.

London was a depressing place to be in until the first shock of war was over, and then began a boom in music and entertainment which pointed then, as it always does, to the tremendous value of this branch of Art in helping to keep up the morale of the people. The enquiry into Sir Edgar Speyer's dealings with the enemy, however, and his consequent disgrace through being deprived of his baronetcy, caused a black outlook for 1915 and the members of the Queen's Hall Orchestra, for without some sort of financial backing another Promenade Season was out of the question. By this time we had returned to our flat and were wondering whether or not we ought to re-let and go into rooms once more. We decided to stay on and see what would happen.

Then Phyl took it into her head to write to Mr. William Boosey, the director of Messrs. Chappell & Co. of New Bond Street (who were the owners of Queen's Hall), to ask him if he would consider taking over the responsibility of the Queen's Hall Orchestra. She received a charming reply from him, and soon afterwards the Promenade Concerts reopened in the summer with the *New* Queen's Hall Orchestra, conductor Sir Henry J. Wood, under the auspices of Messrs. Chappell & Co. Phyl refuses to believe that her letter to William Boosey had anything to do with his taking over the responsibility of these concerts, but I still like to think it went a long way towards bringing the idea to fruition.

William Boosey, or 'The Emperor', as he was styled by Fred E. Weatherly, usually alluded to by us as just plain 'W.B.', was a striking figure of a man, with a dominating personality which made itself felt wherever he went. In some ways he was difficult to approach, but he had a good heart under his imperial appearance, and his word was his bond. He had an uncanny knack of spotting a winner but liked to do the 'spotting' unaided, and woe betide your chances if you took him in a piece of music and let him know you thought it was going to set the Thames on fire, for you would be greeted with: "I can't say I think much of it." It was wiser to go into his room in an apologetic manner and either say timidly: "I'm afraid this is not much use, but I'd like you to hear it," or, better still, say nothing at all. The first mode of approach would in all possibility bring from him the retort: "What's wrong with it? It shall go in to engrave at once," but the second, the one which I always adopted, put him 'on the spot' so to speak, and in this way I received an unbiased opinion and a sure criticism. I have known him to turn down songs which he must have known were 'winners' simply through his antipathy to anyone with an opinion of his own. In my own case he dismissed 'Bird Songs at Eventide' as being worthless, through lack of judgment on the part of the manager of the Professional Department, who did not know his man well enough to realise the correct method of approach when bringing the song up for a hearing. It was not until a year had passed and W.B. had forgotten all about its existence that it was brought up again, this time without comment, and was acclaimed as "just the thing we are looking for!"

I remember how he used to complain about my always writing on orchestral-scoring paper even though it was not an orchestral work, and when he did not care for any part of a composition he would go off into a doze. I have seen him at Queen's Hall sometimes nearly falling off his seat during a deep sleep brought on by some orchestral work which he thought needed a good cutting. How well I know the feeling myself! One night at the Covent Garden Ballet I fell sound asleep through the sheer boredom of trying to watch a *corps de ballet* failing dismally in its efforts to dance to Tschaikowsky's E Minor Symphony; a more unsuitable work to portray choreographically I cannot conceive. 'Présages' they were misguided enough to name it; I should have thought that something like 'Présages d'ennui réalisés' would have been more suitable.

Besides his remarkable sense of picking a popular 'hit', W.B. almost possessed the gift of second-sight where the trend of musical affairs was concerned, and we have to thank him for the part he played in the great fight in this country which resulted in the much-neglected and helpless composer being able to claim his legal rights where copyright, gramophone recordings and performing rights are concerned. When the Performing Right Society was formed over here in 1915 he asked me if I would join and, a request from W.B. being more in the nature of an order than anything else, I became one of the original members of this Society, which, besides its other uses, protects that most unbusinesslike of human creatures, the composer.

My membership, coinciding with the publication of a new orchestral work of mine by Messrs. Boosey & Co., brought a hornet's nest about my ears. Mr. Arthur Boosey, at that time the head of the firm of Boosey & Co., having ideas in opposition to the objects of the Society, gave me to understand that he would hold me responsible for the cost of the already engraved full-score, as nothing would induce him to publish a work by any composer who belonged to a union whose aims were so revolutionary. On top of this bombshell I received letters from all over the country, mainly from military bandmasters, which informed me that my associations with the Society gave them no alternative but to take my works out of any future programmes. Here the 'Emperor' came to the rescue, and by the application of his unfailing tact he arranged with Mr. Oliver Hawkes, of Messrs. Hawkes & Son, the music publishers in Denham Street and members of the Performing Right Society, to take over the engraved plates from Messrs. Boosey. This Oliver Hawkes agreed to do, at the same time making the proviso that he himself had no personal dealings whatsoever with the rival firm of Boosey & Co. of Regent Street. There was no love lost between the houses of Boosey and Hawkes in those days. Regarding the ultimatum from the genii of the military band world, W.B. asked me to hold on, although things looked black for the Performing Right Society, assuring me that all would be well in time. I must admit that I was a bit shaken, but cheered up considerably when on June 1st, 1917, a cheque arrived from the Society for the magnificent sum of fifty pounds, being fees due to me for the period April 5th 1914, to April 5th 1917—three years' performing fees!

He was a grand man, our 'Emperor', and personally I got on well with him, although I admit that on occasions I was a little afraid of him. But weren't we all? I can still see him as chairman of this great Society, standing at the head of the table at one of the official dinners given by the Performing Right Society not long after its inauguration in this country, telling us in his strong, forceful way that it would not be many years before we should be looking to our mechanical rights and performing rights for our chief sources of income. How right he proved to be, although at the time all those composers whose songs were selling in their tens of thousands found it difficult to believe that their sales from sheet music would one day drop and that they would then be thankful to live on their performing rights. The growing popularity of the gramophone started the decline in the sale of sheet music and the advent of the British Broadcasting Corporation in 1922 practically finished it.

* * * * *

During my term as principal viola with the New Queen's Hall Orchestra, I was up against two important factors which interfered a good deal with my chances of advancement as a composer. The first was the disturbing influence which playing other composers' music had upon me; and the second, the difficulty I experienced in obtaining a hearing with my songs at the Chappell Ballad Concerts at Queen's Hall, due to the preponderance at that time of the number of already famous and popular song-writers who held the field, such as Hermann Löhr, Guy d'Hardelot, Teresa del Riego, Haydn Wood, Robert Coningsby Clarke, Liza Lehmann and Maude Valerie White. My chances at the Boosey Ballad Concerts at the Albert Hall were scarcely more promising, with such names as W. H. Squire, Wilfred Sanderson, Amy Woodford Finden and Samuel Liddle to compete with.

It was an uphill fight, for since 'Stonecracker John' in 1909 I had not achieved any great success in the song line, and those orchestral works which I had composed up to the time of which I am writing, although bringing me in hundreds of performances, brought me in no money. This state of affairs left me a little despondent over the possibility of ever being able to give up my viola-playing, and sometimes I saw myself living for the rest of my life with an instrument which was becoming every day more and more of a trial through the ever-growing neuritis in my left arm.

*   *   *   *   *

Three things, however, which were to play an important part in my career and which were the beginning of better days for me as a composer were, firstly, the advent of the Performing Right Society in 1914; secondly, the inauguration of the New Queen's Hall Light Orchestra in 1916, under the conductorship of Alick Maclean, who since 1912 had held the post of Director of Music to the Spa, Scarborough; and thirdly, the taking over in 1918 of the Professional Department at Messrs. Chappell & Co. by Alice Boosey, the charming daughter of the great 'Emperor'.

Writing orchestral music in those days was a labour of love, and glancing back to 1911, the year in which Sir Henry Wood launched my 'Miniature Suite' at the Promenade Concerts, I feel thankful for the desire I always had, and always will have, to express myself through the medium of the orchestra, and more than ever thankful for the 'Emperor', who, through creating the Performing Right Society, was the indirect means of bringing to fruition the efforts of my early work in London.

Before the advent of the Society, many of the successful songwriters of that time said to me that they wondered how I could spend so much thought and energy on writing orchestral works with no hope of financial return, when there was so much money to be made out of songs. To tell the truth, although I have been fortunate enough to have composed several songs which have achieved popularity, I have never been able to get up much enthusiasm over this limited form of expression. I have always 'thought' orchestrally and, as I said previously, even use orchestral-scoring paper when setting words to music, and much as I would have liked to have exchanged banking accounts with any of the composers I have just mentioned, a small voice inside me kept on repeating: "Don't listen to them! The orchestra is your first love! Stick to it!" And so my labour of love continued unabated and unrewarded until that fifty pounds arrived one morning at our flat for 'Three Years' Performing Fees', and from that time onwards finances improved, until some years later I was able to say 'Thank you" to the little, insistent voice which had helped me for so long and given me the courage to stick to my guns.

Although I refer to song-writing as being a limited form of expression it is not an easy thing to write a popular song, for there are several points to consider before you can even put pen to paper. First of all comes the question of a lyric with human appeal, this has to be joined to a melody in which you employ a compass which is within range of the average voice, to this you must add a pianoforte accompaniment which must be such that practically anybody can attempt it, and lastly the finished article must sound pleasant, even to the ears of a musician. Of course there are exceptions to the rule, for if a song or an instrumental piece has achieved tremendous popularity through being sung or played a great deal, the public will buy it and have a shot at it on the piano whatever difficulties it may present.

I had this experience myself over the 'Knightsbridge' movement from my 'London Suite'. In the first instance my publishers considered that none of the smaller orchestras could possibly attempt it, but they *did*, and literally played it to death. In the second place, the pianoforte arrangement was published almost under protest and was looked upon as a failure even before it was in print on account of its unpianistic lay-out, being so essentially an orchestral piece. But, here again, it was bought by the hundreds of thousands and, I am happy to say, even strummed out in public-houses (the criterion, you must admit, of popularity). All the song-writers I have mentioned seemed to have had the knack of sensing the kind of thing the public wanted and, lucky people, they were blessed with such lyric-writers as Fred E. Weatherly, Edward Teschemacher, Harold Simpson, Fred G. Bowles, P. J. O'Reilly and May Eardley-Wilmot. Of these writers there is no doubt that the king was the dapper Fred Weatherly, with his astonishing flair for a story which appealed not only to the more intellectual, but also to the man in the street. Among the composers themselves, Hermann Löhr and Guy d'Hardelot were the most important so far as Messrs. Chappell & Co. were concerned, and as both these writers seemed to have a new song ready for every Ballad Concert, I had to be content with whatever crumbs I could pick up, in the form of a second place on the programmes when I was lucky, but more often than not having to wait until several concerts had passed before I could get a look-in at all. On top of this, these two composers naturally had the pick of the lyric-writers at their beck and call, which meant that the 'also rans' like myself had to put up with taking what they could get in the poem line.

W.B., except for owning the Queen's Hall and running the orchestra, was not in the least orchestrally-minded and thought only in terms of popular song-hits. But one day, while searching for ideas as to how he could revive interest in the Ballad Concerts, which were beginning to show signs of a falling-off in attendance, he had the inspiration of introducing some kind of Light Orchestra to liven up the proceedings. Up to that time the instrumental relief had been supplied by such artists as Fritz Kreisler, Benno Moiseiwitsch and Arthur de Greef. And so, in 1916, the New Queen's Hall *Light Orchestra* of fifty players came into existence, bringing with it a musician who was to become one of my dearest friends and to whom I owe the beginning of better things. Alick Maclean had already been the Musical Director to the Spa, Scarborough, for four years, and his orchestra was considered to be one of the best outside London. He was a fine musician: generous, sensitive, lovable, extremely temperamental, gloriously tactless, and besides being a good conductor was completely unselfish and possessed a heart of gold. We in the orchestra named him the 'Lightning Conductor' on account of the terrific speed he took anything which had a rapid tempo-marking, and later on it came to be said that he had only three tempi: quick—quicker—and damn quick!

At the first rehearsal with the New Queen's Hall Light Orchestra, our conductor, in his vain attempts to get anything out of us in the nature of a rapid crescendo or a violent rubato or a lightning diminuendo, worked himself up into such a state of frenzy that he became completely incoherent. The scene was chaotic. None of us understood what he wanted. The more excited he became the more he bewildered us with his indescribable, monosyllabic outbursts. I remember how nonplussed I was by his hopeless attempts to describe to me the way in which he wanted me to phrase a particular solo passage, and I vividly recall my equally hopeless efforts to understand what he meant, which resulted, after three or four play-overs, in my executing the passage exactly as I had played it in the first place and to my astonishment receiving a nod of commendation. Some years later, when I had the privilege of conducting his orchestra at the Spa, Scarborough, I realised the reason for his demonstration of temperament when he first appeared on the rostrum at Queen's Hall, for compared to his inspired body of players at the Spa we must have seemed like a crowd of amateurs! There is no doubt that playing too much under one conductor had not been good for us, and we had become so used to 'Timber's' regular beat, ever-steady rhythm and never-varying renderings that the advent of this musician with the dyamic energy of a whirlwind proved too much for us, and I regret to say that I, in company with several other members of the orchestra, broke down and laughed helplessly.

Phyl and I, having succumbed to the lure of the West End, had moved to a flat three minutes' walk from Queen's Hall. This fantastic rehearsal, on top of having to 'run for it', thinking I could make it in two minutes instead of in three, came near to finishing my career as principal viola of the New Queen's Hall Light Orchestra. This was firstly on account of my heart reacting badly to any form of violent physical activity, and secondly to the fact that I did not think I could possibly stand up to another ordeal such as that to which I had been subjected that morning with our new conductor.

The extraordinary thing is that, many years later, I was to hear from my friend Alick Maclean himself that *I* had been the cause of his excessive display of temperament on that occasion. He had heard, way up in Scarborough, of the principal viola who wrote popular works for the orchestra, and he had pictured a self-satisfied and extremely spoilt young man who was going to be the very devil of a nuisance to him when he made his first appearance as conductor of the new Light Orchestra. He was determined to have no nonsense and to enforce the strictest discipline and to put the young man in his proper place. I can still see the twinkle in his eye as he told me this, while I was having tea with the maestro and his delightful wife in their flat overlooking the gardens at Scarborough.

* * * * *

At the time when Alick Maclean took over the New Queen's Hall Light Orchestra I was going through a difficult period with my composing. For two years things had been steadily on the downward grade and my royalties from sheet music were at a low ebb. Not only my songs but even my orchestral works were given the cold shoulder where the Chappell Ballad Concerts at the Queen's Hall were concerned.

For a long while Phyl and I had had suspicions that someone was harming me professionally and stopping my performances. As I have said already, I had always experienced a good deal of opposition over my song appearances at the Ballad Concerts, on account of my inability to break through the ring formed by the already established song-writers of that time, and when the New Light Orchestra was introduced at these concerts I thought that now, at last, I should be given an opportunity of showing what I could do, at any rate in the orchestral field. But no! Here again I was up against a stone wall, every avenue appeared to be closed to me—a state of frustration on every hand.

One day I happened by chance to be in the front shop of my publisher's in New Bond Street and heard my name being mentioned.

I pricked up my ears and overheard the following conversation which took place between a well-known tenor and an important director of Messrs. Chappell & Co.:

"I'm looking for a new song for my next concert at Queen's Hall. What about this new one by Eric Coates?" said the high voice.

"Oh, no," said the deep voice, "I should not advise you to take that up—it's no good."

"Well, here's another Eric Coates song," insisted the high voice. "I could make a hit with this!"

Once again persisted the deep voice:

"No, that is no good either. I should choose something by someone else."

And then followed the usual list of songs by Hermann Löhr, Guy d'Hardelot, Coningsby Clarke, Haydn Wood, Teresa de Riego, etc. etc. I could scarcely believe my ears. I thought of my scanty royalties, of my non-appearances at the Ballad Concerts and a hundred and one other things which had been worrying me for so long.

I left the building and ran into Alick Maclean. He was obviously distressed and bewildered. It appeared he had been trying for some time, without success, to get the 'Emperor' to allow him to put down my 'Miniature Suite' for performance at one of the Ballad Concerts.

"But, my dear boy," he exclaimed, "I can't imagine *why* they keep on taking it out of the programmes. It's one of my most popular successes at Scarborough and would be ideal for these concerts. The 'Scene de bal' movement never fails to get an encore!"

I thought of the conversation I had just overheard, and that evening Phyl and I held a lengthy post-mortem over the happenings of the past two years. Our subsequent findings were that the arrival in the firm of a certain gentleman had coincided with the alarming drop in my royalties, so we decided that the only course was for me to crave audience of the 'Emperor' and lay my case tactfully before him. It was an unpleasant thing to have to do and would need handling carefully, so, praying I could get a fair deal without incriminating the two-year-old member of the firm in New Bond Street, I climbed the winding stairs to the first floor, took a deep breath and knocked bravely at W.B's door. The 'Emperor' was sitting at his desk looking more imperial than ever, or was it that the impending encounter which I had not been looking forward to with relish had given him this unusually majestic appearance? I felt rather like the horse to whom all objects appear so much larger than they really are.

The great man rose from his seat and towered over the poor little neglected composer. I realised at that moment why Fred Weatherly, who was several inches smaller than I, had christened him 'The Emperor'. The preliminary handshake over, he gave me to understand, by not inviting me to be seated, that he had important business on hand and the interview would therefore have to be brief.

"Why do we not play your 'Miniature Suite' at the Ballad Concerts?" he replied in answer to my question. "For the simple reason that we (this collective noun business was making me feel smaller and smaller)—*we* are anxious to make a good start with the orchestral side of these concerts and cannot afford to perform anything but the most established and popular works."

I pointed out to him that my 'Miniature Suite' had been published for some years by Messrs. Boosey & Co. and was being played with much success all over the country, at the same time quoting Maclean's remark about its popularity at the Spa, Scarborough.

"But our director, Mr. X, told me this was an unknown work!" And ringing the bell he summoned to the Imperial Presence the last person on earth whom I wished to meet at that moment. Then followed a lively five minutes: my friend of the deep voice insisting that I had told him my Suite had only just been published and I denying that we had ever spoken of it. To cut a long and unpleasant story short, W.B. listened patiently to the two of us and evidently drew his own conclusions, which resulted in my 'Miniature Suite' being put down for performance at the next Ballad Concert and my false friend leaving the publishing house in New Bond Street a few months later. Phyl and I did not feel happy to think that I might have been the cause of his dismissal and we were both relieved to hear from someone in authority that he had already done the same thing with another composer who happened to be friendly with the 'Emperor'. My complaint, coming on top of this, gave W.B. the proof he needed. I remember meeting this one-time member of the staff some years after I had given up my viola-playing, and the look he gave me, when in answer to his enquiries I was able to tell him that I was existing on my composing, was one which I would gladly forget.

And so my 'Miniature Suite' came to Queen's Hall again five years after its first appearance there. I can still see the delighted look on Alick Maclean's face as he turned to the first desk of violas and signed to me to get up from my seat to acknowledge its reception, only to sit down again in order to lead the violas through the encore which followed. This was the beginning of a twenty-years friendship with my newly-found champion. After the trying time I had experienced, his encouragement acted like a tonic and made me feel that, after all, my labours had not been in vain. Many times after this did my Suite appear on the programmes at the Ballad Concerts and in due course other orchestral works in the lighter vein were given their first performance here, including my little Valsette, 'Wood-Nymphs', which became very popular at these concerts and was soon widely played about the country. Maclean had an irresistible way of putting over this type of number, for he would beam all over his face and literally dance as he conducted, carrying the orchestra and the audience with him as he went.

This Valsette never failed to obtain an encore. Whenever we played it, a second play-through was looked upon as a foregone conclusion, and on one occasion we had to repeat it three times, making four performances in all. So often was this piece asked for that Maclean said to me he really thought the orchestra could play it blindfold. However, we little thought that one day we should be called upon to prove this.

It happened in Newcastle, when the lights suddenly failed after we had negotiated the introduction and were well into the valse theme. To the astonishment of the audience and with no less surprise on the part of the orchestra, we played on undeterred by the darkness until the final pizzicato chords brought up the lights again. It was timed to a split second and might have been the result of a carefully rehearsed effect. At any rate, it caused a sensation in the local Press, who, I think, had their doubts about the genuineness of the orchestra's temporary eclipse.

It was at this same concert that Madame d'Alvarez sang Bizet's famous 'Agnus Dei', which performance I shall always remember by reason of the entrance, at a certain point in the aria, of what should have been the sonorous notes of a great organ. Poor Frederick Kiddle, the organist and accompanist at the Queen's Hall, pedalled like one possessed at a small harmonium in his frantic efforts to conjure up in the imagination of the audience the glorious sounds he was wont to bring forth from the great instrument in London. It reminded me of Nelson Keys, in company with Arthur Playfair and Basil Hallam, in a busking scene in one of the 'Passing Shows' at the Palace Theatre in which the tiny comedian, seated at a harmonium, pedalled so zealously that he blew out the bellows with a cloud of dust and brought the scene to a hilarious and sudden end. Fortunately Kiddle's bellows held.

* * * * *

Once the orchestra became accustomed to Maclean's frequently-changing dynamic renderings, some of the performances were unbelievable. Sometimes I think my dear old friend could have produced music out of a stone, so full of artistic feeling was he. His whole nature breathed music and with his music went a kindly, lovable disposition which did not know the meaning of the word 'self'. Only once, during the twenty years it was my privilege to be his friend, do I remember his speaking of his own activities in the sphere of composition, and this was relative to the forthcoming performance of his opera, 'Quentin Durward', at Covent Garden. Even then he quickly changed the subject and drew my attention to some programme or other he was compiling, for which, with his usual unselfishness, he was choosing items which would show up to the best advantage my own small contributions. He took the greatest pains over everything he conducted, but, unlike so many conductors, never *over*-rehearsed, with the result that our performances were ever fresh and gave the feeling of spontaneity. The old hackneyed overtures took on a new life under his bâton; and how he loved his Mozart!

He had an unexpected and irresistible sense of humour, which showed itself in an occasional boyish prank in the middle of conducting a work during a public performance. One instance of this occurred when we were on tour with the New Queen's Hall Light Orchestra, our soloist being Benno Moiseiwitsch, who, as everyone knows, possesses a technique which enables him to surmount the most intricate of passages while assuming an air of indifference. Maclean, of course, never failed to take things up to time, and in the nightly performance of Liszt's E flat Concerto he lived up more and more to his name of 'The Lightning Conductor'. His tempi for some reason or other increased until it seemed impossible that any pianist, even a Moiseiwitsch, could manage to get through the double octave passage in the final Coda. The climax was reached one night, when he conducted this particular section at such a speed that even we in the orchestra were wondering whether the whole thing might not collapse at any moment. At the height of this exhibition of virtuosity and at the risk of losing my place in the music, I glanced over at our soloist and caught a wan smile crossing his somewhat worried countenance as he rushed wildly up and down the keyboard in his efforts not to be left behind by our now quite ungovernable conductor. The final chords over (thank heaven, we finished together!), and after a tremendous demonstration from both the audience and the orchestra, I went round to the artists' room, to find Maclean dissolved in perspiration and Moiseiwitsch, as usual, as cool as a cucumber, quietly reading a programme. I was permitted to enter the inner 'holy of holies' while my friend changed his collar and shirt in readiness for the next 'round', and, during the ceremony of rubbing himself down with a towel, I gleaned that his ferocious display of tempi was responsible for a secret ambition: to make Moiseiwitsch sweat. With one of his short characteristic laughs and a rueful look at his own now crumpled shirt and limp collar, he had to admit that he had failed.

* * * *

It was after I had given up my viola-playing in 1919, and when I was attending an orchestral rehearsal for one of the Ballad Concerts at Queen's Hall, that the maestro buttonholed me on the stairs leading down from the entrance in Riding House Street to the artists' room:

"Would you like to come up to Scarborough during the Summer Season at the Spa and conduct some of your works with my orchestra?"

His face lit up as he continued: "I think you'd enjoy yourself, that is, if we have a calm sea and a low tide. You see"—this with a twinkle in his eye—"we play in the open, but under cover, of course, and the audiences"—he raised his hands and chuckled—"the audiences are a thing to be seen to be believed, and if we are lucky and have a still summer night, it is just like making music in fairyland. Will you come?"

And each year, usually during the last two days of August and the first two in September, up to the time when ill-health prevented him from fulfilling his duties as Musical Director in 1935, I took the turning on the Finchley Road where the sign-post points 'TO THE NORTH' and made music with my friend under conditions which were as near approaching a Continental atmosphere as anything you could find in the British Isles. They were days of romance indeed, and ones which I look back upon with intense pleasure, mingled with regret that they will never be repeated. For with the passing of the lovable, high-shouldered, black-coated, large-brimmed-black-felt-hatted figure which walked to and fro from the bandstand to the dressing-room of the Spa, summer in sumer out for twenty-four years, the attraction that Scarborough held for me seemed to pass.

* * * * *

I remember attending a luncheon given in honour of Sir Henry Wood's seventy-fifth birthday, at which one of the speakers paid tribute to this veteran conductor by saying that it was he who had taught the orchestral musicians how to play. And my thoughts went back to Alick Maclean and all he had done to improve the standard of orchestral playing in his own sphere and the many well-known instrumentalists who had passed through his hands all those years ago.

It is strange that Alick Maclean was never acclaimed as he should have been. I think this is mainly due to a complete selflessness on his part, which caused him to take pleasure in bringing others forward to enjoy a universal success that, through some trick of fate, he himself was denied. Alexander Movaren Maclean. A grand musician with a great heart.

* * * * *

In 1918, the taking over by Alice Boosey, the 'Emperor's' delightful daughter, of the department of my friend of the deep voice meant that at last I had a friend at Chappell's in a position to give me a helping hand where my songs were concerned. I remember so well the first time she asked me to call and see her upstairs in the little room which always gave me the feeling that at any moment it might collapse and carry us down to the floor below, so insecure and sloping was it. Many years ago associated with William Pitt, Earl of Chatham, Chappell's even to-day is a queer mixture of the old and the modern, with its unexpected spiral staircases and underground passages which make an ideal escape from the attentions of someone you may wish to avoid. The room where I used to play over my songs to Alice Boosey, prior to submitting them for final approval to the 'Emperor' himself, was in that part of the building reputed to have been the one-time quarters occupied by the stable-boys, which goes some way towards explaining its uneven and shaky condition. I recollect sitting at an angle of ten degrees at a piano which was propped up against the wall in an endeavour to make it look what it purported to be, an 'upright', trying to do justice to an accompaniment with a technique which I wished to goodness I had taken a little more seriously, when under the tutorship of my old friend 'Hartley's Marmalade' at the Royal Academy of Music. Still, Alice Boosey seemed to understand (with the aid of a good deal of whistling on my part to make up for some of the missing notes) what I was trying to convey, and in this way I managed to convince her that if my songs were given a proper hearing, they might do more than just pay for the cost of the engraving. Alice told me, at this first meeting, that she could not understand why my songs were scarcely ever performed, and after I had related my unpleasant experience of the two previous years, she said she was determined to do her best to see that in future I should have no regrets that Chappell & Co. were my publishers. This is now many years ago, and still I take my walks down New Bond Street and mount the flight of stairs to the publishing department to hand over my latest in the orchestral or the song line, and give into its capable hands the responsibility of producing an edition in keeping with the best traditions of this old and established house.

* * * * *

After this the future began to take on a more roseate hue for Phyl and me (still living in our flat close to the Queen's Hall), though we sometimes looked anxiously through my pass-book. My not being fit for military service during World War I had been the means of my being invited by my old friend, Sir Alexander Mackenzie, to take the place of a Royal Academy of Music professor who had been called up, and the experience I had gained in this way tempted me to consider taking up teaching permanently in order to augment my falling income. Knowing how, in my heart, I detested the idea, Phyl made this the excuse to fulfil an ambition which she had always hoped would materialise, and went on the stage. This saved us from a considerable amount of worry by means of the welcome salary which was brought home to the flat on Friday nights, though I must confess I was rather apprehensive over her determination to swell the Coates banking account, and I do not think that the added financial security made up for the anxiety I felt every evening when she went off to the theatre and I to the Queen's Hall. Luckily my engagements usually finished at an earlier hour than the theatre and so I was able to join the crowd outside the stage door and escort the new 'bread-winner' home.

* * * * *

The end of the run of one of her shows fortunately coincided with my own break between the last concert of the season and the next Promenades. This meant a ten weeks' holiday before I was due to take up my duties as principal viola again, and one lovely morning in the June of 1919 we packed our suitcases, labelled our bicycles, and set off from Liverpool Street Station to the peace of the East Coast and settled into a couple of comfortable rooms overlooking the sea at Southwold. Four and a half years of war (with Phyl down with septic pneumonia and myself with influenza at Armistice time), added to the hard work of keeping our heads above water during these difficult years, had begun to tell on both of us. It was a haven of rest, this little seaside town with its miniature promenade; its old-world atmosphere; its lighthouse conveniently built for its keeper among the houses well back from the sea; the beach from which you could reach deep water in a few strokes; the modest pier round which Phyl swam daily, to the discomfort of the boatman who did not think it was proper for young ladies to achieve anything so spectacular; the lovely walk northwards along the glistening beach to Covehithe, to see the huge church built around a smaller one; the equally delightful walk southwards over the chain-ferry to Walberswick; and, added to all this, the quaint small-gauge railway and its even quainter tank-engine and antiquated coaches which went up hill and down dale, across fields, through woods and over unprotected level-crossings to the main line junction at Halesworth where you picked up the express to London.

July came, and with it the coming of even lovelier weather. We basked in the sun, we bathed, we boated, we cycled, we walked, and were wishing this glorious holiday would never come to an end, when a letter arrived one morning from Robert Newman, the Manager of the Queen's Hall Orchestra, informing me that he regretted Sir Henry Wood would not require my services as principal viola for the forthcoming season of Promenade Concerts. We were aghast. Not even a letter from Sir Henry. There had never been any signs that he had been dissatisfied with my leadership. My thoughts flashed to the deputies I had sent to take my place on the occasions when I had been invited to conduct the London Symphony Orchestra at the Palladium on Sunday afternoons, and to the rehearsals which I had not attended when my arm was troubling me more than usual. I certainly had been growing tired of my orchestral life and had already wondered more than once how I could manage to get away from it, but not in this undignified way. Sacked from the Queen's Hall Orchestra! Sir Henry might have had the decency to give me a satisfactory excuse for my dismissal himself, instead of laying the responsibility on to Robert Newman. I was furious. What a scurvy trick to play on me at the last moment! We consulted the state of the exchequer, vacated our rooms in favour of a tiny cottage overhanging the cliff-side where the spray, on rough days, came right into our rooms, and decided to enjoy the unexpected and enforced holiday far into the autumn. The weather held—we basked in the sun, we boated, we cycled, we walked, and we were the last couple to brave the already dropping temperature of the waters of the North Sea in October. The dwindling figures of my banking account and the first performance of a new Suite of mine

G*

at the Promenade Concerts drew our attention to the fact that all good things must come to an end, and on a chilly morning in October, quite glad to say goodbye to the sea, but not to the bicycles which had taken us so pleasantly to the four quarters of the county, we picked up the London train at Halesworth. Later that afternoon we were having tea in the flat near the Concert Hall which was to be the scene of my activities as principal viola no more. I sighed as I put my viola case away in the box-room, but it was a sigh of relief, for I made up my mind at that instant that I would never play the viola again, and I never did.

* * * * *

I slipped into my dress clothes, strolled along to Queen's Hall, mounted the rostrum, grinned at my successor on my right and conducted the first performance of my 'Summer Days' Suite.

* * * * *

A short interview with Robert Newman, during which I made no secret of the disgusting treatment I felt I had received, brought a letter from Sir Henry in which he eulogised my qualities as principal viola and the fact that during the seven years we had worked together we had never once crossed swords, at the same time stressing that he *must* have a leader who was able to attend *every* rehearsal and *every* concert, and he therefore had no alternative, etc. etc. This took me back to a conversation I had had with Wood in 1908 while walking with him along Elsworthy Road, during which he said he would rather have an orchestra composed of inferior musicians who were reliable in their attendance than one of first-class musicians who were always sending deputies. I comforted myself with the reflection that perhaps I had not been such a bad viola player after all. Some ten years later, while conducting at one of the Bournemouth Festivals, I ran across Sir Henry and Lady Wood having tea under the trees on the lawn of the Royal Exeter Hotel. In response to their invitation to join them I pulled up a chair. Over tea, after discussing the musical activities then in full swing at the Winter Gardens, we got on to the subject of orchestral musicians and, in particular, the principals in the old days at Queen's Hall. It was a pleasant meeting, reviving old memories. As I was taking my leave, Lady Wood asked me if I often played my viola; my reply, that I had not touched it since the day Sir Henry had given me the opportunity of giving it up, caused a flutter.

* * * * *

When I had launched my new Suite, another committee meeting late into the night made it clear that something drastic would have to be done if we wished to continue in our present mode of living. The contract with Messrs. Chappell & Co., which I had found waiting for me on my return from our unexpectedly long holiday, although coming at a time when funds were needed, did not completely make up for the income which I had until recently derived from my viola-playing. Our only other financial acquisition being our flat, we decided after a good deal of deliberation to let it and go into rooms once again. (I can almost hear my reader saying: 'But how can you reconcile all the ups and downs you write about with your statement at the beginning of this chapter that the first nine years of your married life were happy and carefree and without responsibilities?' I confess, at first flush, it does seem to be contradictory and I can only put it down to the confidence of youth. The idea that we had anything serious to worry about never entered our heads. Financial crises came and went, but these never interfered with our happiness. After all, what did it matter so long as we were together?)

So we let our flat yet again and went once more into rooms, this time a large bed-sitting-room, with service, on the top floor of a pleasant house in Frognal. We went out for the day, a few days after our arrival, in order not to witness the unnerving sight of half a dozen perspiring men engineering our Bechstein grand-piano up four flights of creaking stairs, while an anxious landlady stood in the hall below wondering whether her banisters would ever be the same again. We reappeared later on in the day, and asked no questions.

*   *   *   *   *

Our stay with the grand-piano on the top floor, except for meeting for the first time G. H. Clutsam and his wife, was not on the whole a happy one. Clutsam, affectionately known to us as 'Clutty' and composer of that famous song, 'My Curly-headed Baby', lived on a floor somewhere underneath us and he and his wife spent the time, when he was not at his piano, doing the round of all the picture theatres.

I do not know whether Mrs. Clutsam shared his keenness for this form of entertainment. 'Clutty', at any rate, was a complete film fan and his activities in the field of the 'flicks' took the two of them over a far-flung area. We failed to understand what they could possibly find in watching idiotic and silent figures rushing about at a tremendous pace and in a most unnatural way on a badly-lit screen, with an orchestra in the pit below doing its best to portray in music the unspoken dialogue flashed on to a picture which the funny little figures were trying to get over in mime. How their eyes stood up to the strain of these nightly orgies was beyond our comprehension. We tried it once, and once only, and even then we saw spots for many days afterwards.

* * * * *

Clutsam, for some years, was Vice-Chairman on the Board of the Performing Right Society, on which I serve in the humble capacity of a Director. At these meetings there is usually too much serious business to attend to, to allow of any over-display of fun, but on the Special Classification Committee, consisting usually of from four to eight musicians, when 'Clutty' was in the Chair the seriousness of the earlier meeting was amply compensated for by the hilarity which then persisted. This Committee has to deal with placing in categories all kinds of music; a tricky business requiring an expert knowledge of music ranging from symphonies to jazz. Here 'Clutty', with his three pairs of spectacles (or was it four?) of various strengths, to enable him to cope with the sometimes minute notations set before him, was in his element, for there was little you could teach him about any branch of music.

Whether the material we were called upon to deal with inspired him to do so I cannot say, but at that time he was busy compiling a volume showing that if you got down to fundamentals, all tunes were built on a well-worn plan and, if it were not for the originality of the composer, would all sound exactly the same. I forget, for the moment, when original themes ceased to exist, so far as Clutty's calculations were concerned, but I know this depressing musical state was supposed to have come about well over a century ago, and as a good deal of music has been written since that time our Chairman had the time of his life expounding his theory that a certain newly-published song up for classification was in reality composed as long ago as 1860 and was, in fact, according to his book, Prescription No. A24.

* * * * *

The trouble began with three pounds of candles and ended with a penny tin of Colman's mustard; not that the mustard had any connection whatsoever with the candles except helping to aggravate a situation brought about by the former and precipitating our having to look elsewhere for accommodation. It was altogether an unfortunate affair and, on the whole, I think our behaviour was justified. Now, neither of us had anything to complain about over the running of the establishment in Frognal; the place was spotlessly clean, the service excellent and the food, although not abundant, was nicely cooked and presented. But our landlady had a bee in her bonnet which took the form of turning off the electric light at eleven o'clock at night, which meant that any unsuspecting lodger who felt the call to stay out late was forced to go to bed either in the dark or else employ that old-fashioned system of lighting, the candle. This was bad enough but what was even worse was the fact that the electric light was not turned on again until one hour after sunset the next day, so during the time which intervened between the setting of the sun and the switching on of the light, you either had to revert to the antiquated candle or pace about your room making use of unparliamentary language. What happened when one of those yellow fogs, so common in those days, descended on the land, is nobody's business.

In those far-distant times we, being young, spent a good many nights prowling about the West End in search of entertainment, and our return to the fold being made in complete darkness, brought out in us all the qualities of primeval man. We pleaded with the lady of the house, assuring her that we would be only too pleased to pay the extra cost of another few minutes of electric light per day. We (I regret to say) bribed little Agnes, the maid, to see if she could manage to turn on the light again by accident. But all our efforts were in vain, and after having staggered up those four flights of stairs night after night, purposely making the very devil of a noise, opening wrong doors on the upward climb, cursing loudly at every corner and in general making ourselves a nuisance, we paid a visit to the local grocer and invested in three pounds of candles. These we stuck all over our room: on pictures, on ledges, on picture-rails, on chairs, on the dressing-table, on the bed-posts, on the mantelpiece, wherever there was a spot capable of supporting a candle. You should have seen the light! Fifty candle-power! You should have felt the heat! You should have seen the mess! It was *terrific!* Fortunately, little Agnes, who was secretly in league with us, kept to herself the knowledge of the fifty candles which nightly dripped fifty streams of hot wax down fifty different ways, otherwise I am sure we should have been expelled at a moment's notice.

No, it was not the candles but the penny tin of mustard that was our undoing. In the establishment in Frognal no provision was made for those whose business kept them at home during the day —bed, breakfast and dinner being the rule of the house. As I spent most of the day upstairs, either at the table or the Bechstein, we conceived the idea of having a picnic lunch in our room to obviate the trouble of lunching out. Now, I insist, how could we have been expected to eat sausage-rolls or cold ham without mustard? So we persuaded little Agnes to bring us up from the kitchen down below in the basement a neat mustard-pot filled with this most necessary of ingredients. All went well for a time, and then, one day, we were told by the little parlourmaid that she had unfortunately been waylaid on the stairs with mustard-pot in hand and questioned by the irate lady of the house as to who had had the audacity to make use of her belongings. A summons from the lady herself requesting my presence in her sanctum on the ground floor ended in my informing her that she might remember she was dealing with grown-ups and not with children, and that, among other things, she was obviously not fit to run a boarding-house. I left the room feeling I had had the last word, went round once again to my friend the grocer, purchased the smallest tin of Colman's mustard that I could procure (one penny being the cost), sent it down to the incensed lady of the house with my compliments and a note in which I made it quite plain that I considered the tin more than adequate compensation for the amount of mustard we had consumed upstairs. We received a note by return requesting us to leave the house. We left the following morning, our departure, with Bechstein grand-piano, being watched by the lady herself, presumably to see that we did no pilfering on the way out. I must not forget to add that, to the satisfaction of the ejected couple, the piano left its mark upon the banisters. Poor Miss X—she went the way that all good, bad and indifferent landladies go, and her passing occurred shortly after our departure. At first I felt a little sorry over our behaviour when I heard the news, and then the memory of those ghastly climbs up those four flights of pitch-dark stairs hardened my heart.

* * * * *

So once again we 'took the road', with piano, pots and pans, china, cutlery, and all the paraphernalia connected with the making of tea at all hours of the day and night. Our destination was St. John's Wood, where we had been invited by Phyl's mother to live in the top part of a house which proved to be too spacious for her much-depleted family. Frank, the eldest son, had lost his life in the war; Lelant, the second son, passed on shortly afterwards as the result of rheumatic fever; the eldest daughter, Beatrice, had married the year before us; thus leaving them with their youngest daughter, Joan, who had won a scholarship for pianoforte at the Royal College of Music and was studying with Harold Samuel.

The little flat on the top floor of this charming house was just what we had been looking for and was the nearest thing approaching 'home' which we had experienced since we had been obliged to say goodbye to our flat close to Queen's Hall. Proximity with my in-laws made me realise how greatly they disapproved of having a daughter who was associated with the stage, and they were not in the least impressed when Phyl made a 'hit' in the West End and the Press singled her out specially for praise.

And so, while she played, I composed. Two orchestral works were the result of the charming sitting-room which looked down on to the wide road with its abundance of trees where the birds sang all day: a Suite, 'Joyous Youth', and an Overture, 'The Merrymakers'. How clearly I can recall my friend Alick Maclean coming up one morning to hear me try to show him on my piano what he had already put down for 'first performance' with his orchestra at the Chappell Ballad Concerts. It is not easy to make an effect with an orchestral work on the piano unless you are a competent pianist, but fortunately Maclean's keen eye perceived in my full-score what my stumbling fingers were trying so vainly to achieve. How beautifully he used to present my new works and, like the true artist he was, tried to carry out my wishes down to the smallest detail.

*   *   *   *   *

Then came 1922, an eventful year for the young couple who had lived for so long in each other's pockets. For Phyl it was a disaster from a career point of view, for myself it seemed little short of a catastrophe. During the nine years we had been married, if either of us were ill the one always looked after the other. But on this night of April 16th everything seemed to be taken out of my hands. My thoughts went back to Armistice Day when Phyl had lain unconscious with a temperature of 105°, and I had crawled out of bed with a temperature only three degrees less to watch the doctor anxiously trying to coax some life back to the frail little figure lying so still and looking so deathly pale.

What is the old rhyme? 'But the child that is born on a Sabbath day is blithe and bonnie and happy and gay'—and I must say our son has lived up to this old adage to the letter, for a happier, cheerier, more affectionately disposed person I have never known. It was unfortunate for Phyl that Austin took it into his head to arrive at the time when she had made a 'hit' in a production in the West End and offers were pouring in upon her from every quarter; added to this, the blow of knowing we were never going to be alone together again seemed insufferable. Depression settled on us like a blanket, and when an old friend of Phyl's family, having inspected the new arrival, told us that '*now* our happiness was complete', we could quite cheerfully have felled her to the ground. We little knew at the time how soon we were to grow to love the little boy who had come into our lives so unexpectedly.

Having recovered from the shock of knowing that we should now have to reorganise our mode of living, we pulled ourselves together and faced the facts. A four-roomed flat was all very well for two, but what were we to do about the nurse and the baby? Then there was the question of Phyl's theatrical work. Would the managers have forgotten her by the time she was fit to act again?

However, the managers had not forgotten her, for one morning, some three months after Austin's arrival and while she was in the bath, the telephone-bell rang. Leaping out of the bath and pulling a towel around her, Phyl lifted the receiver to hear Robert Courtneidge ask her if she could be at the Savoy Theatre in twenty minutes' time to meet a young author. Rapidly calculating how long it would take her to dry herself, dress and call a taxi, she said she could just manage it—and manage it she did.

She was shown up to 'the Guvnor's' room, where she found him deep in conversation with a slim young man who turned as she entered. "I want you to meet Mr. Noël Coward"—and after a brief interview she was engaged to play an amusing part in his forthcoming production at the Savoy, 'The Young Idea'. In the caste were: Leslie Banks, Herbert Marshall, Naomi Jacob, Ronald Ward, Ann Trevor and the author.

From then onwards Phyl lived a very busy life—practically every West End management and every theatre in London saw her at one time or another and, if it had not been for her being obliged to give up her stage career on account of throat trouble, I might have ended my days as 'Mr. Phyllis Black'.

I always loved watching Phyl on the stage, in fact, I never tired of hearing her play the same part over and over again. She had a grace and charm of her own and acting seemed to come naturally to her.

* * * * *

Those who went through World War I will remember the shortage of small houses which prevailed for several years after the Armistice. Really, Austin had chosen a most unreasonable time to make his entry into the world—if only he could have arranged it a year or so later it might have been easier! So the Coateses travelled the highways and the byways looking for that little house which they knew must be waiting somewhere to receive them.

At long last, after weeks of searching, we heard of a house which sounded all right, but it was in the one place in the world we did not want to have to move to, the wilds of the Hampstead Garden Suburb. By this time we were both worn out with looking over houses: houses with attics, houses with basements, dilapidated houses, houses too large, more houses too large, houses with no central heating, houses with no adequate hot water supply, houses with no decent bathroom and always without a garage—so we got out the little 10 h.p. motor-car we had invested in and journeyed up to the hills beyond Golders Green.

So far as accommodation was concerned, we thought we could just manage to squeeze ourselves in—and there was space at the side of the house to erect a garage. On the latter score, however, our hopes were dashed, for at that time there was a clause in the suburb leases restricting the building of private garages. However, on being told there was an excellent public garage only a few minutes' walk away in the main road, we decided that it was Hobson's Choice and set about the business of raising the necessary money to purchase. Capital we had practically none, and the money had to be found quickly. Full of hope we approached a Building Society, but were soon to discover that this was far too expensive a method of buying a property. Then my father, with his usual generosity, came to the rescue and lent me the necessary money, and within a few weeks we settled in. It was a charming little house set in delightful surroundings, but the moment we arrived we realised the isolation from all things musical. After having lived so close to the Queen's Hall, St. John's Wood had seemed remote, but compared to the ten-minute journey from there to the West End, this forty-minute business from Golders Green was tedious in the extreme. We considered we might just as well have taken up residence at the North Pole. Added to this there was the impossibility of keeping a maid who was willing to run the risk of passing the crematorium after dark! These were the days of what Byron used to allude to as 'bogles', and woe betide any innocent cook who lingered too long down the road, for, as sure as fate, the spirits who lurked in the shadow of the ashes would sweep out through the iron gates and —presto—gone was your cook!

Austin loved it. He roamed the woods with his nurse, played with Mickey the next-door neighbour's dog, talked to the squirrels, fed the birds, and at the age of five discoursed profoundly on matters of religion with the vicar of St. Jude's, who, I feel, must have had visions of his taking to the Church at an early age.

Our young five-year-old never missed an opportunity of evading the eye of his nurse to slip away unobserved and take the narrow path leading up to the church, in the hope of coming across that most fascinating of all beings and Master of Life and Death, the vicar, and on one of these expeditions he injudiciously loitered on the way to watch a tennis match in progress. One of the players noticed the little boy and, leaving the others, he came across and enquired of him if he was Eric Coates's son. On Austin replying in the affirmative, the man volunteered the astounding information that he often saw his father's name in the *Radio Times*. Austin was nonplussed—the idea that his daddy was in the public eye had never occurred to him, and it was a worried little boy who ran back to his mother to enquire if all he had heard was true. He smiled on hearing her reply, hesitated for a moment and then:

"I suppose"—anxious pause—"I suppose Daddy's name would not be in *World Radio*?"

Fortunately she was able to assure him that it was. Austin heaved a sigh of satisfaction and beamed.

He was an unusual little boy. I remember him, at the age of three, being nearly blown off his feet by a violent gust of wind and seeing him face the gale and in a loud and determined voice tell it not to '*push*'. At the age of four he was the cause of my paying a flying visit to Eastbourne to conduct the first performance of my Phantasy 'The Three Bears'—this was the outcome of a request for me to set to music his favourite bedtime story which was read to him with such dramatic effect by his mother before being tucked up for the night. At six he accompanied us to a *thé dansant* at the Savoy Hotel and ate masses of sandwiches and cakes while gazing in open-eyed astonishment at a mummy and daddy practising the latest Charleston steps to the strains of the Savoy Havana Band. At seven, on arrival at his first preparatory school, he enquired of the Head whether he might be allowed to order a paper, and on being asked what daily he would like to take, gave the question considered thought (during which pause the Head visualised *The Times* or the *Telegraph*) and then said with conviction, that he considered *Rainbow* was about as good as anything. "You may fight me with fists but *I* will fight you with words"—this to a little girl whose physical strength outmatched his own. Yes, Austin was an unusual little boy and very determined, from the first showing a marked inclination towards independence. I remember how furious my father became when he wished to take a 'snap' of him when we were spending a few days at his house in Kent, where he had retired. As my father moved to the right, so Austin moved to the left. The climax came when my father, in desperation, took a quick step backwards and nearly took a thirty-foot plunge into the sea, and the language which followed his escape from 'total immersion' was an eye-opener to the little boy who could not for the life of him understand what it was all about.

* * * * *

During the seven years we lived in the Hampstead Garden Suburb, considering the amount of time I spent either following Phyl about the country or else, when she was at home and not playing, dancing my feet away with her nightly at some such place as the Savoy, it was remarkable that I was able to compose as much music as I did. However, I managed to make an Orchestral Phantasy on Oscar Wilde's 'The Selfish Giant' and conducted quite a good first performance of it at an Eastbourne Festival in 1925. But the performance I shall never forget was when Jack Hylton with his band, augmented by his players from the Kit-Kat and Kettner's Clubs (thus bringing the personnel of the orchestra up to the prodigious proportions of *twenty-five* players!), ran it through one morning at the Kit-Kat, to the delight of a crowd of admiring waiters, whose duties were forgotten in their excitement at seeing such a galaxy of jazz musicians under one roof at the same time.

From that moment I began to realise what brass could do when in the hands of capable players, for up to that time my experience had been limited to the sphere of 'straight' orchestral musicians. Candidly, I am of the opinion that this style of playing has had the effect of raising the standard of orchestral technique in general, particularly in the brass, wood-wind and percussion sections, of even our Symphony Orchestras. I do not know what some of my friends in these orchestras would have to say to me about this, but I feel certain I am right. 'The Selfish Giant' was turned down by my publishers as being too great a risk to put into print (who had ever heard of syncopation in an orchestral work!), but, thanks to the enterprise of Ralph Boosey of Messrs. Boosey & Co., it found its way into the catalogue of the old firm in Regent Street which in 1908 had given me my first chance as a composer. This, I thought, was going to be the beginning of new things with my old friends, Boosey & Co., but when my Phantasy 'The Three Bears' was born, the 'Emperor', to whom I was under contract, snatched it from my arms almost in embryo and it was in print before you could say 'Jack Robinson'.*

And so my flirtation with the firm of Messrs. Boosey & Co. was short-lived. Still, I must admit, the 'Emperor' did me well; for

* 'Who's been sitting in *my* chair?' 'The Three Bears', dedicated to Austin on his fourth birthday, April 16th, 1926.

partly to make amends for having turned down 'The Selfish Giant' and partly to make sure I should not turn my face Regent-Streetwards again, he very magnificently engraved the full score, a thing hitherto almost unknown in the annals of Messrs. Chappell & Co., at any rate where the work of a composer of popular orchestral music was concerned.

* * * * *

Then came an invitation from my old friend, Basil Cameron, to write a new work for the Harrogate Festival. I regret to say I was feeling in lazy mood and said that I would write something for him if I could think of anything. But Basil would not accept this and insisted on my getting down to a new work at once; and so, much against my will, I accepted his invitation.

Weeks passed, during which time I journeyed about the country in pursuit of Phyl, utterly oblivious of the fact that the Harrogate Festival was looming near.

Then one morning came a telegram informing me that the Musical Director wished to know the title of the new work, for its inclusion in the preliminary notices. Could I think of a title! Could I think of anything at all to do with music! My mind could only register the times of north-bound trains to outlandish districts, or else jigsaw-like patterns of intricate Charleston steps which I had been taught by my attractive dancing instructress in Kensington and which Phyl and I were bent on trying out the next time we took the floor. I was just on the point of giving up in despair when, suddenly, there came an idea, and off went the telegram: 'New work "Four Ways". When must you have it? Not started yet.' This brought back yet another from Basil, to the effect that the full-score and band parts were wanted far too soon for my liking, and intimating at the same time that I was a lazy devil!

The first performance of 'Four Ways' will always bring back a picture of an audience half rising from its seat to stand to attention, owing to the side-drum roll and cymbal crash in the first bars of the opening movement which unintentionally gave the impression of a 'God Save the King' to follow. At the rehearsal I had a tussle with the Charleston rhythm of the last movement and at one time almost gave up hope of being able to get the brass and percussion to produce the effect I wanted. But at the concert they came up to scratch and the work was well played and, I am thankful to say, well received.

Then came another fairy story, this time 'Cinderella', which meant an excuse for us to stay luxuriously at the Grand Hotel, Eastbourne, for *me* to conduct the first performance at the 1927 Festival and for *both* of us to spend several days and nights doing more intricate Charleston steps all over the floor at the Winter Gardens. Then we returned once again to London, to dinner at the Savoy and to dance to the Savoy Havana Band until the restaurant closed, and then downstairs to the ballroom and the Savoy Orpheans, to carry on our strenuous way until a tired band and even more tired waiters intimated that it was 2 a.m. and time to get our things, pick up the car and drive home to the heights of the suburb through a deserted London—two exhausted but extremely contented people, both feeling that life was well worth while, but with the thought at the back of their minds that, if they were only a little nearer the West End, they could then not only dance every night until the early hours of the morning but in the afternoons as well!

The appearance of the first crooner at the Savoy warned us that our dancing days were in danger. How right we were, for with the coming of this unpleasant cult came the slow, monotonous beat of the blues, the slow foxtrot and the nauseating sentimental love croon. Gone was the happy, carefree rhythm which made going out a delight, gone were the lovely dancing melodies which, even at the thought of them, set our feet a-tingling. No more driving at a snail's pace at half-past two in the morning round that corner where Baker Street runs into Regent's Park, and where on November nights the fog settles down like a thick yellow blanket and your partner has to forget all about her pretty dancing shoes to climb out on to the muddy road to guide you into the haven of Park Road. No more changing tyres at three o'clock in the morning on the summit of Child's Hill, when your opera hat falls off on to the rain-sodden road and the mud on your shirt-front makes you thankful you are homeward bound. Gone were all these things, but—and this is most important—the *money* we saved!

* * * * *

One of the bright spots of our stay in the wilds of Hampstead was when, on a Sunday morning (providing it was sunny), I would get out the car, drive down to Duke Street and bring Ernest Kuhe, at that time music critic to the *Daily Telegraph*, back to our garden, where he loved to sit in the sun in a deck-chair and purr like a cat while being plied with all the good things that are associated with Sunday afternoon tea at home. E.K., as he was affectionately called, possessed a fascinating lisp, adored the sun, loathed all things gramophonic and detested anything to do with radio sets or the kind of people who love making the air hideous with music sounds out of doors. What he would have done if he had lived to see these days of jet aircraft overhead and wireless sets on the ground, I shudder to think. We both hold very pleasant memories of this kindliest of men—kindly in his ways and kindly in his criticisms, a rare attribute in that strangest animal of all, the music critic, who so often tends to destroy rather than to construct.

Writing of E.K. reminds me of the English Musical Festivals which were so popular about this time. Those were the days when music was not put into categories as it is to-day, or laid out on the operating table for dissection, but was looked upon simply as music to delight and elevate. They were interesting occasions, both musically and socially, for people flocked from far and wide to hear and see the famous composers and executants who had been engaged to appear. The most notable of these Festivals was the one which took place annually at Bournemouth, where Sir Dan Godfrey officiated in the dual capacity of Musical Director and Manager. Here it was that I first met Sir Edward Elgar, who told me that he always bought my gramophone recordings, his favourite at that time being my 'Summer Days' Suite, which, he said, he had literally worn out. In later years I was told by one of the Directors that Elgar had had a standing order with the gramophone company to supply him with each of my new recordings as they were issued. Many people said they found Elgar difficult, but I always found him charming. It was he who scared me out of my life at Eastbourne by appearing in the artists' room just as I was about to go on to the platform to conduct my 'Three Bears' and who insisted on sitting behind the drums. He was quite oblivious of the fact that his entry into the orchestra had created a minor sensation among the audience and that during the performance he nearly dried me up by tapping his feet and waggling his head from side to side, to such effect that it was only with the greatest difficulty I managed to keep my mind on directing the orchestra through the crossrhythm of the foxtrot section in my Phantasy. Along with Elgar's restlessness and nerviness went a keen sense of humour. I remember a rehearsal at Queen's Hall when he climbed down from the rostrum to give place to Henry Wood. 'Timber', as usual, always in a panic at the thought of wasting one second of a rehearsal, hurried on to the platform and stumbled as he pushed his way between the principal first violin and the off-coming conductor; quick as lightning, Elgar (very aware of Wood's weakness for decorating every page of a work with blue-pencil markings) turned, and with a malicious twinkle called out: "Now then, Henry! That's not in the score!"

As I have said before, Elgar was not very satisfactory as a conductor; with stick in hand, he did not seem able to indicate to the orchestra all that was in the score. That he himself was aware of this shortcoming seems to be borne out by the story of his turning to a famous 'cellist, who was just about to play Elgar's Violincello Concerto with him one day at Bournemouth, and saying: "I'm going to leave this to you. I simply can't make head or tail of it!"

* * * * *

It was in Dan Godfrey's room at the Winter Gardens, Bournemouth, that the famous composer of 'Gerontius' turned his attention to something far removed from the religious. I will try to tell the story as Dan Godfrey told it to me. Elgar was very mystified at the frequent and sudden entrances to and exits from the room of a small page-boy, who was continually handing Godfrey little slips of paper in exchange for sums of money, some small and some large. He was even more mystified when he heard 'two-thirties' and 'three o'clocks' and 'three-thirties' and such enigmatical expressions as 'both ways', 'ten to one', 'fifty to three', 'non-starters', 'odds', 'form', 'in the know' and so on. He thought of time-tables and of the booking of seats in trains, hotels and theatres and then the idea of concerts and rehearsals flashed through his mind. 'Odds', 'form', 'in the know'! These were not musical terms and neither had they anything to do with trains, hotels or theatres—what *could* Godfrey be playing at? Unable to check his curiosity any longer, he politely enquired of the musical director what it was all about. Horses! Preposterous! It was shocking! Bound to bring about a man's downfall sooner or later! The ruin of thousands! And so forth and so on. Dan Godfrey first of all laughed and then played the part of tempter. Elgar would not hear of it. Five shillings on 'so-and-so'? Certainly not! He had never heard of such a thing! It was altogether against his principles! Half-a-crown, then? He wavered. Well, perhaps—five shillings on the horse Steve Donoghue was riding. And then, rather ashamed but a little excited, he waited for the result while Godfrey's small page-boy bustled in and out with little bits of paper and expert directions from his master. Twenty-five shillings for *five* shillings! It was unbelievable—*much* simpler than filling those thirty-stave sheets of music paper with dots and dashes. This time ten shillings was speculated, with an even more profitable return, and at the end of the afternoon it was a bewildered and slightly conscience-stricken composer who went back to the hotel with his afternoon's earnings burning a hole in his pocket. Some weeks later, a telegram was delivered to Dan Godfrey at the Winter Gardens suggesting 'so-and-so' for the 'two-thirty' as being a sure thing. It was from Elgar! D.G. had done his work well.

* * * * *

It was also at Bournemouth that I first met Sir Edward German, the composer whom Elgar said was the most English of all our writers. From a young man, German had been my idol and it was just like meeting someone whom I had known for a long time. We were standing together at the back of the stalls at a rehearsal in the Winter Gardens, waiting to hear a new work conducted by its composer, one of our younger musicians. After the first few bars of introduction the opening theme struck an unmistakably familiar note. German turned to me and with a wry look said:
"I seem to have heard that somewhere before!"
My reply, that we had all come to him at one time or another, left no doubt in his mind that I knew practically every note he had written. But the Valse Song from 'Merrie England' is still as lovely and as fresh as it ever was, while the poor imitation we listened to together that morning was never heard again. Edward German was always sympathetic towards me and my music, and often showed his pleasure at my success.

The last time I saw him was in New Bond Street (he was wearing his habitual morning coat and black felt hat) and on my telling him with what intense pleasure we had listened to his Incidental Music to 'Romeo and Juliet' only a day or so previously, he gave me one of his pleasant smiles and said:
"Don't let's talk about my music. It's your day to-day, my boy!"

In my opinion Edward German has immortalised this England of ours as no other composer has ever succeeded in doing, and his delightful melodies will still be giving us joy when the works of many of our 'moderns' are long dead and forgotten. I heard a pathetic story from a friend of mine about German. It was a few years before he died and my friend was urging him to put pen to paper and give the world some more of his inimitable music. German shook his head sadly and glanced at his wireless set—"To tell you the truth," he said, "I'm afraid to write any more, they would only laugh at me."

* * * * *

Dan Godfrey, who always said that Phyl and I spent far too much time dancing the hours away nightly in town, and that sooner or later my health would suffer for it, would probably have put down to our nocturnal exploits the nasty attack of bronchial pneumonia which kept me to my bed for several weeks. Whatever the cause may have been, it was an unpleasant experience and at one time caused Phyl a considerable amount of anxiety. However, good nursing with sundry cups of boiling hot tea brewed at all hours of the day and night when my cough nearly laid me out, and a glass of champagne with my meals when I was able to sit up, brought me back to life, and the soft, fresh air of Sussex did the rest.

Take the road which runs south out of Chichester and in fifteen to twenty minutes you will come to one of the most barren spots on the South Coast where the trees, what is left of them, turn in supplication away from the ravages of the prevailing south-west gales. But how often have we blessed the day when we discovered this unpretentious village, with its bathing, its glorious beaches and its life-giving air, which three features are beyond the powers of man to despoil. Our house in the main street was looked upon by us as the 'bathing-box', for from here on lovely summer days, clad in our bathing attire, the three of us would leisurely walk the two minutes to the beach and bathe in waters as clear and almost as warm as you would find in any South Sea lagoon.

When we first came to this little place in 1922, such things as charabancs and trippers had not as yet discovered its attraction. The only thing the village had to offer was bathing, fishing and riding, and if you were not interested in these three forms of sport, then the only thing to do was to go into Chichester and do some shopping. The local omnibus to Chichester was a never-ending source of delight to Phyl, who vastly preferred journeying into this old cathedral city on the top deck of this slow-moving conveyance to making the trip in under half the time in our fast twelve-cylinder 'Yank'.

I don't know what the attraction was, but I think it alternated between the fine view of the countryside which she received from her perch ten feet above the ground, and listening to the 'back-chat' between the conductor, the driver and some of the quaint characters who boarded the bus during its majestic course through the various villages *en route*. I must admit that this omnibus service had its uses, for besides acting as an excellent though somewhat ponderous method of transport for humans, it more or less undertook to do the household shopping as well, at any rate it fetched and carried parcels in the most obliging manner. Which reminds me of the antiquated one-track railway which twisted its eccentric way over dykes, through meadows, across land habitually waterlogged during the spring tides; the little tank-engine and its strange conglomeration of coaches frequently leaving the metals in favour of the more inviting meadowland beside the track. A most perilous journey which only the uninitiated would hazard. The one and only guard the railway company possessed was even more obliging than the omnibus service, for he made it his business to call at the Station Hotel to arouse from their slumbers any intending passengers for the early morning train, the engine-driver and his mate not daring to start before his flock was safely on board.

It was a remarkable railway and I think the notice at the bottom of the 'Time of Departure of Trains' board outside the entrance to the station, announcing, in effect, that the trains would not depart *before* the scheduled time, speaks for itself. This little one-track railway is to-day a thing of the past, but if you leave the Chichester road and make your way over the marshy land that leads across to the sea, you may find here and there, hidden in the long grass, remains of rusty narrow-gauge metals, a pathetic reminder of an heroic little system that could not survive the advent of the modern motor-car. . . .

* * * * *

The call of 'Sussex by the Sea' is an insistent one, of which anyone who has lived for any length of time in this gracious county is well aware. The gentle slopes of the South Downs shelter many a pretty hamlet, while glorious Goodwood House stands in stately aloofness, contemplating, amidst its leafy surroundings, the flatness which leads by the silvery spire of Chichester down to where the wind blows fresh across the Isle of Wight from the open Channel beyond. A lovely county, this 'Sussex by the Sea', and one which grows on you the longer you stay in it. They say it takes seven years for the natives of these parts to accept you as a friend, but we have not found it thus; from the first we seemed to become a part of this county of our adoption with its soft, life-giving air, where the summers are never too warm and in winter the snow is as rare as it is in the West Country. And although I love London with its busy thoroughfares and its gay restaurants (for this is where the ideas for my best work have come to me), I never mind leaving it to go to the peace and quiet of the house we have made our home. Here I can live my own life without being thought eccentric, knowing, at the back of my mind, that there is always the flat on the top floor to return to at will whenever the desire for change comes over me.

FOURTH MOVEMENT

RONDO

FOURTH MOVEMENT

RONDO

IT was in August, 1930, that we felt we could put up no longer with the isolation of surburban life, especially in the winter months when fog and snow made the journey up and down to the West End very difficult. By this time Austin was installed at his preparatory school on the Solent facing the Isle of Wight and we decided to move from the suburb and take up residence in what at that time was called a 'luxury' flat in Baker Street. The house in Sussex, with the sea only a couple of minutes away, was an ideal place for Austin's holidays and more than made up for the loss of the pretty garden in Hampstead. The flat on the top floor was delightful, perhaps a little on the small side, but with Austin away at school in term-time and in Sussex during the holidays, and therefore only having our two selves to consider, the accommodation was ample. The view across Regent's Park was lovely in all seasons, delightful in its greenery and equally picturesque in its bareness—a paradise in the leafy spring and summer seasons, and a place of enchantment in winter under its mantle of snow—always a place of mystery at night, whether in the heat of August or the cold of January, with its myriads of little lights showing here and there among the branches of the trees, and from one corner of the sitting-room could be seen the still, blue waters of the lake.

Here in my writing-room, looking out over this peaceful scene, I felt I was going to make up for the seven years of isolation which I had spent in company with Phyl in the remote regions of Hampstead. *We were back in London at last.* It was wonderful to be in the centre of things again, and from the moment we settled in I knew we were going to appreciate every minute of our existence.

I remember sitting in my writing-room overlooking the Park and glancing back over the seven years we had spent in the Garden Suburb. I realised with rather a shock that, apart from conducting my works a good deal about the country and doing some broadcasts for the B.B.C. at Savoy Hill, my output had scarcely been prolific, which went to prove what I had always thought regarding my lack of desire to compose when away from the actual metropolis.

Speaking of broadcasting for the B.B.C. at Savoy Hill makes me realise how times have changed since then. Dear old 2LO, Savoy Hill, 1922, in the days when you almost arranged your *own* appearances. It was quite a common occurrence to be asked by the director say, at the close of a broadcast on Monday, whether you could come along and do another broadcast on the Thursday. It was all so delightfully informal and, now I come to think of it, was tremendous fun.

* * * * *

It was not until we came to live in the heart of London that I was able to shake off my ever-present desire to be wandering about the highways and the byways of my native Nottinghamshire. It had been a restless, unsettling feeling, this temptation to get the car out and take the road to the north. But the flat and the view began to take hold of me, and when one day I went up on to the flat roof and saw the vast expanse of the great city spread around me I realised that I had found a new home.

* * * * *

I now settled down to do some writing. The first experiment in this direction was a short Valse Serenade which I called 'By the Sleepy Lagoon'. Phyl was certain this was going to become the rage, and as she was always right in her prognostications over the ultimate outcome of my compositions, it was somewhat alarming to discover that she was not infallible, in fact she had let me down badly. However, ten years later, in 1940, we suddenly realised that 'Sleepy Lagoon' was being played and sung all over the place, in fact it became a No. 1 'hit' not only in this country and the Dominions but also in the United States of America, and was crooned incessantly by male sopranos and female baritones to the accompaniment of sobbing strings and doleful saxophones.

Next came an invitation from André Charlot to compose a Ballet for the opening of the new Cambridge Theatre, which resulted in my setting to music the story of 'Snow White and the Seven Dwarfs'. There was some opposition at first over the choice of subject, as Charlot had a private superstition that dwarfs were an ill omen to a production. On top of this, the situation in the story where the Queen smashes the mirror on finding that her reflection is not as lovely as that of Snow White was an even more unfortunate incident, which no producer would stand for. However, these difficulties were overcome at last, and whether the dwarfs and a synthetic looking-glass introduced an unlucky element into the theatre, I cannot say, but Charlot's first venture at the Cambridge Theatre did not achieve a spectacular or a lasting success. 'Snow White and the Seven Dwarfs', being instrumentated for a special orchestra of twelve solo players, was of no use to me outside the theatre and, apart from two or three broadcasts given by the popular B.B.C. Conductor, Stanford Robinson, with the B.B.C. Theatre Orchestra, the unusual orchestration bade fair to limit its chances of future performances.

Stanford Robinson suggested I should rewrite the work for full orchestra and thus make it suitable for concert purposes, but as by that time I had already started work on something else, the idea of putting aside what I was doing and getting down to re-orchestrating a work on which I had already spent several weeks concentration, did not fill me with enthusiasm. So, much to Robbie's disgust, I put the Ballet away in my desk and only gave it a thought when he occasionally twitted me with being afraid of doing too much.

This went on for nearly eight years, during which time, to give the lie to the idea that I was lazy, I hasten to state that I wrote ten orchestral works and a number of songs. However, Robbie would not leave the matter alone and continued chipping me over my lack of enterprise; this, and an invitation from the Swedish Broadcasting Company to write them a new work, decided me, and I began sketching out plans for a full orchestral version of 'Snow White and the Seven Dwarfs'. Imagine my dismay when Walt Disney brought out his masterpiece 'Snow White', and thus destroyed any hope of my being able to bring my work to fruition. Then Phyl, as usual, came to the rescue by taking pen and paper and writing me a story woven round the lovely garden of our house near Chichester—the story of a Prince and a Princess and of the birds which sang in the garden all the day and of the little furry creatures which roamed there by night. Into the story I wove my music—and 'Snow White and the Seven Dwarfs' became 'The Enchanted Garden'. It was conducted by myself later on in the year at the Radiotjänst in Stockholm, although the actual first performance took place at the B.B.C., where it was produced by Clarence Raybould, who took my place at a moment's notice through my being laid up with 'flu.

I should like to recount an unusual phenomenon resulting from this performance. Shortly after the broadcast I received a letter from a lady in Holland (a complete stranger to me) in which she said that, on hearing 'The Enchanted Garden', she had received a vivid mental picture of 'Snow White and the Seven Dwarfs'. It was all the more strange as she knew nothing whatsoever about the rewriting of my Ballet or the change of title, neither did she know anything about the original version at the Cambridge Theatre.

* * * * *

Our happiness at living once more so near to the heart of things was short-lived, for in January, 1931, Austin went down in an epidemic which swept the South Coast. It was a dreadful scourge, chiefly measles followed by all kinds of dangerous complications too horrible to write about, and which caused most of the schools to be closed. At first Phyl and I did not realise the full implications of the communication which told us that Austin was ill, but the urgent telephone call late one night asking our permission to perform an operation was the cause of our packing our suitcases and leaving post-haste for the South Coast. Phyl put up at an hotel near the nursing home to which Austin, in company with about forty other boys, had been taken. For a long time his life hung by a thread and there were times when it was thought he would never pull through. But thanks to a brilliant surgeon and Phyl's tireless devotion and ceaseless vigilance, and the special nurse sent down from London, the day came when we were able to wrap him up and take him in the car to our house on the South Coast.

The soft, life-giving air of Sussex did for Austin's depleted lungs what it did for mine after my attack of pneumonia in 1929, but in his case the cure took much longer to achieve. Here, for nearly two years, he spent a carefree existence in company with his mother, whose happy outlook soon dispelled the unpleasant memories of the past few months. The little nine-year-old boy, as soon as his strength returned, would spend his days sometimes picnicking with his mother when it was bathing weather and at other times cycling about the winding Sussex lanes or running wild on his pony.

In between my professional commitments I took every opportunity to pay flying, and sometimes longer, visits to those whom I always think of as 'The Other Two', sometimes getting up as early as four o'clock on summer mornings to motor down to the whitewashed house near the sea in time for an early breakfast, and occasionally, when I looked like making the seventy-five miles in under the usual time and arriving before the front door was ajar, spending a few enchanting moments on the top of Duncton Hill to watch the sun rise. Those early morning journeys were fascinating. The characteristic odour of the London streets after a hot summer night changed to the sweet smell of wood-smoke and damp roads, and the climb up over the South Downs to the freshening breeze brought with it the tang of the sea, and two familiar figures at the end of the journey, one very small, in the road waving me a welcome—these things will always linger in my memory.

The days became weeks, the weeks months, during which 'The Other Two' spent the time between the house and the beach, or on long summer days making an 'expotition', as Pooh would say, to a lonely spot on the other side of the Point, where the sea at high tides laughed at the puny efforts of man-made defences and invaded what was once upon a time green pasture-land.

At the side of the swirling waters, warmed by the sun, was a quiet pool, and here Austin would play with the tiny crabs or make towers with the shining white pebbles, or paddle in the shallow places or bathe where it was deeper, while his mother, under her shady hat, would pass the hours away reading until the sun showed it was time to go home. Sometimes when I could get away from London for a more lengthy period, the three of us would spend days at this unfrequented place, bathing in the pool when the tide was full, and, if it looked inviting, following the sea as it receded to enjoy the fresher waters of the open. "Is it a Cove day?" was the question which was always on our lips when we came down in the mornings to see the early mist still clinging to the apple trees—and it usually was.

It was not an easy matter, during this time, to turn my attention to writing, but notwithstanding the difficulties I experienced in trying to be in two places at the same time, I managed to compose an Orchestral Suite which I called 'From Meadow to Mayfair' and which, as I had adopted London as my home, was intended to be a kind of farewell to my native Nottinghamshire and the pastoral scenes which up till then I had felt the urge to describe in music.

The same year I was invited by the Director of Music to write something for the forthcoming Festival at Eastbourne, the outcome of this being a Concert Valse, which I called 'Dancing Nights', and a visit to this delightful town on the South Coast. Then came an invitation from the Musical Director at Torquay to give him a new work for his Spring Festival the following year. I was by this time stuck for ideas, but Phyl, as usual, came to the rescue with a story of a Jester's hopeless love for a Princess. It was the ideal subject for musical treatment and some of my happiest recollections are of the weeks I spent working on the score and playing over to her the themes and the general lay-out, followed by a visit to Devonshire for the first performance. I have a particular affection for 'The Jester at the Wedding', much the same as I hold for my later work, 'The Enchanted Garden'. The reason for this is possibly that in some measure it was the joint effort of both of us, although I know that Phyl, notwithstanding the fact that she had been the inspiration at the back of it, would assure me I was being ridiculous.

It was early in 1933. Austin, now fully recovered, but still showing the scars of his long illness, was back at school and Phyl's long and enforced stay in Sussex was at an end. Then, following on the success of an orchestral transcription of Richard Rodgers's popular song 'With a Song in my Heart' (my one and only arrangement), came a further request from the Columbia Gramophone Company for me to do a special transcription of three of my better known songs: 'I Pitch my Lonely Caravan', 'I Heard you Singing', and 'Bird Songs at Eventide'. At this time I was putting the finishing touches to an Orchestral Suite, the subject of which had been suggested to me by the view across London from the flat in which I lived, and in which I described some of the familiar points that I could pick out in the panorama which lay before me: Covent Garden, Westminster, Knightsbridge. I was anxious to get a recording of my new work, and the invitation from the Columbia Company, meaning that I should have a whole session at my disposal, seemed to be a golden opportunity to record the new suite at the same time as the commissioned transcription.

The first performance of my 'London Suite' took place at the B.B.C., where it was conducted by that popular conductor and champion of British music, Joseph Lewis. I had asked Arthur Brooks, at that time the recording manager of the Columbia Company, if he would listen to the broadcast with a view to including the work in the forthcoming session at Abbey Road. Great was my chagrin, on ringing him up the morning after the performance, to be told that he did not think much of the new work. After a long argument, during which I told him it was not fair to criticise a first performance over the air, it was decided that I was to bring the manuscript parts of the 'London Suite' along with me to the session and if there was time to spare (which he doubted), he would allow me to make a recording.

It was the London Philharmonic Orchestra which I found waiting for me when I arrived at the recording studios, Paul Beard leading. When I glanced round at the familiar faces I could see I had a body of musicians under me who worked quickly, and, as I crossed my fingers and prayed that there would be no wrong notes and no split waxes, the recording commenced. By twelve o'clock noon my 'Two Symphonic Rhapsodies' were completed. Then followed the usual fifteen-minute break for cups of tea, coffee and cigarettes.

Those who have attended a gramophone session will know the immense amount of bell-ringing and 'Gentlemen—please' which has to be resorted to before the members of a large orchestra can be persuaded to leave the warm, inviting canteen and return to the cold, uninviting recording room with its suspended microphones, its 'buzzer' which gives two signals for 'Stand by', the little lamp which gives the word 'Go' when it glows red, and that most unnerving of all mechanical things, the large white-faced clock whose long second hand, like the hand of fate, silently and inexorably shows you when you are exceeding the time-limit which a record is capable of playing.

A wrong note from the brass, the oboe too close to the microphone, an overdone double-bass pizzicato, any of these things can spoil a wax and waste valuable minutes, which may result in an unfinished recording when the clock points to one and the three-hour session comes instantly to an end. At last, after much ringing of bells, more insistent shouts of "Gentlemen, *please*," the musicians were once again in their places. The clock showed 12.20. Two minutes more to restore silence and at 12.22 we started on the first movement of the 'London Suite'. All went fairly smoothly and we managed to get the first two movements completed by just on ten minutes to one. We now had only the last movement to record, the 'Knightsbridge March'. At 12.53 we started recording. At 12.54 someone blew a wrong note. At 12.55 we started again. At 12.57 a wax split. I was in despair. Something inside me told me it was absolutely imperative that I should get the disc somehow, and I knew it was now out of the question to achieve a recording before one o'clock. I also knew it was of no use appealing to the recording manager for a few minutes' grace, for every minute overtime meant a considerable increase in the expense of the recording session; and besides, had he not said to me that he did not think much of the new work? So I took my courage in both hands and asked the musicians if they would, as a personal favour to me, spare me a minute or so longer to give me the chance of getting the record. Two signals on the buzzer—we held our breath—the red light glowed and, at three minutes past one o'clock, thanks to a sturdy wax and the good-natured gesture on the part of the orchestra, the 'Knightsbridge March', which was to prove to be the biggest seller the Columbia Gramophone Company had ever had, was made.

As I have already said, my publishers were somewhat averse to printing the new Suite, and it was only after a considerable amount of pressure on my part that they consented to do so. Everybody was of the opinion that no orchestra but the very best could hope to make an effect with the 'Knightsbridge' movement, on account of the difficult staccato bowing for the first violins. They felt that the second movement, 'Westminster', was the one that would become popular, and they even considered publishing this separately. The issuing of the pianoforte solo edition was the next difficulty. I admit that anything in march form is almost impossible on the piano, unless you have a Moiseiwitsch at your disposal, and when I attempted to play over my own arrangement on my little upright I began to think that perhaps, after all, my publishers were right.

At last, however, the band parts and the pianoforte solo were duly printed and issued for sale. The weeks passed. 'The London Suite', in company with my earlier works, went steadily on its way.

But one Saturday evening, deeply absorbed with my camera, I heard Phyl calling me. Reluctantly I dragged myself away from my dark-room and went to see what it was all about. They were playing something on the radio. It was a blare of trumpets. It sounded familiar. We exchanged glances. It was the brass introduction to the Trio of the Knightsbridge March, my own recording. Looking in the *Radio Times* we discovered the announcement of a new weekly feature entitled 'In Town To-night', in which people in the news were brought to the microphone and interviewed. We listened to the broadcast until the fanfare of my march and the few bars of the melody faded out and the half-hour came to a close. "At any rate," we agreed, "it cannot do the Suite any harm."

The telephone now started to ring. It appeared that listeners had been in touch with Broadcasting House to ask the title of the tantalising few bars which they had just heard on the radio, and having been told it was by me, they had rung through to the flat to ask for further information about the music. No sooner was the receiver down than the bell rang again. Another telephone call was immediately followed by another and yet another. I resigned myself to coping with the eulogies of complete strangers, ranging from old ladies of eighty down to young ladies in their 'teens, while Phyl looked on and laughed.

Twenty thousand letters arrived at Broadcasting House within the following two weeks, asking for the name of the composer and the title of the signature-tune to 'In Town To-night', and a harassed and overworked staff had to resort to the expedient of printing special slips giving the necessary information. Special editions of the march bearing the title of 'In Town To-night March' were issued by my publishers. A simplified arrangement was published, which, strange to say, was not the one that the public bought; they preferred my own unpianistic version. The Columbia Gramophone Company could not press the recordings fast enough; the band-parts and the piano solo were in such demand that the band department staff in the basement at No. 50, New Bond Street, worked overtime to cope with the orders. Orchestras large and small; brass bands; military bands; dance bands; barrel organs; fairground organs; mechanical pianos; pianolas; accordions; even electric penny-in-the-slot pianos waxed hot in their endeavour to overcome the difficulties of that provoking and tricky staccato. Everywhere you went you heard it.

I think my publishers were a little disappointed when I refused to conduct at the numerous functions to which I was invited, but I well remember the one occasion when I broke my rule and turned up on the stage of a famous super-cinema in the East End in company with Alex James, the well-known footballer (who, incidentally, kicked a football from the stage up into the back of the gallery); Jimmy Wilde, the famous light-weight boxing champion, whose small stature tempted me to see if he was really the stuff he was supposed to be made of; and, most distinguished of all, the Fastest Greyhound in the World. . . .

It is extraordinary the way in which the 'Knightsbridge March' never fails to rouse the dullest of audiences. I cannot understand the reason for it, but over and over again, when I have been conducting it in public both in this country and abroad, the moment the double-basses begin the reiterated quaver beats at the opening I can feel a sensation of excited anticipation coming from the audience and striking me in the back of the head.

The story goes of the would-be passenger who could not remember the name of the station he wanted to get to, and his humming the first few notes of the refrain of the march produced a ticket for Knightsbridge from the smiling booking-clerk. I remember one night hearing a bishop in the lavatory in Leicester Square singing to himself as he stood in his stall. I could not make out at first what tune he was trying to execute, and then it dawned on me that the doleful sound he was producing was intended to be 'Knightsbridge'. Tactfully turning towards him, I said: "Excuse me, sir—it goes like this", and gave him a note-perfect presentation of a few bars of my hackneyed march. This was too much for the old clergyman: "You'll be telling me you wrote it yourself next!" On my assuring him that such was the case he gave me a frightened look and beat a hasty retreat, no doubt congratulating himself that he had been delivered out of the clutches of a dangerous lunatic.

Three letters reached me about the same time. The first was from an admirer in Czecho-Slovakia: now, 'Great Maestro', 'Revered and honoured Master', and 'The greatest composer in Europe—nay, in the whole world', are music to the ears of a musician (*crescendo*)— the second letter came from the North of England and was addressed to me c/o The B.B.C., Newcastle: 'I have written the libretto of a Light Opera and as I have received good reports about your music, although I have not actually heard any of it myself, I think that you might be suitable for making a musical setting of my script' (*diminuendo*)—and the third was from a remote village in Lancashire: 'I wish to have my poems set to music and it has been suggested that I send them to you—I cannot understand why, unless you are a composer' (*lunga pausa!*).

* * * * *

The other day I came across a cutting from the London *Daily Express*, dated April 13th, 1937, in which Mr. James Agate declared that, if he were king, it would be to this, among all modern English airs, that he would soonest march down the aisle at his coronation. Notwithstanding that the chances of 'Knightsbridge' being used as anything so spectacular are extremely slender, the march has nevertheless been played in unusual and even dramatic circumstances. It has frequently figured at weddings, and on one notable occasion it was played at the funeral of a prominent member of the Turf who wished to take the last fence in good spirits; it is used to this day as a tonic by invalids; it was suggested from Holland as a Victory March to which to enter Berlin during World War II. It was blared out by loud-speakers in the Square in Copenhagen during the German occupation as a sign of the Danes' sympathy with London, and it took a Nazi machine-gun crew to silence it. It has been played well, indifferently and badly at one time and another by practically every orchestra and band in existence. It was recorded through the good behaviour of a sturdy wax and the kindly co-operation of the members of the London Philharmonic Orchestra, against the good judgment of the Columbia Gramophone Company, and published almost under protest by Messrs. Chappell & Co. It was picked out at random from a pile of recordings in Broadcasting House and chosen by Eric Maschwitz as signature-tune for 'In Town To-night', in which feature it has been coming regularly 'over the air' since its inauguration in 1933.

All these memories of 'Knightsbridge' were revived for me when, in the autumn of 1950, 'In Town To-night' reached its five hundredth edition. A B.B.C. feature that had weathered five hundred performances was something worth celebrating, and Peter Duncan, the producer of 'In Town To-night', had gathered round him a galaxy of famous people for the occasion and had insisted on my starting the ball rolling by coming to the microphone to tell John Ellison and the listeners the story of 'Knightsbridge'.

The success of the programme was assured from the outset. It could not have failed with such names as Greer Garson (at that time filming the sequel to 'Mrs. Miniver'), my dear friend Christopher

Stone, Lord Brabazon, Dame Felicity Hanbury and Annette Mills, with Frank Phillips announcing. At the conclusion of the broadcast they all came to supper with us at the Dorchester, where Greer Garson, at the height of the party, produced and played a few notes on a charm in the shape of a tiny mouth-organ given to her by Larry Adler.

* * * * *

"Nay, me deer Coates, ye'll never induce me to listen to the wireless. It's an abomination above all abominations." With these words my old Principal, Sir Alexander Mackenzie, settled himself in his arm-chair, adjusted his carpet-slippers, pulled his alpaca coat about him, set his pince-nez on the tip of his nose, and giving me one of his delightful smiles added: "The only time a wireless set was ever brought into my house it refused to work, and so I made up my mind that the thing didn't like me, and the feeling was mutual." I was a fairly regular visitor at No. 20 Taviton Street, usually turning up after my old friend had had his afternoon's rest. We were sitting in the comfortable writing-room at the front of the house. I had found the distinguished musician at his desk in the window working on some unfinished score.

It was about ten years since he had retired from the position of Principal at the Royal Academy of Music, a post which he had held for thirty-six years. As we talked, I could see that the years had not diminished his affection for the place where, for so long a time, he had shaped the destinies of many hundreds of future musicians, and where he had been so loved by many, so feared by some, but respected by all.

We talked of the old students who had passed through his hands, some now famous and others forgotten; of the rambling building in Tenterden Street which had given way to the 'monstrous edifice' (he called it) at York Gate, Marylebone Road, then looking conspicuously unmellowed with its walls of crude red brick and its inartistic design; of my motor-car standing at the kerb outside his front door and in which, when the weather was warmer, he promised himself he would accompany me on a run out into the country; of modern music, which even then was a thorn in his flesh; of his own activities in this direction—his 'Pibroch Suite' for Violin and Orchestra, his Violin Concerto, his Pianoforte Quartet (a signed copy of which he presented 'to his old friend' as a souvenir of the many times I used to play the lovely viola solo in the first movement in the far-away days of the Lena Ashwell Season at the Kingsway Theatre); of his incidental music to 'Ravenswood', which led him to tell the story of the evening prior to the opening night of the production, when he had asked the stage carpenter what he thought of the chances of the show being a success, and which brought from his 'oracle of the theatre' the veiled pronouncement: "Well—there's Sir Henry Irving acts, Sir Edward Burne-Jones paints the scenery and Sir Alexander Mackenzie writes the music. Three ruddy knights—and that's about all it will get," ("And that," said Sir Alexander, wreathed in smiles, "was about all it *did* get"); of the club to which he belonged said to be the smallest in existence, consisting of himself, Edward German, Herman Finck (Herman Finck of Finckley Road) and Mackenzie-Rogan, which met only on birthdays and which had to be discontinued on account of the birthdays becoming too frequent.

He rippled on in that fascinating Scottish accent which had attracted me so greatly the first time I met him, thirty years before, upstairs in his room in Tenterden Street. He was still just the same, only looking a good deal older, and his eyes troubled him. Then we got on to the topic of broadcasting, which he detested. I pointed out to him that perhaps he had never listened with a decent radio set. No, he had *not*, and anyhow he had no intention of wasting his time attempting to listen to the nonsense which, judging by the programmes advertised in the daily papers, poured out unceasingly from that dreadful B.B.C. It was more than useless to argue with the Principal when he had made up his mind. He came to the front door and watched me down the stone steps, looking a little wistful as I stepped into the car, as if he were thinking he would wish he were coming with me, even in his alpaca coat and his carpet-slippers. I called out to him that I would bring along a portable radio one day when there was something really worth listening to, started up the engine, let in the clutch, and moved off. I looked back—the bent figure was still in the doorway. I waved, and drove on.

I was determined to break down his prejudice against the wireless. "Is that Sir Alexander? They are broadcasting your Pianoforte Concerto from Bournemouth on Wednesday. Would you like to hear it?" There was a long pause—and then: "All right, my boy. But I warn ye, you're running the risk of your wireless breaking down if ye bring it to my house!" I put down the receiver and took the risk. As I watched my old friend, sitting on the settee, his head on one side, listening intently to the performance coming to us over the radio, I pictured him thinking of the dozens of times he had led the Royal Academy of Music Orchestra, plus a struggling piano student, through this lovely work, and wondered what were his emotions on hearing, probably for the first time for many years, both the orchestral and the solo passages being executed with such brilliance.

The old man was obviously moved. A tear ran down his cheek. The music ceased. I left the switch on for him to hear the enthusiastic reception which followed. Ten years later I was to recall the memory of that warm summer afternoon and my old Principal sitting so quietly listening to my portable radio set. It was the occasion of the closing night of a Promenade Concert Season at the Albert Hall; the solo pianist, joined by the combined orchestras of the B.B.C. Symphony, the London Symphony and the London Philharmonic, was giving a performance of the 'Scottish' Concerto to a packed house. It was a fitting tribute to a great musician and scholar.

I thought I had broken down Mackenzie's prejudice to the B.B.C. and, although his long antipathy to the Corporation, probably added to his Scottish thriftiness, prevented him from going in for one himself, from that day my portable radio was a welcome guest at No. 20 Taviton Street. On one memorable occasion, when his dances to 'The Little Minister' were being broadcast, it was even taken round by request. But one afternoon I found him deeply engrossed, poring over a familiar-looking magazine. He looked up as I entered and with a malicious smile greeted me with: "This really is the most *terrible* paper I have ever seen! Of all the unmitigated twaddle—but, d'ye know, Coates" (breaking into an even more malicious grin), "I read every word of it, it *fascinates* me!" I looked over his shoulder to see what he was reading—it was the *Radio Times*.

Early in 1935 I sat by his bedside and held the wrinkled old hand while we spoke again of past times and mutual friends. It was the last time I was to see him, for on April 28th, he passed over, and with his going went one of my oldest friends.

* * * * *

An invitation from Eric Maschwitz to write a new work for a special concert of my music at Broadcasting House had done the trick. The blank patch was over. I had only recently attended a concert at the B.B.C. given in honour of the famous Hungarian composer, Emmerich Kalman, who had come over to England specially to conduct the augmented Theatre Orchestra in a programme of his music. I had always been a great admirer of this composer of so many lovely Light Operas and I spent a delightful evening, not the least pleasant part of it being my meeting with the maestro himself in the artists' room at the close of the performance, when he proudly presented me to his new young wife. Of course, I was naturally very pleased to be asked to appear at a series of concerts devoted to the works of those musicians who had become famous through their writing, and when I heard that Franz Lehar was to be the guest conductor at the concert following my own, I felt flattered at being included among such distinguished company.

It was at the close of 1934 and the winter had set in. I had decided on the idea of describing in music three personalities whom we all of us know: The Countryman, the Townsman and the Seaman. 'The Man from the Country' came out in the form of a rhythmic country-dance jig; in 'The Man-about-Town', introducing a tenor saxophone, I hit upon a nostalgic kind of melody which lent itself well to syncopated treatment in the middle section, and in 'The Man from the Sea' I employed the old sea shanty, 'When Johnnie comes down to Hilo', to give local colour to my mariner. I remember what a hullaballoo broke out when I wrote a short fugal exposition on the last three notes of the shanty, which were so identical with the last three notes of 'Three Blind Mice' that I could not resist the temptation to employ the old nursery song in full. The hullaballoo came from the Royal and the Merchant Navies, who informed me that mice were *never* found on board any ship, for the very reason that no rats would ever put up with their presence for one moment and would promptly devour them. On my pointing out to them that the allusion was intended as a joke and that anyhow I considered that mice had the *entrée* anywhere, the incident closed amicably with an amusing caricature in the *Radio Times* of an A.B. on the deck of a battleship, scrutinising a mouse at point-blank range with an enormous telescope.

* * * * *

It was the result of an invitation from Godfrey Brown, at that time Director of Music to the B.B.C. in Northern Ireland, that I found myself seated in an extremely small and uncomfortable aeroplane *en route* to Belfast, to fulfil an engagement to appear as guest conductor in the Town Hall.

I had already seen 'The Three Men' on their way, composed something specially for King George V's Jubilee, paid a flying visit to Hucknall to open the Annual Carnival and conducted performances of the 'London Suite' in most of the towns in England which boasted an orchestra. It was early in 1936 and the memory of my first journey by air is still fresh in my mind. A far too small aeroplane, a gusty February morning inducing a series of unpleasant 'air-pockets', especially over the Isle of Man, and it was an extremely airsick and exhausted composer who stepped out on to Irish soil.

My discomfort was not decreased by hearing, on my arrival, that a man had been shot the night before outside the Town Hall and his body tactfully thrown into the vestibule as the audience was leaving the building, and when I saw for the first time the fine film-star police patrolling the streets with revolvers stuck in their holsters, I began to wonder whether I had been judicious in accepting the invitation. However, apart from an anxious moment when the soloist of the evening was only just prevented from going on and playing as an encore the banned 'Londonderry Air', the concert was a great success and the warmth of the audience, added to my meeting for the first time the shock-headed virtuoso of the saxophone, soon made me forget all about my unpleasant journey and my uneasy feelings.

I had already heard a good deal about this famous saxophonist and his amazing facility, and when I listened to him rehearsing with the orchestra in the morning my expectations were fully realised. A lovely tune allied to perfect phrasing and a flawless technique summed up Sigurd Rascher, the artist; Sigurd Rascher, the man, was just as unusual a figure as he was an instrumentalist. First and foremost you noticed his amazing crop of hair, which, somehow or other, he contrived to deposit in the limited space afforded by the tiniest of berets. This minor miracle was achieved in a manner known only to himself, for any other man would have needed a far more voluminous headgear than a beret with which to perform such an astonishing hat-trick. With his hair went a tremendous vitality and a perpetual urge to practise his beloved saxophone (affectionately alluded to by himself as his 'pipe'). In this latter respect, time and place were of little consequence and many were the complications brought about by over-indulging with his 'pipe' at a time when most good citizens were taking their rest. As anyone knows, the saxophone possesses a particularly penetrating tone, especially in the higher register, and as Sigurd Rascher produced notes which no other player had ever succeeded in producing, it is easy to imagine the effect this would have upon the residents of some sleepy country hotel at two o'clock in the morning.

The introduction of the tenor saxophone into the second movement of 'The Three Men' Suite had not passed unnoticed by the Danish virtuoso, who took me to task the moment I came off the platform and insisted that I should write something specially for him to play on his 'pipe'. As usual, I was preoccupied with plans for wasting a little time with my camera, and, giving him a half-hearted promise that if I could think of anything suitable I would get in touch with him, I boarded the steamer for Heysham, in preference to being knocked about in a railway company's uncomfortable aeroplane, and did not give the matter another thought.

Then came a letter from the Musical Director at Folkestone asking me to write him a new work for the forthcoming Festival. By this time I was feeling more than ever in lazy mood and more than ever determined to waste time with my camera; but not liking to say 'no' outright and knowing that Sigurd Rascher was safely tucked away in Southern Sweden, I promised the Director that if he could manage to engage my friend specially for the Festival I would write something for him. Feeling perfectly certain that I was safe to carry on my leisurely way, I was about to turn my attention to the engrossing pastime of spending a morning at Messrs. Wallace Heaton's in New Bond Street, in order to compare the features of the latest in Leicas, Contaxes, Contaflexes, or Rolleiflexes, when it was suggested to me by one of the B.B.C. directors that I should accompany him to Stockholm, whither he was bent on official matters relating to the B.B.C., and that while there I should conduct a broadcast of my music for the Svensk Radiotjänst.

My friend, Kenneth Wright, had been responsible for the forthcoming visit of the Swedish conductor, Adolf Wiklund, to England where he was due to conduct a Symphony Concert at the B.B.C. studios. It was arranged that my visit to Sweden should coincide with Wiklund's return to Stockholm after the broadcast and that, in fact, we should all travel by the same steamer. My visit to the shop opposite my publisher's in New Bond Street now had a purpose, for my trip to Sweden was an excellent excuse to try out a new camera I had had my eye on for some time.

It was June and the weather was perfect. The boat was the little *Möde* of the Svensk Svea Shipping Line. We sailed from Millwall Dock at three o'clock in the morning, Wiklund consenting to share a two-berth cabin with me, after I had assured him in my best Swedish that I did not snore.

We went across the North Sea to Wilhelmshaven; through the Kiel Canal; out into the Baltic, whose blue waters reminded me of tropical days at sea many years previously; past Gothland and the lovely Visby whose ruined cathedrals could be seen standing out naked to the sky; and up through the picturesque archipelago, which we reached as the fourth day was drawing to its close. We spent the last few hours sitting on deck as we made our way silently and smoothly among the hundreds of little islands which crowd the approaches to Stockholm, while craft of every kind slipped here and there in the twilight, looking not unlike little grey ghosts with glow-worms for lanterns; and then regretfully I left the enchanting scene and climbed up into my bunk. I woke to find the little *Möde* moored safely at the quayside and a reporter from the *Svenska Aftonblatt* breaking the early morning stillness with shouts of: "Is Eric Coates on board?"

From then on began one long round of sightseeing; entertainment; visits to Skansen to see the Zoo; to Drottningholm (shades of Versailles and a voluble guide expounding the virtues of Louis Quatorze!) to see the Palace and the eighteenth-century theatre; to Djursholm to spend a delightful evening with the Director of Music to the Svensk Radiotjänst (Swedish Broadcasting Company); dinner on the shores of Lake Malar; visits to the fine Picture Gallery; to the magnificent Town Hall; to restaurants; to more restaurants; just finding time to conduct a rehearsal and broadcast with the Radiotjänst Symphony Orchestra at Konserthuset (the Concert Hall) in Kungsgatan; and throughout all these excursions and alarums the temperature was always in the neighbourhood of one hundred degrees fahrenheit and always was there *smörgäs*.

I shall always remember the farewell party, in true Swedish style, given in my honour by Adolf Wiklund and his wife, at the height of which Wiklund made a speech eulogising a remark I had made in Swedish on board the *Möde*, apropos of the apparently never-ending succession of meals, in which I innocently made use of a word with a *double entendre* of such magnitude that it was some considerable time before I was allowed to forget it. Here they sang us their old national songs and we sang them ours, over much filling of glasses and '*skols*' and '*var so gods*' and '*tak sa myckets*' and '*jas sos*', while we made the most of the dishes laid out so temptingly before us, dishes which only Sweden understands how to prepare.

Saying "*Tak for i dag*" to my newly-found Swedish friends and with a promise that the next time I visited Stockholm I would bring a new work specially for them, I caught the Saturday morning train to Göteborg, climbed on board the s.s. *Britannia* and arrived back in London early on Monday, very brown and feeling extremely well, to find a letter and a postcard awaiting me, the former from Folkestone telling me that Sigurd Rascher had been engaged for the Festival in September, and the latter from Sigurd Rascher from Sweden asking for the solo saxophone part of the new work to be sent to him immediately, as he wished to 'make good the practice'. In a mild form of panic I got down to 'make good the writing', hoping that the fates would come to my aid and give me something to write about, which they did, and I was able to send the shock-headed virtuoso the saxophone solo part to my 'Saxo-Rhapsody' (I remember how disappointed he was at not receiving a full orchestral score); and judging by the splendid performance he gave at the Folkestone Festival in September, he must have 'made good the practice' indeed.

We were at our house in Sussex—it was April, and Phyl, who had been out on one of her voyages of discovery (by which I mean either poking about inside antique furniture shops or prowling about outside and inside empty houses), came back in a high state of excitement to tell me that she had found a house which I simply *must* come and look at. It was quite possible I should not like it, but she thought it was only right to tell me about it, just in case. When she had run the place down sufficiently for me to make some show of intelligent interest and was still warning me that I must not be disappointed at what I was about to see, I got the car out and we drove together about four miles inland to where there is a turning on the left in the first village on the road to Chichester, and there, about a couple of hundred yards up on the left, hidden away among trees and covered, in places, two feet thick with ivy, was the house of our dreams.

The whole place was so overgrown that it was only with difficulty we were able to find our way up the gloomy drive, to where the house gave on to a triangular lawn bathed in sunshine. Our arrival was the signal for hundreds of birds, which were congregated in the branches of every tree, to set up a chattering protest against the two humans who had dared to invade the privacy of their verdant sanctuary, before flying away into the tree-tops at the bottom of the garden.

We wandered round the house, peeping in at the windows where the ivy permitted, admiring the lovely old mellowed roof with the moss-covered north side, making plans as to where we would add windows to let in the south sun, exploring the old chaise-house at the kitchen entrance and trying the pump in the dairy to see if it worked and wondering whether the water, which sparkled like diamonds, was fit to drink. Then returning once again to the garden, while risking the displeasure of some birds which, bolder than the rest, had taken up their stand again in the trees close to the house, we found that the V-shaped lawn gave on to a profuse vegetable garden, followed by a fruit garden, followed yet again by an orchard, and lastly by a copse carpeted with bluebells which (we discovered later) had taken the place of earlier violets: and throughout were trees and flowering shrubs of every kind. Here were white chestnut, pink chestnut, oak, elm, ash, walnut, laburnum, lilac, glauca, silver poplar, japonica, wistaria, honeysuckle, gorse, while rose trees apparently unattended and unchecked climbed here and there in wild confusion.

The house was lovely in all weathers, even when the rare snow lay around and about, for the cheery log fires and the soft light thrown by the oil lamps (electric light had not yet come to these parts) gave a sense of cosiness which no other form of lighting and heating can convey.

In the spring the garden was a veritable paradise, for Joe, who was part and parcel of the place, was blessed with the 'green finger', and anyone who owns a garden knows what that means. Phyl adored Joe, and if I missed her about the house, I only had to wander out on to the lawn and through the winding pathway which led to the vegetable garden and, sure enough, there she would be, discussing the merits of the seeds just delivered by carrier from Chichester or making plans for a new herbaceous border or the laying down of a lawn on the south side of the house. There is no doubt that she was as clay in Joe's hands—it was sufficient for him to suggest her climbing down into some deep and muddy ditch, and down she would go, and I verily believe she would have scaled the highest elm if Joe had told her there was something to be gained by so doing.

So far as I was concerned, it took Joe some considerable time before he was able to reconcile himself to the idea that I ever did an honest day's work—to him, work meant digging, hoeing, mowing, hedging, ditching, lopping, or clipping. He certainly associated me with doing something in my writing-room which somehow or other came out over his battery radio set in his tiny back parlour, but as for its being anything in the nature of work, I'm sure the idea to him was absurd.

One of Joe's recreations took the form of playing darts, at which ancient sport he excelled; the other pastime, which besides being a form of recreation had its lucrative side as well, was the even more ancient sport of donning sea-boots, arming himself with a voluminous sack and, when the tide was at its lowest, ruthlessly raiding the winkle beds. We knew it was quite useless to expect Joe to turn up on time when the tide was at the ebb, for winkling was a far more fascinating business than looking after gardens, but by keeping a tide-table on hand we were able to tell the days when he would arrive late and also the days when he would go early.

It is strange the way in which old houses, especially those of character, have a way of possessing you. We both of us felt the old place owned us rather than that we ourselves were the owners. It was as if the pretty front door with its protecting porch was saying: 'Come along in and stay with me,' just as if it knew that, once inside, we would never have the heart to tear ourselves away again. It was a curious sensation of possessiveness of which not only we were conscious, for Austin felt it just as acutely. He used to tell us he would like to live there for ever and ever, and just write his plays and his books as he felt inclined, and I think he was very disappointed at our decision that it was not practicable to own a house in the country which attracted us so greatly and which, in some ways, interfered with my professional work. It is very difficult to remain in London when you are conscious all the time of the call of an old house in Sussex and, although I did some of my best orchestration in the window of the upstairs room looking on to the triangular lawn, it was not without some measure of relief that in the late summer of 1939, just before the outbreak of World War II, it passed out of our possession into the hands of the charming people who are the present owners.

* * * * *

It was the autumn of 1939. Another visit to Scandinavia had come and gone, this time Copenhagen, Oslo and Stockholm, followed by a flying visit to Amsterdam. I went to Copenhagen by air with a temperature of 100°, following a chill I had contracted while in Paris. At that fascinating city of waterways, the Statsradiofonien Symphony Orchestra and a friendly audience gave me a welcome I shall long remember—'touche', I think they call it. After my broadcast I had supper with Kapellmeister Erik Tuxen and his wife in their delightful flat in Havngade, from the windows of which I watched, fascinated, the little white steamers setting out in the moonlight for Malmö. At Oslo my visit unfortunately coincided with a hotel strike, and the 'frukost', which I needed so badly (after sweating the nightlong through from many doses of 'codyl' prescribed for me by a famous physician in Copenhagen) was not forthcoming. Hugo Kramm, the Director of Music to the Norsk Rikskringkasting, very kindly saved me from starvation by sending round to the hotel a thermos and a pile of sandwiches; charming Fru Kramm also added greatly to my comfort by supplying me with a hot-water bottle to accompany me in the 'sleeper' which carried me away to Stockholm after the broadcast. While I was with the Kramms I was amused to find that the chief excitement at the house during supper seemed to be the tuning-on of the radio to listen to a commentator giving a description of a football match taking place in Newcastle. I am afraid I associate this visit to Oslo with cold hotels, no food and no service, although I can remember how lovely the sea looked outside the harbour the morning I strolled down to the quayside and, heedless of the cold, watched the many steamers coming and going across the pale waters of the motionless fjord. Next came Stockholm, with the friendly 'portvakt' at the K.A.K. (and memories of the little *Möde*), where I conducted the first performance in

Scandinavia of my Ballet 'The Enchanted Garden'. Next, Amsterdam, another city of waterways just as lovely as those in Copenhagen, where the people remind you of our own folk, so homely are they and so kind. It was here that I arrived at Schipol by K.L.M. and had to crave a glass of water before I was able to make myself understood by the Director-General of the AVRO, on account of my tongue cleaving to the roof of my mouth through much usage of Vasano (as administered to our Mr. Chamberlain on his historic flight to Munich).

The same year there were pleasant recollections of a three weeks' engagement on the cinema stage in the West End, alluded to by 'The Other Two' as my 'glory' on account of the electric signs outside the theatres, blazing out to an anticipating public the announcement of my first appearance in the 'show business'. Here I conducted half an hour of my music with a Symphony Orchestra three times daily, between the showing of the chief film 'feature', at the Gaumont Cinema, Hammersmith, the New Victoria and the Dominion Theatre in Tottenham Court Road, which culminated in my being given the place of honour at Radio-Olympia with the same orchestra, plus the Dagenham Girl Pipers and a couple of Hammond organs, where we played the same programme at intervals throughout the day to an audience composed of five thousand radio enthusiasts.

* * * * *

Once again we were in Sussex, and my thoughts went back to another holiday by the sea twenty-five years earlier which had also been marred by rumours of war. Once again we refused to believe that such a calamity could happen, but the rumours persisted. A journey to Scarborough, only to find the orchestra disbanded and the Spa deserted, made me fear the worst. Motoring back to London the following morning with loud-speakers at every petrol station on the road polluting the lovely autumn air with news of the latest outrage from Germany, added to the filthy 'pool' petrol which was poured under protest into the tank when I stopped to fill up, brought home to me the unpleasant realisation that before many hours had passed we should be at war.

* * * * *

I sat on the balcony outside Phyl's bedroom window and looked south-east across London to where the summer lightning played fitfully in the gathering dusk. How little did I realise that soon those silent flashes would give place to the flash of anti-aircraft batteries, warning us of the approach of Nazi airmen intent on dealing death and destruction in the city of my adoption! But sure enough, as each evening drew in, they came in their hundreds, coming earlier with every earlier setting of the sun, and each morning we climbed up on to the roof to see what landmarks still remained from the night before. We saw the east covered in a pall of smoke, mounting higher and higher to screen the rising sun, and each morning our landmarks held—Westminster, St. Paul's, Tower Bridge, the B.B.C. The sound of fire-engines pumping—pumping, the sight of a tiny figure abreast some tottering wall, pouring a jet of water from some puny hose-pipe into a raging inferno below, the scream of falling bombs, the roar of aircraft overhead (are they *theirs* or are they *ours*?)—guns, guns, more guns—that dreadful red glow eastwards, is it our Queen's Hall or is it Broadcasting House?—what's the use of thinking?—and through it all the sound of fire-engines pumping —pumping. And then suddenly—unexpectedly—silence—broken only by the scrunch of feet on glass and the unmistakably friendly sound of the chinking of cups and saucers being handed out by the staunch proprietor of the coffee-stall which, raid in, raid out, took its stand each evening at the corner of the street one hundred feet below Phyl's bedroom window. A lorry driver pulls up at the side of the pavement and with a "Warm night, chum!" drinks the proffered cup of coffee—a warden calls out to a passing motor-car to "Put out those lights!"—an ambulance goes silently by on its errand of mercy —wandering searchlights roam ceaselessly about the sky—a red glow on every hand and the acrid smell of burning.

They're an unaccountable lot, Londoners, and although those first years of the war were anything but pleasant to live through, least of all on a top floor, I feel sorry for those who left London at the first sign of a raid, for they missed the experience of seeing how the Cockney reacted in a crisis, and, believe me, it was magnificent.

Lovely autumn days, reminding one of the end of many holidays in peaceful Sussex, with a scent in the air, this time not of wood-smoke but of the charred remains of some burnt-out building— lovely, still autumn days, savouring of a country at peace, were it not for the unreal atmosphere pervading everything, an atmosphere of apprehension at the evenings, now drawing in rapidly, and the knowledge that the first signs of dusk would bring the wailing of air-raid sirens.

Austin had left Stowe in 1938 and had managed to squeeze in some months with a tutor in Paris before the war started. He had then gone to the Royal Academy of Dramatic Art (pending his call-up) to get first-hand knowledge of how plays were written, acted and produced, after which he had journeyed up to Perth to gain experience in stage-craft. The daily papers giving news of a block of flats in North-West London destroyed by enemy action brought him back post-haste to see what had happened to his father and mother, and his return coincided with one of our worst air-raids. We sat, the three of us (with the windows slightly open to obviate, as we had been told by an expert, the danger of breaking glass), quietly partaking of our dinner and trying to make ourselves heard above the bark of guns and the screaming of bombs, slowly rocking from side to side when something dropped nearer than usual. It was a fantastic dinner, with no one to wait on us (after all, who would want to experience air-raids in a top-floor flat one hundred feet from the ground if they were not obliged to? It was different for us —it was our *home*.) The meal was made all the more unreal by the knowledge that all the flats below us had long ago been vacated, so that we seemed very much alone and, as it were, naked to the elements and the war. Most fantastic of all was the fact that none of us referred to what was going on around us, and I don't think we should have thought it in the least out of place if we had been in full evening dress, which forces me to the conclusion that we have more of the Englishman's characteristic sense of orthodoxy in us than I thought!

Writing music in those early days of the war was not a job which received encouragement from official quarters, and the Government's characteristically short-sighted decision to disband all military bands confirmed my fears that, as in the last war, music, for a space, was going to be looked upon merely as a means of livelihood for 'rogues and vagabonds', a hindrance, rather than a help, to the war effort. However, as in 1914, the Powers That Be were soon obliged to change their attitude and admit, if not openly, that even musicians had their uses. For my own part, the muse seemed to have deserted me altogether. I had struck another blank patch, which this time persisted for several months—but, once again, Phyl came to the rescue with the suggestion that I should write something specially for the Red Cross Depôt whither she went daily to treadle her way with a sewing-machine through miles of hospital supplies. So I sat me down at my desk in the window, looking far away across London to the twin towers of the Crystal Palace (before the shortage of metal required them for more useful purposes than ornamenting the skyline), and wrote what Phyl still calls *her* 'signature-tune'. We experienced some difficulty over the question of title and after numerous abortive efforts to find one, a gangster film with G-men tapping out the usual 'calling all cars' supplied the solution, and 'Calling All Workers' it was.

I remember waiting to hear Stanford Robinson with the B.B.C. Theatre Orchestra broadcast the first performance of the march from Cheltenham in the autumn of 1940, soon after it was composed, and the anxiety we both went through, wondering whether the coming of the customary evening air-raid warning would mean the cutting down of the transmission with consequent weak reception. Some weeks later Phyl's 'signature-tune' was adopted by the B.B.C. to announce, in the course of time, the opening and the close of many thousands of 'Music While you Work' programmes.

About this time came the unexpected news from the United States of America that my Valse Serenade, 'By the Sleepy Lagoon', composed as long ago as 1930, had been published out there as a Valse Song under its new name of 'Sleepy Lagoon' and was selling in its tens of thousands. This was followed by the issuing in England of my Valse Serenade in its new dress, which also sold in its tens of thousands. Soon after, I was to receive a cable from the New York house of Messrs. Chappell & Co., congratulating me on being the composer of a number one song-hit in the U.S.A., which showed that the sales had grown still more—in fact, it was soon being played all over the world.

November came, with an invitation from Jack Hylton to journey up to the North to conduct programmes of my music with the London Philharmonic Orchestra. The orchestra had fallen on bad times and Hylton had come forward with the then novel suggestion that, under his guidance, it should make a tour of the provincial music-halls, playing to audiences which normally went to this type of theatre to hear the latest in comedians or the hottest in dance bands. It was a daring experiment to fill the bill with a Symphony Orchestra, but it proved highly successful and was the beginning of bringing the best in orchestral music to the masses.

It was eight o'clock in the evening, dark, pouring with rain and there was one of the nastiest of air-raids in progress. We managed to find a taxi-driver who scorned such things as enemy aircraft and, with lights extinguished, drove through the dark, wet streets to the accompaniment of anti-aircraft batteries spitting their explosive loads up into a pitch-black sky, in defiance of the scream of falling bombs from Nazi bombers which roared and zoomed their destructive way overhead. We were both thankful when the uncomfortable journey to King's Cross was over and we were able to put ourselves in the protection of the porter who took us under his wing and shepherded us to our 'sleeper', nursing us along the dark departure platform, warning us when we approached a more than usually deep puddle or were about to break our ankles where the flooring had collapsed.

They were wonderful, these railwaymen—thinking only of our safety and our comfort, with never one word of complaint about the conditions under which they were working. If it had not been for the barking of guns, and Nazi planes wheeling and roaring over the station, we might have been in an ordinary holiday crowd going away to the seaside. It was a relief to close the windows and shut out the dreadful night and even more of a relief when we moved slowly out of the station into the comparative quiet of the tunnel, for here were no guns or bombs or diving planes. Back there, on the platform which we had just left, was the same porter, calmly finding his way back to the front of the station to shepherd another traveller across the same puddles and the same loose boards.

My impression of the days we spent with the London Philharmonic Orchestra are, for the most part, of a crowd of smiling faces in front of me and of a warm, responsive audience behind me; the rest is a jumble of railway stations, hotels, darkened streets, air-raid warnings and precarious railway journeys.

Notwithstanding that it meant returning to the land of incessant air-raids, we were glad to board the 9.15 p.m. from Glasgow, although we did not anticipate it was to be 2.30 the following afternoon before we were in sight of London. I hold vivid recollections of this journey and of the steward, just as dawn was breaking, coming into our 'sleeper' with a welcome cup of tea and a biscuit, at the same time pointing to an angry red glow in the eastern sky with the significant remark: "I don't know what's happening, but that's Coventry!" Here again I would like to take my hat off to our railwaymen and the way in which they carried on under almost impossible conditions. Trains may have run behind schedule but the destination was always reached. I have often wondered what it must have felt like to be in the cab of a great locomotive drawing one of our famous expresses during this dreadful time. It would have been an experience to remember, and would have brought home to one how much we owe to these men of the footplate.

It was the May of 1941 and we had been through practically every raid on London, when a Government representative called on us and very courteously gave us fourteen days in which to find a new home. They wished to take over the south and best side of the building to house the greatly enlarged staff of a certain department. I remember asking the representative what they were proposing to do with our three luxurious bathrooms, and with a sense of humour not always associated with government officials he replied that he had not the remotest idea, as the encouragement of cleanliness on the part of the staff did not come in the regulations.

However, our ejection turned out to be a blessing in disguise, for we were fortunate in finding a charming house in Buckinghamshire which possessed a 'writey' small room on the first floor. Here I was able to get down to orchestrating a work which had come into my mind during the raids on London.

As soon as we had moved into the house we realised what a relief it was to us to be able to go to bed without the usual suitcase ready in case of emergency, and to know that we could sleep without the fear of being awakened at all hours of the night by the sound of falling bombs. In fact it seemed we had at last found a neighbourhood where we could relax for a space and where I should be able to get down to my new orchestral work without fear of interruption.

Writing music is a strange business and there does not seem to be any explanation of why certain conditions bring about in me what Phyl calls my 'broody state'. I believe I said earlier on in this narrative that the drinking of tea has the effect of making me want to write—also, if I become bored in a crowd or listen to many people talking at once, my 'muse' becomes active, and any excessive noise has the effect of stimulating my imagination to such an extent that it would require a mechanical hand to put my ideas down on music-paper, so rapidly do they come to me.

Only those who know me intimately can tell when this state is upon me and sometimes I have known Phyl, while we are together in some noisy restaurant, to wave a hand across my face with the words: "Come back, you're not here!" There is a small dark room somewhere in my head that only I myself am acquainted with, and once I open the door and close it gently behind me, I can always be assured of being safe from interference. I go inside, but instead of turning on the light I turn on the music—and it rarely fails.

So whenever an air-raid warning sounded, or three rings from the bell told me that enemy aircraft were heading this way, or the guns in Hyde Park set up their staccato racket, I knew that the little dark room was waiting to receive me and give me its wealth of musical sounds which, in the sanctuary of its peaceful protection, I was free to collect and commit to my manuscript paper.

The long delay before I was able to put my ideas down on paper had been the means of 'Four Centuries' growing in my mind so completely that the actual orchestrating was not unlike musical dictation. The writing-room in our temporary house in Buckinghamshire, after we had been there for a couple of weeks and I had become accustomed to its atmosphere, was literally impregnated with musical sounds, and the next two months saw me, day in, day out, working on the score in which I have endeavoured to describe music of the seventeenth, eighteenth, nineteenth and twentieth centuries, beginning with the Fugue, leading through the Pavane and Tamourin to the Valse and concluding with present-day Jazz.

It was writing in ideal surroundings. And so the work which I had dreamed about under the stress of air-raids came to life in the quiet of this peaceful place.

It was eight months before it was possible to arrange a first performance, but the wait was well worth while. I can still see Stanford Robinson smiling darkly at me over the full-score and the top of my grand-piano, as I struggled with the intricacies of the syncopation of the last movement in a thumb-and-first-finger attempt to give him some idea of how it went, but the broadcast which was to follow showed that I must have acquitted myself better than I had thought. The performance was brilliant, but then, when Robbie presents a work for the first time you may be sure he will never let it down, his one thought being to present the music exactly as the composer intended.

There was some talk of my conducting the first performance myself, but Robbie suggested his taking over the actual 'first' and my doing a 'second'—"You know, Eric," he said, "it's good for you to hear what your work sounds like over the radio in somebody else's hands, and then you'll know how it goes!" There was sense in what he said, so I stayed at home and listened, somewhat relieved to be rid of the responsibility which always attends the launching of a new work, although I think if it had been otherwise I should have been spared the helpless suffocation which attacked me the moment the announcer came to the microphone. Some months later I ran into Robbie's principal flautist and congratulated him on his lovely tone and the way in which he played the opening cadenza to the first movement, and was delighted to hear he had taken his first lessons on the flute with the old friend who, all those years ago in Nottingham, had initiated me into the mysteries of the Boehm System and who had started me on my short career as a flautist.

Some three years later, 'Four Centuries', in a small way, was to make musical history in this country. It was the occasion of my conducting the National Symphony Orchestra in a recording session at the Kingsway Hall. My old friend, Victor Olof, who was in charge of the orchestra as well as the balancing, had enlisted for the last movement the services of a well-known team of saxophonists and also special trumpet players who, at one time or another, had had dance band experience. I believe it was the first time that a recognised Symphony Orchestra in this country had departed from the 'straight' and gone over to the 'dance', but it was remarkable (after half an hour's rehearsing to become acquainted with the unfamiliar medium) how quickly the musicians picked up the style. Where jazz is concerned, the tendency over here, on the part of some members of a Symphony Orchestra, is to sit back and smile at something which they think is beneath their notice and needs no rehearsing—so for the first few minutes of the session I had the gravest doubts as to whether I should achieve a recording, for some of the players showed only too openly their desire to fool about. However, after explaining at some length that the movement was intended as a joke and that the effect of a good story was spoilt if you laughed in the telling, they entered into the spirit of the thing and gave me a performance with which I do not think Whiteman could have found much fault. Which brings me to the subject of the saxophone.

Unfortunately the penetrating tone-colour of this mainstay of the modern dance orchestra, unless used with great discretion, can change the character of a work so completely as to make it almost unrecognisable. The danger is that, unless used with meticulous care, its entrance into a piece has the effect of conjuring up in the minds of an audience the conglomeration of trap-drum paraphernalia with which it is normally associated.

I remember how Henry Wood, rather foolishly I thought, detested the saxophone; although his antipathy to this instrument was in a way excusable at the time, as he only heard it played on the annual occasion when the bass-clarinet player in the old Queen's Hall Orchestra unearthed, from out its locker underneath the platform, his neglected specimen of the Firm of Sax, and gave a performance of the famous melody in Bizet's incidental music to 'L'Arlésienne' in a pitch that was contrary to the rest of the orchestra. Later, however, I often wondered, on watching Wood take the B.B.C. Symphony Orchestra through a dramatic performance of Ravel's 'Bolero', what he must have been thinking, with a complete team of saxophones lending their penetrating tone to the tremendous build-up. Perhaps by that time he had succumbed to popular taste and had fallen a victim to the saxophone's allure!

* * * * *

Once again we were on the move, this time to the hills of Hampstead. We had toyed with the idea of buying the house in which I had worked so hard and which Phyl loved on account of its sunny south and west aspect, with its views over the Buckinghamshire hills, and its prolific garden. But the coming of autumn with its chilly nights made us realise that, with the fuel restrictions then in force, it would not be a pleasant place in which to spend a winter. Our new home in Old Hampstead was what the agents described as 'An Eighteenth-Century Gem'. When we were first shown over it we could not help but be astonished at the artistic care and thought which had been lavished on every part of the delightful place. At first we were not sure whether we could put up with the old original sloping floors upstairs (harbourers of mice and moths), but the idea that the cottage was at one time the stables of an old house which had sheltered Queen Anne, and which was still approached through a wrought-iron gate at the side of the garage, appealed so greatly to historically-minded Austin that we did not like to disappoint him. This, and the knowledge that the twenty-five-foot garage would house the twelve-cylinder 'Yank' so beautifully, decided it.

Our stay in Hampstead was not a success. My piano refused to take the stairs up to my writing-room, which meant that I was obliged to work in the drawing-room, conscious that Austin in the room above me was unconsciously listening to me each time I went to the piano to try out a theme and that I was not only preventing him from working on his books, but causing him to refrain from putting a recording on his gramophone out of respect for my sensitive ears below. It was an impossible situation and between the two of us any sort of serious work was out of the question. The journeys into the West End (quite bad enough with the motor-car in commission), with the coming of more drastic petrol restrictions, became impossible, and the eventual laying up of the vehicle altogether, added to an intensely cold winter which laid me out completely for some months, finished us so far as Hampstead was concerned.

The cottage, lovely as it was, was so difficult of approach that we could not expect our friends to come to see us, let alone *find* us, and, so far as I can recollect, the only people who ever braved the heights of the desolation of our surroundings were G. H. Clutsam ('Clutty'), Victor Olof, Harriet Cohen, Lionel Tertis (*he* came by car), W. H. Squire, Sir Granville Bantock, Stanford Robinson and Frederick Grisewood.

Freddie Grisewood's visit came on top of a nasty bout of bronchitis which was the beginning of several more attacks to follow and which eventually drove us back again to the warmer if perhaps less salubrious air of Baker Street. Freddie came to discuss the details of a broadcast of my music which was being given by Stanford Robinson, and found me sitting close to a roaring fire with a warm Jaeger shawl, known as the 'life-preserver', pulled snugly round my shoulders. The cold, as I said earlier, I consider to be an abomination and Hampstead had shown us that, in this respect, we might just as well have remained in Buckinghamshire. The 'life-preserver' had earned its name through, at one time or another, being worn by the members of the family on the occasions when any of them were laid up, but from a certain date it had been appropriated and used exclusively and more or less permanently by myself. This article of apparel evidently made such an impression on Freddie that in the broadcast a few days later he drew a vivid picture of the composer sitting on the settee with the shawl round his shoulders.

At that very moment this was exactly what I and the shawl were doing, and I was astonished at what appeared to be an unusual display of second-sight on Freddie's part.

The letters which dropped into the letter-box a couple of days later were even more astonishing: remedies from firms which dealt exclusively in 'cures' for bronchial ailments; prescriptions from ladies old and young; hand-knitted scarves; flannel jackets; pages of advice from all over the country and sundry boxes of pills. The intervention on the part of my doctor and a specialist, advising me to return to the warmth of a centrally-heated flat, saved me from the temptation of trying out each 'cure' in turn.

Bar a couple of orchestral marches, 1943 was practically a blank so far as writing music was concerned.

Casting about for ideas for another orchestral work, I was just about to begin making some pencil notes when an invitation came from Lord Kindersley and Sir Harold Mackintosh (later Lord Mackintosh) to write another march, this time for the 'Salute the Soldier' Campaign. Another march! I hesitated and said I would like a week in which to think about it, but the cause won me over and when Sir Harold called at the flat a week later I was able to show him the completed full-score and give him some idea of how it sounded, by playing it over to him on the piano. As he took his leave he handed us a box of his delicious Toffee de Luxe with the words: "You can't get *these* in London!" Didn't we know!

'Would I conduct the march on the opening day of the Campaign in Trafalgar Square?' It would be the full band of His Majesty's Scots Guards. Visions of a cold east wind made me think of the 'life-preserver' and the scarf. Should I be able to wear these? And then the idea of a conductor appearing in public looking like an old gentleman who had just got out of bed led to its being agreed that if there was any element which might prove dangerous to the state of my chest, my appearance would be cancelled. March 25th, 1944, the opening day of the 'Salute the Soldier' Campaign, turned out to be perfect. It was mild, with scarcely a breeze, and the sun shone on the thousands who had flocked to the great Square to welcome the famous men and women gathered on the beflagged platform. It was a wonderful send-off to a campaign which was to prove one of the most successful of the war.

*   *   *   *   *

In the raids of 1941 you were able to snatch some sleep during the day in preparation for what the evening was to bring, but with the flying-bombs (aptly nicknamed 'doodle-bugs' by our American friends), coming at all hours of the day and night, even this unnatural form of rest was more or less out of the question. It was an exhausting kind of existence and I became so tired that I had not the strength or even the desire to open the door which led into the peace and quiet of my little dark room—the little dark room about which I told you earlier on in this story.

What was the good of trying to write music?

We had been in London for five years almost without a break, we who had been used to moving about so freely with never more than a few weeks passing without a glimpse of the sea. I knew it must be possible to write music in war-time, even under shellfire, for had not a Russian composer achieved this remarkable, if not altogether artistic, feat? It was no use, I could not write a note, the incessant air-raid warnings and the 'doodle-bugs' saw to that, and even the little dark room had shut its door in my face. It was all too patent that my writing days were over.

*   *   *   *   *

In answer to a ring at the bell I went to the door and with a heavy heart took a letter out of the letter-box. Another income tax form, or an A.R.P. notice, or someone asking for an autograph. I opened the letter and read: 'Dear Sir, As a constant admirer of your very charming and essentially English light orchestral music, I am venturing to suggest to you a theme for a new Suite——'

Hardly a week passed without my receiving a letter from someone or other, suggesting an idea for musical treatment, ranging from an air-raid warning to a football final, and one enterprising correspondent had even gone so far as to think that a musical impression of a baby having its bath would make a wide appeal.

As the first idea was being done to death far too realistically at the moment, and football had never appealed to me, and Richard Strauss had already given us a vivid picture of His Majesty the Baby's bath-time in his 'Symphonia Domestica', I was spared a great deal of trouble.

I glanced at the letter, still unread before me, and with a resigned "Here we go again" prepared myself for the inevitable. Then suddenly I became interested, my attention focused and I read to the end. "Well," I said, turning to Phyl, "that's the best idea that anyone has ever given me."

Gone was my feeling of exhaustion, gone was my fear that I should write no more, forgotten were the air-raid warnings and the 'doodle-bugs'. My imagination was fired. The door into my little dark room opened wide of its own accord. The suggestion came from a clergyman,* a complete stranger to me, and was for an Orchestral Suite, to be called 'The Three Elizabeths': Elizabeth Tudor, Elizabeth of Glamis and the Princess Elizabeth. It was a perfect theme for musical treatment. So I sat down at my desk and began to sketch out some ideas.

At first the flying-bomb attacks on London were only sporadic, but as the days passed they became more and more frequent. During this time, however, the pencilled sketch of 'The Three Elizabeths, was completed, and thinking it would be a good idea to get down to the orchestration in a district which did not indulge in such luxuries as 'doodle-bugs', we packed our bags and boarded the 1.45 train from Paddington to the peace of the lovely Vale of Evesham.

Our bedroom looked across the Avon to the old abbey on the hill and through the great avenue of trees to where the grateful slopes of Bredon lay bathed in the glow of the setting sun. The only links with war were aircraft practising overhead, the occasional passing of a column of American tanks along the road underneath our window, and a weekly demonstration with the air-raid siren, which, the first time we heard it and notwithstanding that it failed to reach the peak of its compass, sent crowds of evacuees in search of shelter. It was the fruit season, of which we made the most, for at that time London was scantily served in this respect. We had not seen so many plums since the first days of the war, and the apples which came along in due course were equally plentiful. So prolific, in fact, was this land of plenty that when we despatched a basket of 25lbs. of plums to our friends in London we were told it would have been much simpler to have sent off a truck-load.

Life from then onwards consisted of orchestrating the new work, taking morning coffee in the town, sitting in the sun under the walls of the old abbey, or walking in the fields to where you could see the outline of the Malvern hills, with an occasional visit to Tewkes-

*The Rev. Arthur L. Hall, Vicar of Barnes.

bury, or Gloucester, or Cheltenham thrown in. Everything, however, revolved round the orchestrating of 'The Three Elizabeths', made as easy as possible by the kindly proprietor and his wife and the staff at the little hotel which was to be our home for nearly three months. Nothing was a trouble to them—we had come from London where the raids were, and that was enough.

The hotel being full, there was no sitting-room available, so each morning I took my manuscript into the downstairs lounge and tried to orchestrate, and at the same time carry on a disjointed conversation with whoever happened to come in and out.

I experience no difficulty in writing during a conversation, provided it is not directed at me, and have even worked in a room occupied by a crowd of bridge players holding noisy post-mortems every few minutes. I suppose the idea of being at close quarters with a composer in the throes may have been a little intriguing, but so far as I was concerned it did not help matters and might have had disastrous consequences to the ultimate shape and sound of the new work had it not been for the timely intervention of the barman, who volunteered the helpful and original suggestion that I should take my score into the seclusion of the bar, where I could work undisturbed until the opening ceremony at twelve noon. It was a most successful move, and here, each morning, I settled myself at one of the round beer tables, while my friend, vaguely conscious that what I was doing needed concentration, ignored me completely and attended to his own business of laying in sufficient liquor for the mid-day rush.

I don't believe the natives of these parts had the remotest idea of the ordeal through which Londoners had been going and which had now started up again in the shape of the flying-bomb, for if you were ever so injudicious as to mention the fact, you were usually rewarded with an incredulous look as if to say: 'You can't get away with *that* sort of thing down here,' and then would follow at length the dramatic story of the one *real* air attack which the district had suffered in the early stages of the war and which, in reality, had been a harassed Nazi pilot, jettisoning his bomb-load in a frantic attempt to escape our fighters. So we spoke no more of war and concentrated on orchestration and the cultivation of fruit. Phyl, after five years confined to London, almost forgot about the call of 'Sussex by the sea' and spent many hours scrutinising the bills displayed outside the local auctioneer's advertising 'attractive rural properties for sale', with a resolve to take up farming at once.

This craze for the acquiring of house property has always been a weakness of hers and must have been handed down to her from her mother, who at one time had an uncanny and most lucrative knack of buying houses, living in them for a while, and then selling them at a gratifying profit; very often, I regret to say, to the discomfort of any member of the family who may have been staying with her at the time. It is not conducive to a life of peace and quiet to be conscious that at any moment you may find yourself without a roof over your head, for my mother-in-law would sell her houses with never a thought as to her future place of residence. It was always: "My *dear* child, I shall find something quite easily," and although we always thought she never would, she always did. Houses, occupied and unoccupied (preferably the latter); old furniture shops; sales of every description, except motor-cars (farm tractors and bulldozers, while the farm urge was upon her, being the exception to the rule); junk shops of every kind; even blocks of modern flats and, in some cases where the possibilities of bringing them up-to-date did not present insurmountable difficulties, the old-fashioned large-roomed high-windowed type with no lifts and no central heating: all these things held a fascination for Phyl and, I must admit, up to a point I grew to share her interest, especially in the renovating and modernising of old houses. But, thank heaven, up to the present she has not succumbed to the temptation of investing in an hotel.

In all fairness to Phyl, however, I must say that her buying and selling adventures have developed in her a kind of sixth sense which on many occasions has proved itself to be an attribute well worth the possessing. We want an old oak bureau: now oak bureaux at any time, and especially old ones, are very difficult to come by, but she goes down an unfrequented side street in wherever she happens to be at the moment, and there it is sitting conveniently in a shop window.

We want a cottage in Sussex: now cottages in Sussex, especially those on the coast, are practically impossible to buy, but she strolls quietly down a lane leading to the sea in the little village which we had not seen since 1939, and there, staring her in the face and only one and a half minutes from a perfect bathing beach, is the cottage. I tell her she has missed her vocation in not setting up as a clairvoyante house agent, but she tells me she's afraid that if she fell to the depths of commercialising her gift she might lose it altogether, and then, what should we do?

* * * * *

We were once more in London, sorry that the completion of the full-score meant saying goodbye to lovely Worcestershire, but glad to be back amongst our belongings, despite the fact that the flying-bombs were still coming over. Her Majesty the Queen had very graciously accepted the dedication of my new work, and Dr. Victor Hely-Hutchinson, Arthur Bliss's successor at the B.B.C., had arranged a first performance to take place on Christmas Eve in the 'Music For All' Series at Bedford, with the B.B.C. Symphony Orchestra and myself conducting.

So the day before Christmas Eve we journeyed in the snow down to Bedford, where the B.B.C. Symphony Orchestra, for want of a Concert Hall in London, had made its home for the time being. I had been warned that the Symphony Orchestra was too cumbersome a body to attempt anything in the popular vein, but the morning of the rehearsal was to prove how wrong these cynics were, for the musicians (and there were ninety-five of 'em) played with as much 'snap' and rhythm as any orchestra it has been my good fortune to conduct. As I took them through the first movement of 'The Three Elizabeths' I caught a fleeting impression of the atmosphere which pervaded the Spa, Scarborough, in the days when Alick Maclean held sway, for there, seated on my left, still leading the orchestra as he did in those almost legendary times and looking scarcely a day older, was Paul Beard.

* * * * *

The 'doodle-bugs' had now been practically displaced by an even more terrible and barbarous German 'horror', the rocket, and once again we experienced a sense of relief at being fifty miles away from the target zone. So peaceful was it at the hotel by the old bridge, and so welcome were we made by the charming manager and his wife and the attentive and obliging staff, that we decided to make it our home for the next three months, and here I edited the printed band-parts of the new work, while Phyl enjoyed a well-earned respite, interspersed with much entertaining in the hotel and periodical visits to London to see if the flat still stood.

I could write a book about the diversity of people who came in and out of this homely place: B.B.C. artists drifting in for an early meal before a broadcast; R.A.F. pilots coming in 'after hours' for a well-earned 'refresher', following a raid over Berlin; romances materialising under one's nose, some delightful and others too often sordid; little 'Wrens' making themselves up in their rooms in Toc H. just across the road from our bedroom window, in preparation for spending the evening with the smart-looking, soft-spoken young American soldiers waiting for them on the pavement below; burly and fully-armed American M.P.s coming over to the hotel, in response to an S.O.S. from the manager, to prevent the bar from being smashed up by a crowd of excited 'Yanks' who had discovered that our 'Export' beer was too strong for them; the standing invitation to Frederick Grisewood to join us for lunch when he came down from London to compère the 'Music For All' programme every other Sunday, and the stories which followed, one on top of another, which usually meant the time passing so quickly that he stayed on to tea.

They are happy memories, these memories of our stay by the Ouse—and where in the world could you find a hotel in war-time in which you could be ill (as I was) more comfortably than in any nursing home and which possessed a head-waitress who could produce tea and biscuits in your bedroom at all hours of the day and night?

* * * * *

The war was over, and our first thought was to get down to the sea once again. We had the twelve-cylinder 'Yank' taken out of store and, motoring down to the little village on the Sussex coast, we stayed in rooms not far from the Point and Phyl scoured the district in search of a house. As usual, she found the ideal place, and here we stayed on and off until the summer of 1946, when I was invited by the Chairman of the Performing Right Society to be a member of a delegation which was going over to the United States to attend an International Congress of Composers and Authors at Washington. I accepted the invitation on condition that Phyl should accompany me, and one still autumn afternoon we found ourselves in the Pullman borne away to Southampton, where the *Aquitania* was waiting to take us over to Halifax, whence we were to take train to New York.

The *Aquitania* was still in commission as a troopship and we were both very worried as to whether I should be quartered with the men and Phyl with the women. However, all was well, for when we climbed up the gangway it was to take up combined quarters in a comfortable state-room with bathroom.

We were a party of four, the other two being C. F. James and G. H. Hatchman, respectively general manager and assistant general manager to the Performing Right Society, affectionately known to us as Jimmy and Gerald. The rest of the delegates were going by air later.

* * * * *

The weather favoured us—the Atlantic was as smooth as a millpond and, according to the staff, the smoothest crossing they had ever experienced. Nevertheless, just to be on the safe side, the three of us persisted with precautionary seasickness remedies; and even if they did nothing else, I expect they helped to sleep off the results of the sort of meals which, until we got on board, had been denied us for nearly five years.

Halifax was reached without event and here we boarded the train for New York—Phyl and I enjoying the luxury of a private 'drawing-room' in which we could go to bed at whatever hour we pleased, without having to don night attire behind recalcitrant curtains while a discreet car attendant waited patiently to put out the lights.

I remember how impressed we were with the beauties of the St. Lawrence River, along whose banks the train wended its tortuous way, and the regret we felt on leaving the rocky country for the flat plains ahead, although these too were not without their charm. It was a novelty for Phyl to be waited on by coloured attendants—boys who brought back memories to me of long train journeys in far-away days in South Africa—and she was so intrigued with their simple unaffected ways that at one time I thought it not beyond the bounds of possibility that we might be saddled with one as a permanent servant. However, we reached New York without encumbrance and were soon settled in a comfortable hotel where, on coming down to dinner on our first evening, we were greeted over the radio with the strains of 'Sleepy Lagoon'.

I love New York with its endless rush of streamline motor-cars, its skyscrapers, its elevators, its coloured drugstore assistants, and even Broadway with its myriads of multi-coloured flashing advertisements, so characteristic of the life of this great city. One hears much about the so-called garishness of New York, but I must say it never seems so to me. Neither do I find the skyscrapers anything but things of beauty to delight the eye. To look down on New York of an evening from the summit of one of these gigantic towers is a thing to remember, and I am sure that if Turner had been alive to see the loveliness of a sunset turning the thousands of windows in the Chrysler and R.C.A. buildings into tiny balls of burnished gold, he would never have left his easel until he had immortalised the scene in his inimitable way.

* * * * *

Prior to going on to Washington to attend the Congress (which, as a special honour, was to be held in the Library of Congress) the American Society of Composers, Authors and Publishers (the sister society to the P.R.S. in London) had arranged a round of luncheon parties and receptions which kept us in New York for nearly a week.

This was an opportunity for us to pay our respects to Max Dreyfus, Louis Dreyfus's elder brother and the head of the firm of Messrs. Chappell & Co., Inc. in New York and commonly known in the extensive offices in the R.K.O. Building as 'the Boss'.

I think we must have lived six months during those six hectic days: shopping; lunching and dining in drugstores and expensive restaurants; going to theatres, music-halls and night-clubs; drinking gins and tonics and consuming salted peanuts into the early hours of the morning in the bar at our hotel (the only times we could ever get alone together); attending official luncheons and receptions and, through it all, trying to get used to the over-efficient central heating with New York in the throes of a heat wave.

* * * * *

Once again we were on the move, the foursome of the *Aquitania* being joined by delegates from nearly every country in the world: Britons, Danes, Swedes, Norwegians, Dutch, French, Belgians, Canadians, Argentinos, Brazilians, Spanish and Portuguese—and all *en route* for Washington to discuss all things relating to the important matters of Performing Rights.

* * * * *

We stayed at the Shoreham Hotel, where we were allotted a delightful suite looking on to the gardens at the rear. Our stay in what is considered to be the second finest hotel in the world was somewhat spoiled by practically the whole of the hotel staff being on strike, and instead of enjoying breakfast in bed we had to resort to getting what we could in the drugstore attached to the building. However, the drugstore turned out to be excellent and, apart from official and private luncheons in the city, most of our meals were taken here.

Then began the serious business of the meetings in the Library of Congress, interspersed with visits to Arlington and the Tomb of the Unknown Warrior, or along the banks of the Potomac to Mount Vernon and the charming home of George Washington, or to Georgetown with its lovely eighteenth-century houses; and at the close of each day there were supper parties in most of the famous restaurants, one of which stands out in my memory as being just like the dinner party the night before I left Stockholm on my first visit there in 1936, except that the traditional Swedish songs had given place to the tango and the rumba.

The climax to the Congress came with a banquet given in honour of the delegates at the Ritz Carlton in New York. Everyone of note in the musical and literary life of New York seemed to be there, including some celebrities from other countries. I was very intrigued when, each time the band played some popular number by one of the composer guests, the applause that followed was the signal for the composer himself to rise from his seat at the table to bow his acknowledgments. So fascinated was I watching composers bobbing up and down and wondering where the next bob was coming from that, not only did I almost forget to eat what was put before me, but it was only by the merest chance that I pulled myself together sufficiently to rise to my feet at the close of 'Sleepy Lagoon'.

One of my pleasantest recollections of our visit was conducting the Columbia Broadcasting System's orchestra in New York in a broadcast of my music in a series entitled 'Invitation to Music'. This was my first encounter with an American orchestra and I was a little apprehensive as to how the musicians would receive me. I need not have worried, for they were with me from the start, and when it came to the interval and they crowded round the rostrum, asking me 'how were the boys in London', it was just as if I were talking to our own musicians at a rehearsal at Broadcasting House.

Just before the actual transmission, I was very amused when the Director rushed in to the studio and wrathfully told us that a rival station had 'done it again!', meaning that another broadcasting company had got in before us and had broadcast my entire programme on records. What it is to live in a land of competition!

So we said goodbye to our hospitable American hosts and boarded the *Aquitania* once again, this time in New York, after having been informed by the Customs officials that America wanted 'guys' like me and that the next time I paid them a visit they would see to it that I had a permit to stay for two years.

* * * * *

I do not know whether it was the unexpected heat wave in the States or the over-efficient central heating in hotels and places of amusement or the going up from our warm state-room in the *Aquitania* to the icy wind on the upper deck, but once again my chest began to trouble me and by the time we were back at the flat I was literally gasping with an acute attack of bronchial asthma. What was even worse was that I was due to fly over to Copenhagen in a week's time to conduct for the Danish Broadcasting Corporation.

A long consultation with my doctor ended in my making up my mind to take the risk. To this day I do not know how I managed to go through with it. I think the Danish Press had a suspicion that my arrival at the airport smothered in scarves was a 'stunt', the scarves being alluded to as 'a picturesque sight', and, judging by the advance reports, my so-called asthma was nothing more serious than a 'cold'. The fact that the Broadcasting Hall had been sold out in a matter of minutes, when my Danish friends knew I was making my first appearance there since the war, apparently did not impress certain sections of the Press, and I do not think I can resist the temptation of quoting verbatim some of the outspoken allusions, not only to myself and my music but also to the audience, that appeared in the papers the morning after the concert: 'Coates can be adapted to anything, from a large orchestra to a single harmonium; this is a practical but somewhat wearisome method when one has to spend an evening listening to a series of works in which the instruments merely duplicate one another . . . excellent entertainment for the dense audience, which was in high spirits and clapped loudly.' '. . . bouquets and a fanfare for the famous guest of the evening.' '. . . one was compelled to sit and listen to all of his insipid waltzes, facile suites and quick marches, the whole being slightly *passé* . . . conducted with routine superiority by Coates, who received a tremendous ovation from his delighted audience.' 'Coates is indeed without any kind of artifice, conventional and polished like a man of the world and yet—behind the impeccable shirt-front there is after all a heart beating, and the elegant monocle cannot conceal the fact that his eyes are smiling. His society is therefore pleasant, in spite of everything.'

So, late the following afternoon, I said goodbye to my warm-hearted Danish friends and, still smothered in scarves and feeling very ill, I boarded the airliner which was to bring me back to London. After the almost vibrationless flight out in the luxuriously-appointed Danish Dakota the contrastingly noisy journey home was compensated for by my being invited by the friendly pilot to sit in the cockpit. Here, over the darkness of the North Sea, he did his best to teach me in fifteen minutes a profession in which it must have taken him years to become an expert.

Another contrast, on arriving over London, was to see nothing but gloom on every hand, only a few dismal street-lamps being visible—so different from the hundreds of thousands of twinkling lights that, even in 1946, turned Copenhagen into a city of enchantment by night.

Determined to take myself in hand, I started on a concentrated course of breathing exercises under the direction of our next-door neighbour, before the war a well-known professor of singing and elocution in Vienna. Scientific deep breathing and the consumption of vast quantities of Scott's Emulsion (the latter sceptically smiled upon by my doctor) put me into a better state of health, and by the early spring of 1947 I was feeling more my old self.

With the advent of June came our friends from across the Atlantic to attend the 14th Congress of the International Confederation of Composers and Authors, which was to be held in London. It was now our turn to see what we could do to repay our hosts of the previous year for the lavish way in which they had entertained us during our stay in the States. The Chancellor of the Exchequer, Sir Stafford Cripps, performed the opening ceremony at Lancaster House (where the meetings were to be held) and from then onwards, and when official functions permitted, a round of entertainment had been arranged by the Performing Right Society, including visits to the Houses of Parliament, Windsor Castle, Eton, Greenwich, Glyndebourne (to hear Benjamin Britten's latest opera), and a banquet at the Mansion House very kindly given by the Lord Mayor of London.

The month lived up to its name of 'flaming June'; the weather was glorious and everything went with a swing. Added to the official luncheons and dinner parties, Phyl and I had arranged private parties of our own for our 'specials', some of whom stayed on in London after the Congress was over. The night before the departure of any big liner from Southampton was usually an excuse to make our adieux to some of our one-time hosts, in the form of a supper party at the Savoy, where we had a table on the floor close to Carroll Gibbons, who entertained us with some of his inimitable rhythm versions of the classics.

Our last guests were Deems Taylor and his charming wife, Lou. Deems Taylor was at that time the President of the American Society of Composers, Authors and Publishers, and besides being a famous radio commentator in the States, a composer of repute. I remember how astonished he was at himself to find that his musical susceptibilities were not outraged when the clientèle at the Savoy danced to the music of the Great Masters; even fragments of Beethoven's 'Sonata Pathétique' failing to rouse him to criticism. Whether this was due to Carroll Gibbons's sensitive 'jazzing' of the Masters or the Bollinger non-vintage champagne, we were never able to discover.

* * * * *

The winter of 1947-48 was marked by my not having to take to my bed with my habitual bronchial bouts and I thought that, at long last, I had rid myself of the trouble for good. However, in the summer of 1948 once again I contracted a nasty cough that nothing seemed able to move. Then what looked like a heaven-sent opportunity to 'build myself up' came in the form of another invitation from the Chairman of the Performing Right Society, for Phyl and me to attend a Congress in Buenos Aires. We accepted with alacrity, and on September 18th we found ourselves on board the m.v. *Highland Brigade* with the prospect of three weeks' relaxation ahead of us. Gerald Hatchman (of the foursome of the *Aquitania*) was with us and also Sir Alan Herbert (representing Literature). A.P., as we have always called him, proved to be an insatiable worker and, if he was not buried in his Spanish text-book he was either writing poems and articles for the London Press or taking navigational bearings at all hours of the day and night with an instrument that only he seemed to understand. The ship being filled to capacity, he and Gerald shared a cabin and, judging by what the latter recounted to us of repeated visits to the upper deck in the middle of the night for A.P. to point out to him some constellation which was not visible in the Northern Hemisphere, it was not to be wondered at that he spent a good deal of the day making up for the sleep which had been denied him at night. The three weeks' relaxation turned out to be twenty-four days of cocktail parties and sightseeing and, on crossing the Line, the inevitable King Neptune ceremony with all its attendant ritual. Phyl and I shared the pleasures of the cocktail parties and the sightseeing and she entered into the fun of the Neptune ceremony despite the fact that she was in the grip of a feverish cold. I was officially exempt from the Neptune proceedings by virtue of having crossed the Line when on my way to South Africa in 1908. I must add that Phyl, hoping to avoid a compulsory immersion by the three bears who were waiting for her in the bathing-pool below, executed one of the neatest dives I have ever seen, only to be 'ducked' for her trouble. I enjoyed the calls the ship made at the various ports *en route*—Vigo, Lisbon, Las Palmas and Rio—but as the temperature rose the further south we journeyed, so my breathing became worse.

About an hour before we sailed from Rio, a couple of ladies came on board to see me—they were mother and daughter. The mother asked me if I could cast my mind back to the old days with 'the Hamilton' in Clifton Gardens. We had been boarders there together over forty years ago!

A day and a half was spent in Santos. Here we were taken by the Consul up into the mountains to São Paulo, and after lunching with the local celebrities, we visited the famous Snake Farm and had to look down the throats of wicked-looking reptiles, which had been picked out specially for our benefit from a writhing mass on the floor of the pit by an unruffled but carefully gaitered keeper. The Broadcasting Station in São Paulo had arranged a couple of broadcasts of my music on records and, to liven up the proceedings, I was interviewed at the microphone and asked leading questions on the subject of my brother composers in England, personal questions about myself, the European situation and, what I thought of Brazil!

One more port of call before we reached Buenos Aires—this being Montevideo, where I was invited by the charming Head of the English School to give a talk on my music, with gramophone illustrations, to his 400 pupils. At first I was inclined to refuse on account of my asthmatic trouble, but in the end I consented, and when I saw the delighted faces of my young audience, I was glad I had done so.

At last, early on a Tuesday morning, three days late, we turned in to the River Plate and in the space of a few hours we had reached our destination. I don't think that either of us had ever felt as tired in our lives as when, eventually, we tied up at the quayside. I had felt ill practically the whole way out and Phyl had not stood up to the journey very well, partly because of the excessive changes of temperature and partly because of her anxiety for me. At any rate we were *thankful* that, the voyage over, we could get to our hotel, unpack our trunks and enjoy a good sleep.

We were soon to be disillusioned. The Press, the British Broadcasting Corporation's representative, the representatives of the Performing Right Society, the British Council and our South American hosts were all there to greet us and, before we knew where we were, we were in the midst of introductions, interviews and flashlight pictures and finally we were rushed into streamlined motor-cars and taken by our enthusiastic hosts to a race-meeting, where, until late afternoon, we were backing, with borrowed pesos, horses which up to that moment we had never heard of.

* * * * *

I will not bore my reader with matters relating to the Congress—suffice it to say that, under the leadership of our Chairman, Leslie Boosey (the head of the firm of Boosey & Hawkes and son of the late Arthur Boosey, who gave me my first chance by publishing my early songs), it proved to be a great success. The satisfactory outcome of the negotiations with the Argentinos was to a great extent due to his untiring energy, added to the friendly co-operation of *el Presidente*, Peron.

* * * * *

It was like an early autumn in England. We stayed at a modern hotel in Tucuman, only a few yards distant from the famous Florida (the shopping centre so akin to our own Bond Street in London), and in glorious sunshine we would wander of an early morning up and down its winding length, in company with the crowds that thronged this fascinating thoroughfare. And I suddenly realised that my bronchial asthma had left me. I could scarcely believe it when I found I could stride along at Phyl's side without having to stop every few yards to regain my breath. What had brought about this sudden change in me I could not imagine, but at any rate it enabled me to do some broadcasting: a concert and broadcast for the Radio Provincia in La Plata and a studio broadcast for the Radio del Estado in Buenos Aires. The broadcast in La Plata was a novel experience.

In Argentina it is the custom to advertise a concert only two days before the event. My concert at La Plata happened to follow a two days' holiday in celebration of Peron's liberation from prison, prior to his rise to power, and, no newspapers having been issued during these two days and correspondingly no advance notices of my appearance, the prospect of playing to an empty house was alarming. We arrived at the State Theatre to find a symphony orchestra of about ninety players already seated on the stage in readiness for the final rehearsal and concert (which ran concurrently) only to be met by the director of the theatre with a veritable tirade in a language of which one of the only words I know is *mañana*, and when I distinguished this word recurring again and again I feared the worst. Fortunately, George Hills, the B.B.C. representative in Buenos Aires, was with us and, his Spanish being fluent, he was able to handle a situation that was becoming complicated.

I was for going back to Buenos Aires, to dinner and to bed, but it appeared that if I did not conduct either that night or the next (*mañana*) I should offend the State, and as I was due to broadcast in Buenos Aires the following night there was no getting out of it. George Hills showed a resource that was worthy of the Duke of Wellington. He commandeered motor-cars and, with loud-speakers proclaiming the 'first appearance in Argentina of the famous English composer *in person*, etc. etc.', they paraded the streets of La Plata and produced an audience that would have done credit to any orchestral concert in London.

As in New York, I was apprehensive as to how the orchestral musicians would react to an Englishman coming into their midst, especially as I had heard that the only music they accepted alternated between the classics and the tango, the popular orchestral works only being heard through the medium of recordings over the radio. I need not have worried, for I was soon to discover what an enthusiastic and responsive lot they were—and they gave me of their best.

At the rehearsals it was difficult at first to make myself understood, but with the aid of Italian musical terms, a few words of Spanish and the good offices of George Hills, added to a clear beat, all went smoothly, the performance that followed being little short of remarkable. After the first rehearsal the principal viola (who had seemed vaguely familiar to me) came into my dressing-room and, holding out his hands, "Señor," he cried, "do you remember me? I met you in the artists' room: Durban, 1908—the Hambourg String Quartet!"

The broadcast at Buenos Aires the next evening went off satisfactorily, but we were amused to find that, at the last moment, it was put back half an hour later than the advertised time. Time means nothing in Argentina.

* * * * *

Shortly after our arrival in Buenos Aires we were joined by William Walton, fresh from a holiday in Italy, whence he had come direct to Argentina. We saw a good deal of him during the Congress as we were staying in the same hotel in Tucuman. I remember he was in the throes of trying to find inspiration for a violin sonata which was overdue for delivery, and he had a nasty cold and (one thing we had in common) he carried a clinical thermometer about with him. I can still see him sitting with us late into the night, looking the picture of distress, while he opened his heart to us over his inability to choose the right woman to take as his wife. I am rather inclined to think that he had known all along he had made up his mind to marry the attractive South American who is now Lady Walton. But then, William Walton is like his music: quicksilver.

* * * * *

When I think of all that we did during our short stay in Argentina it makes me realise what steaks and good Argentine wine did for us. All the same, these advantages did not tempt me to accept an offer to remain in Argentina for three months to tour the country conducting my music. The lavish hospitality the South Americans had extended to us in ten days had convinced me that, had it continued for another twelve weeks, I should not have been alive to have told the tale.

Towards the end of our stay, we were taken to lunch at La Cabaña Restaurant by our friend George Hills and I shall always remember the special dishes that were set before us by a *maître* anxious to please an old and valued client and his two 'distinuigshed English guests'. As we were leaving the restaurant the *maître* asked me if, when I returned to England, I would send him a copy of 'Sleepy Lagoon'. On my assuring him that I would do so he gave me his best smile and, leading us to the door, gracefully bowed us out with: "An Englishman, like a Basque, keeps his word", which saying was written on the copy I sent him a few weeks later.

The 15th Congress of the International Confederation of Composers and Authors came to an end, and on October 21st we were on the deck of the r.m.s. *Andes* saying goodbye to our many friends, some old and some new, who had done so much to make our all-too-short stay in Argentina so enjoyable. With shouts of *'hasta luego'*, *'hasta pronto'* and *'hasta proximo'* ringing in our ears and much sounding of sirens and the flashing of searchlights, we moved slowly off—and as we slipped away into the gathering dusk we leaned over the rail to catch one last glimpse of our little group of 'specials' standing on the quayside affectionately waving their farewells.

*　*　*　*　*

As I sit at my desk writing, it has struck me how strange a thing is this 'call' for a country or a city or a countryside. England, with all its drawbacks, has the most insistent call of all for me, for no matter what part of the world I am in and however lovely and colourful it may be, it is always a relief to return to England. Even when we came away from the brilliance of the Broadway lights to find ourselves in the darkness of Leicester Square and Piccadilly Circus in the autumn of 1946 we were thrilled to be home, and after the glorious colours of the South American Continent it was good to be amongst green fields again.

I believe our friends across the water say that we haven't got a climate over here—we've only got 'weather'. After my experiences abroad I think I vastly prefer 'weather' to 'climate', if the samples which it has been my lot to encounter come under the latter heading.

When I look out of my writing-room window on a foggy morning in April and am inclined to complain at having to switch on the light, I think of the ceaseless glare of a tropical sun, and if at the height of our English summer I feel the need of a shawl about my shoulders, I cast my mind back to the discomfort of trying to keep cool in the centre of the South Atlantic.

No, give me England with its glorious uncertainty and you can have your countries where the weather comes round in regular cycles, for what is more lovely than the early spring that brings the flowers, the temperate warmth of summer, the mellowness of autumn, or the winter that gives us days remindful of another season?

* * * * *

It was a glorious morning in early autumn—we were on the road soon after breakfast and with Cheltenham behind us drove westwards through Gloucester and over the heights of Mitcheldean to Monmouth. Here we turned left to Raglan and then, turning left again in the town and taking an unclassed road, we went on until we came to the tiny hamlet which, once upon a time, I used to know so well.

We pulled up here at the very small petrol filling-station (worked by hand), where we took in a couple of gallons of petrol and asked to be directed to the rectory. While the proprietor of the garage ministered to my wants and a small crowd of villagers gathered round the Lincoln, I volunteered the information that I used to visit the rectory over fifty years ago, when I stayed with my aunt in Usk. This called forth from the owner the remark that that was about the time the rector had christened him.

When I told him that the Reverend Gentleman was my uncle, the old fellow looked up at me (he was very small) and in his lilting Welsh accent told me he could distinguish the family likeness. So, leaving the car close by the garage, we walked the few yards to the little lane that led up to my mother's old home. At the top of the hill stood the rectory, washed white and looking spotless. We approached the gateway leading to the drive up to the house and we stopped and looked and went no further. As we looked, I know that I, at any rate, saw a host of ghosts coming down the drive to meet us: my dear mother, Aunt Eliza Anne, Aunt Sarah Emma (Aunt Marjorie), Uncle James, Uncle Reginald, Uncle William, and Grandfather and Grandmother (whom I had never actually met when I was a child). They were all there, so much so that I had not the stomach to go up to the front door and ask the present rector if I might take some photographs of the house and garden —it seemed like sacrilege.

So we stood for a moment longer, Phyl obviously just as moved as I, then, turning and walking slowly down the hill back to the car, we reluctantly continued on our way to Usk, leaving behind us the scenes of my mother's childhood, both of us determined to return there at some future date to explore not only the rectory but also the little church the other side of the lane where so many of my forebears are buried.

It was a perfect day and the Welsh mountains kept rising up out of the distance as we drove quietly along the winding roads. Usk did not seem to have altered one whit since the time when I used to stay with my Religious Aunt at the charming house with the garden that led down to the river, where lived the cat that used to lop out fish with its paws.

We drove down the lane at the back of the house and saw the coach-house where Aunt Marjorie used to keep her Heath-Robinson contraption of a tricycle. We then crossed over the bridge and had a look at the house from the other side of the river, and very pretty it looked—just as it used to be, except that now it was coloured buff, whereas I had thought it was washed white—or perhaps I was wrong.

We then turned and called at the little grocer's in the main street to enquire who lived at the house by the old bridge. When the assistant (who, by the way, was a newcomer to Usk) said that the place had been converted into flats, I thought how horrified my Religious Aunt would have been if she could have known what the ravages of civilisation had brought about to her delightful home.

* * * * *

It seems a long cry to my childhood days in my old home in Nottinghamshire, although in many ways those peaceful times in the dusty lanes round Hucknall might have been but yesterday. Much has happened to me since I packed my bag that spring morning and, together with my viola, took the train which was to bear me southwards away from my native town to the adventures that lay ahead of me in the great city which was to be the inspiration for so much of my music. *'Exit hopeful musician with small viola case and big ideas.'* Little did I know how soon my hopes were to be realised and how blessed I was to be in my work.

The little bank on the road to Derby was soon nothing more than a distant reminder of what might have been my fate had I not had the good fortune to 'make good' in London. The 'small viola case' was soon to be laid on one side, never to be taken up again. There was a time when I yearned for the familiar sights of my native county; the scent of wood-smoke; of new-mown hay, or dusty roads after rain; the cuckoo's note in the wood beyond the fields; the song of the lark; the rusty call of the corn-crake; the soft hoot of the owl up on the Ramper road which runs from Nottingham to Mansfield; the bats flitting round my bicycle-lamp as I make my way slowly home after a long day in the pretty winding lanes, lovely in all weathers; unforgettable days with my father in Southwell; the little train far away in the distance wending its way across fields shimmering in the noon-day heat while everything around me is hushed in the silence which presages the impending storm.

Happy memories, these memories of my old home, but not untinged with regret. Regret that so many of the old familiar faces are missing and that the pretty winding lanes which my mother and I loved to explore together have, for the most part, been replaced by more modern roads to deal with the fast-moving traffic of to-day. Here and there, you may perhaps come across some spot hidden from the casual eye which recalls the peace and quiet which, once upon a time, permeated this lovely countryside. If you wend your way north-west you will still find the unspoilt beauty of Sherwood Forest waiting, in all its greenery, to give sanctuary to the tired wanderer—where the ancient oaks still look like little old gentlemen holding up their arms in supplication to a cloudless sky and the deer still browse in the shelter of its endless glades, while cool streams find their way across the grass as they flow gently down to their mother-stream the other side of the shire.

These memories of my early youth cause in me a feeling of nostalgia which brings in its train a drowsy desire to take my leave of noisy streets and go to the place which I used to know as my home. But I know full well that, however persistently I travelled the highways and the byways in search of the romance that once lingered there, my quest would only be doomed to disappointment.

So I turn once again to the city of my adoption and to the endless streets which have been such a source of inspiration to me—to my daily walks from Baker Street along Harley Street en route to my publishers in New Bond Street, which, in reference to an article that appeared in the *Daily Mail* some years ago stating that I got my musical ideas from a certain lamp-post in this famous thoroughfare, brought forth a host of letters from composers anxious for details as to the whereabouts of this theme-inspiring beacon.

I remember how, to relieve the monotony of the walks, I would go further afield by way of our beloved Queen's Hall, which would bring to my mind hot summer nights at the Promenade Concerts and the ache in my left hand telling me in no uncertain manner that before many months had passed my viola-playing days would be over. Or it might be a picture of Ysaye and Lionel Tertis giving a performance of Mozart's Double Concerto for Violin and Viola, Ysaye's towering frame overshadowing the smaller figure of his companion, but whose tone could not compare with that of Tertis in his prime.

Then the first appearance in London of Fritz Kreisler on the night I had paid my half-crown to sit behind the orchestra; or the début in this country of Jascha Heifetz, the 'violinists' violinist', and a host of bewildered instrumentalists, after the concert, threatening to take up some other profession.

Queen's Hall and memories of my first appearance as composer-conductor after having received my *congé* from Robert Newman; and holidays between the end of the Winter Season and the commencement of the Proms in August, holidays where Phyl and I were at one time haunted by landladies who would persist in possessing names associated with the sign Pisces: Miss Turtle, Mrs. Cuttle, Mrs. Salmon, Mrs. Crabbe, the dainty Miss Dabb and the Queen of them all, Mrs. Fish.

Queen's Hall— which, whenever I passed it, brought a sickening sensation to the pit of my stomach and made me conscious of the great strain to which I had been subjected during my seven years as principal viola in the old days of the Queen's Hall Orchestra.

* * * * *

So I turn once again to the city of my adoption, realising that it is the future that matters more than delving back into the days that used to be.

* * * * *

"Speak well back in your throat, Eric, and remember you are descended from the Welsh Kings." Poor Aunt Eliza Anne—how disappointed she would be if she were alive to-day and we had still not established our claim to the Welsh Throne. How clearly I can hear these words of counsel being delivered in that deep, aristocratic voice, followed by my brother's timely warning!

Several times during my life I have been tempted to take up the matter of my ancestors on my mother's side, the last time being not so long ago when we came upon the whitewashed rectory on the Welsh border with its windows looking across to where the mountains loomed dark in the distance. However, up to now I have let well alone and I shall continue to do so—just in case!

* * * * *

It is not an easy thing for the ordinary man to put his thoughts down on paper and, as I am a *very* ordinary man, the task of writing this autobiography has been all the more difficult. Set before me some music-paper or put a bâton in my hand and I feel instantly at home, but ask me to compose a difficult letter or make an impromptu speech and the little door, about which I have written previously, shuts in my face. Sometimes I feel singularly lacking when I find that others can do with ease the things I find impossible, but then I wonder what they would do with those same sheets of music-paper before them or that same bâton in their hands.

* * * * *

And so the time has come to say farewell. I have enjoyed reminiscing, especially about my childhood days in Nottinghamshire and my early days in London, and if I have reminisced too much or, from want of experience, have expressed myself inadequately, I trust my reader will make allowances for me, bearing in mind that the writing of words does not come so easily to me as the writing of music.

Had I known, when I began this book, the time and patience that would be needed in committing my thoughts to paper, I might have thought twice before embarking on such an undertaking. However, I have learnt my lesson and do not intend to be caught again, so lest the reader may think I have pretentions to blossoming out as an author, he need have no fears, for in future I shall stick to my music.

INDEX

'ABSENT - MINDED Beggar, The' (Sullivan), 29
Academy of Music, Royal, 42, 53, 54, 57–83 *pass.*, 86, 90–1, 101–6 *pass.*, 110–15, 129, 153, 159–63, 167–70, 191, 192, 223–4; C.'s scholarship at, 93, 95, 103
Ackté, 140
Adler, Larry, 223
Aeolian Hall, 110, 114
Agate, James, 222
'Agnus Dei' (Bizet), 188
Albert Hall, 119, 150, 181, 225
'Algerian Suite' (Saint-Saëns), 145
America, 214, 248–51
Amsterdam, 143, 232–3
Andes, r.m.s., 258
'Après - midi d'un faune, L' ' (Debussy), 47, 123, 151
Aquitania, s.s., 248, 251
Argentina, 254–8
'Ariadne auf Naxos' (R. Strauss), 121
'Arlésienne, L',' Suite (Bizet), 240
Ashwell, Lena, 120, 129–30, 223
Asthma, 251–2, 253–4, 255, 256
'Aus meinen leben' Quartet (Smetana), 47, 126
'Ave Maria' (Bruch), 176
AVRO (Amsterdam radio), 143, 223

BACH, J. S.: B Minor Mass, 137; St. Matthew Passion, 136–7, 144
Baker St., W., 213, 241
'Ballad for String Orchestra' (Coates), 42–3
Balloon, encounter with, 11
'Band-room technique', 75–6
Banking career, narrow escape from, 48, 51–4, 58, 93
Banks, Leslie, 200
Bantock, Sir Granville, 149, 241
Barbirolli, Sir John, 135
Barmouth, 22–3, 177–8
Bax, Sir Arnold, 47, 64, 79, 112, 113, 163
B.B.C., 181, 213–14, 218, 220, 222, 224–6, 228, 251, 255, 256 (*see also* Broadcasting)
B.B.C. Symphony Orchestra, 225, 240, 247

B.B.C. Theatre Orchestra, 215, 225, 236
Beard, Mr., 43, 46
Beard, Paul, 43, 218, 247
Beare, Arthur, 81
Bedford, 247
Beecham, Sir Thomas, 45, 120, 121–5, 127, 131, 136, 137, 152
Beethoven: Sonata Pathétique, 253; Violin Concerto, 47
Belfast, 226–7
Bernhardt, Sarah, 151
'Bird Songs at Eventide' (Coates), 179, 218
Birth, C.'s, 3–4
Black, Mrs., 164, 167, 169–71, 198, 245–6
Black, Phyllis, *see* Coates, Phyllis
Blakemore, Arthur, 135
Blenheim Restaurant, 63, 98, 101, 159, 164, 167, 168
Boer War, 29–30
Bohemian String Quartet, 41, 47, 73
'Bolero' (Ravel), 240
Boosey & Co., 110, 131, 180–1, 187, 203, 255
Boosey Ballad Concerts, 181, 191
Boosey, Alice, 182
Boosey, Arthur, 119, 180, 255
Boosey, Leslie, 255
Boosey, Ralph, 203
Boosey, William, 179–83, 186–7, 191, 203
Borsdorf, Oskar, 135
Bournemouth, 22, 128, 194, 206–7, 224
Bowen, York, 64, 79, 114
Bowler, Mr., 27–8, 97
Bowles, F. G., 183
Boyhood, 30–49
Brabazon, Lord, 223
Brahms: Clarinet Quintet in B Minor, 39–40, 47; F Major Quintet, 41; G Major Quintet, 41
Brain, Alfred and Aubrey, 135
Braithwaite, Hartley, 58, 64, 191
Brewer, Herbert, 50, 166
Bridge, Frank, 114–15, 154
Bridge, Sir Frederick, 28, 153–4

INDEX

Broadcasting by C., 135, 143, 213–14, 222–3, 228–9, 232–3, 251–2, 255, 256–7
Brooks, Arthur, 218
Brown, Godfrey, 226
Buckinghamshire, 238, 240, 242
Buenos Aires, 254–7
Bulldogs, 4, 8–9, 18–20, 104
Burke, Billie, 90
Burne-Jones, Sir Edward, 224
Burns, Robert, C.'s song-cycle from, 58
Buscher, de, 135
Busoni, 140
Butt, Clara, 140
Butterworth, Clara, 79
Byron, Lord, 16

'CALLING All Workers' March (Coates), 235–6
Calvé, 140
Cambridge Theatre, 214
Cameron, Basil, 94, 135, 143–4, 146, 203–4
Campbell, Mrs. Patrick, 151
Caruso, 140
Casals, Pablo, 129, 139, 140
Cathie, Philip, 125
Catterall, Arthur, 134, 140
'Cavalleria Rusticana' (Mascagni), 144–5
Cellier, François, 94–6
Cellists, 22, 27, 38, 40, 43, 79, 84–5, 102, 134, 139, 141
Celtic Quartet, 83–6, 102, 123, 125
Chamber music, 32, 33, 38–42, 47, 72–3, 80–6, 95, 102–10, 114, 125, 153
Chapman, Mr. (R.A.M. librarian), 77–8, 80
Chappell & Co., 179, 182–3, 191, 194, 203, 219–22, 236, 250
Chappell Ballad Concerts, 181, 183, 185–7, 190, 199
Charlot, André, 214
Cherniawsky Trio, 110
Chichester, 208–10, 230–1
Child, Annie, 162, 170
Childhood, 4–30
Churcham, 49–52, 165–7
Cinemas, appearances at, 233
Clarinet players, 39, 47, 123, 135
Clarke, Robert Coningsby, 181, 186
Clifton Gdns., W., 102–4, 114, 115 *ff.*, 254
Clutsam, G. H., 195–6, 241
Clutsam, Mrs., 195
Coates, Austin (son), 199–202, 209, 213, 216–17, 230–5, 241

Coates, Dorothy (sister), 6, 24–6, 28, 35
Coates, Gladys (sister), 6, 35
Coates, Gwyn (brother), 3, 6, 9, 10, 20, 34, 52
Coates, John, 128
Coates, Mary (mother), 4–6, 8, 11–12, 14, 21–4, 31, 33, 34–7, 48, 52, 96–7, 98, 100, 104–5, 259, 261
Coates, Meta (sister), 6, 24–6, 29, 35
Coates, Phyllis (wife), 4, 34, 119, 149, 159–79 *pass.*, 184–7, 192–202 *pass.*, 204–5, 208–10, 213–17, 220, 230–8, 240–1, 244–51, 253–62 *pass.*
Coates, W. H. (father), 4, 5, 7, 8, 10–24, 27, 28, 29, 30, 31, 32–5, 37, 43–6, 48, 52–4, 78, 81, 93, 97, 100, 104–5, 164, 169, 201–2, 260
Cohen, Harriet, 140, 241
Coleridge-Taylor, Samuel, 154
Colonne Orchestra, 145
Columbia Broadcasting System, 251
Columbia Gramophone Co., 218–20, 222
Composer, C., as, 27–8, 32–3, 42–3, 57–8, 67–8, 70, 75, 93, 96–7, 110, 112–14, 117–19, 130–2, 143, 145, 146, 149, 152, 163–4, 166, 168, 170–1, 175, 177–83, 185–8, 190–1, 193–4, 198–9, 202–4, 206, 208, 210, 213–15, 217–22, 225–9, 232, 235–6, 238–45, 252, 255, 261, 262–3
Composition, lessons in, 31, 32–3, 43, 48, 53, 62, 63–4, 68, 101, 103
Conductor, C. as, 135, 138, 143–4, 149, 177, 184, 190, 193–4, 202–4, 213, 215, 221, 225–9, 232–4, 236, 239, 242, 247, 251–2, 256–7, 262–3
Conductors, 45, 66, 87–9, 91, 94, 122–4, 126–8, 136–8, 139, 144, 147–55, 177, 184, 187–9, 199, 206
'Conversations' (Walford Davies), 149
Copenhagen, 135, 232, 251–2
Corder, Frederick, 53, 58, 59, 61–3, 71–2, 78, 97, 103, 106, 111, 112–13, 127, 159, 170
Cortot, Alfred, 129, 140
Courtneidge, Robert, 200
Covent Garden Theatre, 122, 189
Coward, Noël, 200
Cowen, Sir Frederic, 150
Cripps, Sir Stafford, 253
Cycling, 33–8, 97, 135–6, 260

Daily Express, 53, 222

INDEX

Daily News, 134
Daily Telegraph, 205
Dale, Benjamin, 64
Dale, Louise, 140
d'Alvarez, Marguerite, 140, 188
Daly's Theatre, 92
Dancing, ball-room, 202, 204–5, 208
'Dancing Nights' (Coates), 217
Davies, Ben, 129, 140
Davies, Fanny, 140
Davies, Sir Walford, 149
Davis, J. D., 114
Dawson, Peter, 129, 140
Dearth, Harry, 119, 128
Debussy, Claude, 47, 123, 150–1
Delius, Frederick, 129, 148
Devant, David, 128
D'Hardelot, Guy, 181, 183, 186
'Dinder Courtship, A' (Coates), 129
Dobbs, 49–52, 165, 167
Dog-shows, 17–18
'Dominoes', orchestral, 142–3, 177
'Don Juan' (R. Strauss), 150
'Don Quixote' (R. Strauss), 138–9, 145, 176
Draper, Haydn, 135
Dresden Opera Orchestra, 150
Dreyfus, Max and Louis, 250
Duncan, Peter, 222
Dunn, John, 41
Dvorák, Anton, 42, 63
Dyson, Arthur, 86–8, 90

Eardley-Wilmot, May, 183
Eastbourne, 149, 152, 153, 202, 203, 204, 206, 217
'Elektra' (R. Strauss), 122–3
Elgar, Sir Edward, 51, 147, 206–7
Elgar: 'Dream of Gerontius', 128; First Symphony, 123–4; 'In the South', 147; Serenades, 42; Violin Concerto, 206
Eliza Anne, Aunt, 3, 6, 22, 27–8, 259, 262
Elizabeth the Queen Mother, 247
'Elizabeths, The Three' Suite (Coates), 244–5, 247
Ellenberger, Georg, 30–3, 38–43, 47, 48, 52, 54, 71, 97
Ellenberger, Mrs. G., 30, 32, 38–40
Ellis, John Edward, 21
Ellison, John, 222
Elman, Mischa, 129, 140
Elsie, Lily, 91
Elwes, Gervase, 129, 132
'En Saga' (Sibelius), 145
'Enchanted Garden, The' (Coates), 215, 217, 233
Enesco, Georges, 145

Evesham, 244
Eyres, Arthur, 64

Fauré, Gabriel, 151
Finck, Herman, 129, 224
Finden, Amy Woodford, 181
'Fingal's Cave' Overture (Mendelssohn), 155
Flautist, C. as, 44–5, 48, 239
Flautists, 4, 44–5, 46, 80, 135, 239
'Florodora' (Stuart), 27–8
Folkestone, 228, 229
Forrest, Ada, 132
Forster, Dorothy, 79
'Fortnightlies', R.A.M., 78–9, 95, 115, 159, 167
'Four Centuries' Suite (Coates), 238–40
'Four Old English Songs' (Coates), 97, 106, 111, 112–13, 117, 130, 132
'Four Ways' (Coates), 204
Fransella, Albert, 80, 135
'Friday Concerts' at R.A.M., 64–5
Frognal, 195–8
Fur coat, advantages and disadvantages of a, 131–2

Galsworthy, John, 111
Garson, Greer, 222–3
Gauntlett, Ambrose, 135
Gerhardt, Elena, 140
German, Sir Edward, 62, 63, 80, 87, 111, 129, 147–8, 207–8
Gibbons, Carroll, 253
Gilbert, Sir W. S., 95–6
Gilbert and Sullivan Operas, 62, 93–5
Glazounov, Alexandre, 153
Gloucester, 50, 166
Godfrey, Sir Dan, 22, 44, 45, 128, 206–8
Goossens, Eugène, 135, 144
Goossens, Léon, 135
Goring-Thomas, 62, 63
Grainger, Percy, 129, 140
Gramophone, recording for, 218–19, 239–40
Greef, Arthur de, 140, 183
Green (R.A.M. factotum), 63, 65, 72, 76, 103, 113, 159
Greene, H. Plunket, 129, 140
Greenish, Dr., 162, 170
Grieg, Edvard, 42, 63, 129–30
Grisewood, Frederick, 241–2, 248
Gutteridge, 135

Hall, Rev. A. L., 244 *n.*
Hall, Vine, 48, 51–4, 97
Hallé Orchestra, 46

Hallett (R.A.M. hall porter), 101, 111–12, 159, 161–4, 169
Hambourg, Boris, 102–3, 108, 116, 125
Hambourg, Jan, 102–3, 116, 125
Hambourg, Mark, 103, 110, 129, 140
Hambourg, Prof., 103, 115
Hambourg String Quartet, 102–10, 114, 115–16, 125, 257
'Hamilton, the,' 115–17, 133, 254
Hampstead, 200–2, 213, 240–2
Hanbury, Dame Felicity, 223
Hansom-cabs, 69–70, 144
Harding, Rev. W. H., 49–52, 165–7
Harlech, 23–4, 177
Harps and harpists, 57, 65, 67, 135, 141–2
Harrison, Beatrice and May, 140
Harrogate, 203–4
Harty, Sir Hamilton, 45, 114–15, 130, 153
Hatch, Daniel, 110, 119
Hatchman, G. H., 248, 254
Hawkes, Oliver, 180
Hawley, Stanley, 120, 129–30
Hawtrey, Sir Charles, 90
Hazleford Ferry, 36, 97
Heifetz, Jascha, 262
Hellmesberger, 137
Hely-Hutchinson, Dr. V., 247
Henley-on-Thames, 5
Henschel, Sir George, 154
Henschel (singer), 140
Herbert, Sir Alan, 254
Hess, Myra, 64, 79, 140
Hess, Willy, 41
Hickin, Welton, 58
Highland Brigade, m.v., 254
Hill, Carmen, 79
Hills, George, 256–7
Hilversum, 143
His Majesty's Theatre, 152
Hobbs, Miss, 8, 9
Hobday, Claude, 135
Hodgkinson, Fred, 38–40, 43, 53
Holst, Gustav, 148–9
Horner, Dr. Ralph, 31–3, 42–3, 48, 52, 54, 59, 97
Horse-buses, 68–9
Howitt, Mr., 27–8
Hucknall, 4, 9, 11–14, 24–31 *pass.*, 54, 96–7, 104, 153, 226, 260
Hudson, Eli, 46
Hundt, Hugo, 134
Hylton, Jack, 203, 236

'I HEARD you Singing' (Coates), 218
'I Pitch my Lonely Caravan' (Coates), 218
'Impressions d'Italie' (Charpentier), 145
'In Town To-night', 220, 222
'Iolanthe' (Sullivan), 95
Ireland, John, 154
Irving, Sir Henry, 224

JACOB, Naomi, 200
James, Alex, 221
James brothers (bassoon players), 135
James, C. F., 248
Jeremy, Raymond, 135
'Jester at the Wedding, The' (Coates), 217
Joachim, Joseph, 30, 31, 32, 47
Joachim String Quartet, 47
Johns, Barter, 91
Jones, Edward, 87–91 *pass.*
Jones, Guy, 86
Jones, Sidney, 86–7
'Joyous Youth' Suite (Coates), 199

KALISCH, Alfred, 134
Kalman, Emmerich, 225
Kastner, Alfred, 135
Kearton, Cherry, 132
Keys, Nelson, 188
Kiddle, Frederick B., 50, 188
Kilburn High Rd., 58–9, 68, 97
Kindersley, Lord, 242
Kinfauns Castle, s.s., 106–8
Kingsway Hall, 239
Kingsway Theatre, 120, 129–30, 223
Kipling, Rudyard, 27, 29, 101
Kit-Kat Club, 203
'Knightsbridge' March (Coates), 183, 219–22
Knoblock, Edward, 120–2
Kramm, Hugo and Fru, 232
Kreisler, Fritz, 41, 47, 129, 140, 146, 183, 261
Kreutzberger, Prof., 103, 105
Kubelik, Jan, 41, 46, 140
Kuhe, Ernest, 205

LANDSEER, Sir Edwin, 23
La Plata, 256
Lehar, Franz, 91, 226
Lehmann, Liza, 181
Lewis, Joseph, 218
Liddle, Samuel, 181
Liszt: Concerto in E Flat, 189
Lockyer, J. B., 135
'Locums' for the family practice, 21, 22, 24–5
Lodge, Herbert, 135
Löhr, Hermann, 181, 183, 186
London Philharmonic Orchestra, 41, 218, 222, 225, 236–7

INDEX

'London Suite' (Coates), 183, 218–20, 226
London Symphony Orchestra, 146, 152, 193, 225
'Londonderry Air', 114, 227
Lotter, Adolf, 134–5
Loudoun Rd., N.W., 117, 120, 130–1
Lunn, Kirkby, 140
Lyell-Tayler, H., 43

McCormack, John, 129
Macfarren, Sir George, 170
Mackenzie, Sir Alexander, 57–8, 63, 64–8, 72, 86, 103, 106, 113, 127, 129, 153, 154, 159, 160, 192, 223–5
Mackenzie, Lady, 159
Mackintosh, Lord, 242
Maclean, Alick, 182, 184–91, 199, 247
'Manon' (Massenet), 32
'Marjorie, Aunt', 4–5, 36–7, 259–60
Marriage, C.'s, 172
Marshall, Herbert, 200
Mascagni, Pietro, 144–5
Maschini, 129
Maschwitz, Eric, 222, 225
'Meadow to Mayfair, From' Suite (Coates), 217
Melba, Nellie, 132–3
Mendelssohn: 'Fingal's Cave' Overture, 155
Mengelberg, Willem, 129, 143, 154–5
'Mermaid, The' (Tennyson), 159, 160
'Merrie England' (German), 208
'Merry Widow, The' (Lehar), 91
'Merrymakers, The' Overture (Coates), 199
Messager, André and Mme., 151
'Mikado, The' (Sullivan), 62
Mills, Annette, 223
'Miniature Suite' (Coates), 146, 182, 186–7
Moiseiwitsch, Benno, 129, 140, 183, 189
Montevideo, 255
Motoring, 132, 209, 216, 223–4, 241, 248, 259–60
Moustache misadventures, 44–5, 79–80
Mozart: Double Concerto for Violin and Viola, 261; F Major Quartet, 103; G Major Quartet, 32
Muhlfeld, 47
Munks, John, 8, 28, 97
Murchie, Robert, 135
'My love is like the red, red rose' (Coates), 58

National Symphony Orchestra, 239–40
Nedbal, Oscar, 47, 73
Neuritis of the hand and arm, 94–5, 96, 100, 102–5 pass., 110, 125–6, 142, 146, 182, 193, 261
New York, 248–51
New York Symphony Orchestra, 135
Newman, Robert, 193, 194, 262
Newstead Abbey, 11, 15, 36
Nicholls, Agnes, 130
Nikisch, Arthur, 129, 143, 154–5
'Nocturnes' (Debussy), 150–1
Nottingham, 14, 20, 27, 30–2, 48, 94, 97, 151, 239; Albert Hall, 43, 46; Sacred Harmonic Orchestral Society, 43, 46; String Orchestra, 42–3
Nottinghamshire country, 9, 20, 33–6, 260–1
'Novelleten' (Glazounov), 153
Novello, Ivor, 134
Novello, Marie, 134

O'Donnell, B. Walton, 66–7, 79
Olof, Victor, 239, 241
'Omar Khayyam' (Bantock), 150
O'Neill, Norman, 129, 154
Orchestral Association, Gerrard St., 91, 99, 101
Orchestral training, 42–6, 64–8, 95, 101
Orchestration, the art of, 33, 44–5, 86, 92–3, 112, 115, 148, 152, 182, 203, 215, 232, 238, 244–5
O'Reilly, P. J., 183
Orellana, I. A. de, 92
Organists, 28, 50, 154, 166, 188
'Orpheus with his lute' (Coates), 111, 132
Oslo, 232

Pachmann, 129, 139, 140
Pagani's, 128–9
Park Rd., Regent's Park, 97–101 pass., 115
Parry, Sir Hubert, 51, 127, 153
'Pelléas et Mélisande' (Debussy), 151
Performing Right Society, 180–2, 195–6, 248–50, 253, 254–5
Peron, President, 255–6
'Peter Pan' Quartet (Walford Davies), 149
Peyton, Pen, 6–8
Peyton, Sir Richard, 6, 7
Philadelphia Symphony Orchestra, 135
Philharmonic Society, Royal, 129–30
Phillips, Montague, 64, 66, 79, 80–1

INDEX

Photography, amateur, 4, 11–12, 15, 16, 17, 23, 220, 228
Pianist, C. as, 8, 9, 27, 32, 51, 58, 59, 64
Pianists, 22, 63, 134, 140, 149
Pierné, Gabrielle, 145
'Poet and Peasant' Overture (Suppé), 141
Portsdown Rd., W., 133, 170
'Présages' (Tschaikowsky), 180
Primrose, William, 32
Promenade Concerts, 117, 132, 134, 140, 141, 142, 146, 150, 154, 164, 168, 176–9, 182, 193, 225, 261–2
Pryor (trombone-player), 47
Pugno, Raoul, 129, 140

QUEEN's Hall, 41, 47, 50, 74, 75, 80, 95, 106, 110, 113, 117, 123, 128, 129, 181, 183, 185, 261–2
Queen's Hall Orchestra, 47, 68, 117, 120, 134–55 *pass.*, 161, 164, 170–1, 174, 176–81, 193–4, 206, 240, 262; New Light, 182–90, 199
'Quentin Durward' (Maclean), 189
Quilter, Roger, 129

RACHMANINOFF, 129, 140
R.A.D.A., 234
Radio Times, 220, 225, 226
Rascher, Sigurd, 227–9
Ravel, Maurice, 154
'Ravenswood' (Mackenzie), 223–4
Raybould, Clarence, 215
Recitations, 79, 159–61
Reed, Willy, 152
Renard, Jacques, 134, 139
Revolver escapade, 76–8
Richter, Hans, 46
Riego, Teresa del, 181, 186
Robinson, Stanford, 215, 236, 239, 241
Rogue Herries (Walpole), 13
Rodgers, Richard, 218
Rogan, Lt.-Col. J. Mackenzie, 224
Ronald, Sir Landon, 127, 154
Rosenthal, Moriz, 129, 140
'Roumanian Rhapsody in A Minor' (Enesco), 145
Rube Prize, 80–3

ST. PETERSBURG String Quartet, 41
Sainton, Philip, 135
Saint-Saëns, Camille, 123, 145
'Salute the Soldier' Campaign, 242
Samuel, Harold, 119, 146, 198
São Paulo, 254
Sanderson, Wilfred, 181
Santley, Charles, 129, 140

Sapellnikoff, Wassily, 140
Saracen's Head, Southwell, 15, 16
Sauret, Emile, 41
Savoy Hill, 213–14
Savoy Theatre, 93–6, 200
Saxophone, the, 229, 239–40
'Saxo-Rhapsody' (Coates), 229
Scarborough, 182, 184–7, 233, 247
Schönberg, Arnold, 154
Schumann: Piano Quartet, 41; Piano Quintet, 41
Scott, Cyril, 129
'Sea Songs, Fantasy on British' (Henry Wood), 45
Seattle Symphony Orchestra, 144
Seidl, 45
'Selfish Giant, The' (Coates), 203
Sharpe, Cedric, 135
Shepperd, Beth, 20
Sherwood Forest, 35–6, 261
Sibelius, Jean, 145
Sight-singing, 64
Simpson, Harold, 183
Singers, 79, 113, 132–3, 140, 188
Sketch Club, 128
'Sleepy Lagoon, By the' (Coates), 214, 236, 249, 251, 258
Smith, Wilfred, 176
Smyth, Dame Ethel, 152–3
'Snow White' Ballet (Coates), 214–15
Solomon (pianist), 129, 140
Sons, Maurice, 41, 134, 140, 143
Sousa, J. P., 46
South Africa, tour in, 107–10
Southwell, 14–16, 17, 36, 97, 260
Southwold, 192–3
Speyer, Sir Edgar, 178
Squire, W. H., 181, 241
Stanford, Sir Charles, 127, 153
Statsradiofonien (Copenhagen), 135, 232, 251–2
Stockholm, 228–9, 232
Stokowski, Leopold, 45, 177
Stone, Christopher, 223
'Stonecracker John' (Coates), 118–19, 128–9, 131, 146, 168, 181
Stowe School, 234
Strauss, Richard, 93, 121, 122–3, 136, 138–9, 145, 150, 176, 178
Suggia, 140
Sullivan, Sir Arthur, 29, 62, 95
'Summer Days' Suite (Coates), 193–4, 206
Sussex, 208–10, 213, 215–17, 230–2, 233, 234, 246, 248
Sweden, 228–9, 232
Swedish Broadcasting Company, 215, 228–9
Szolt, Nandor, 135

INDEX

TALBOT, Howard, 91, 101
Taylor, Deems, 253
Telepathy, marital, 174
Telephones, primitive, 9–10
Tenter Hill, Hucknall, 9, 24–5, 48, 53, 96
Tenterden St., W., 57, 223
Tertis, Lionel, 32, 42, 53, 58, 59–61, 64, 65, 71, 73–5, 76, 81, 102, 115, 122, 241, 261
Teschemacher, Edward, 183
Tetrazzini, 140
Teyte, Maggie, 140
Theatre orchestras, C. plays in, 86–91, 93–6, 100–1, 151
Thibaud, Jacques, 41, 129, 140
'Three Bears, The' (Coates), 144, 149, 202, 203, 206
'Three Blind Mice', 226
'Three Elizabeths, The' Suite (Coates), 244–5, 247
'Three Men, The' Suite (Coates), 226, 227
Torquay, 144, 146, 217
Toscanini, Arturo, 138
Tree, Sir Herbert Beerbohm, 121
Trépied (Pas de Calais), 170–2
Trevor, Ann, 200
Trombone players, 29, 47, 76, 135
Tschaikowsky: Serenades, 42; Symphony in E Minor, 180
Tubb, Carrie, 140
Tuxen, Erik, 135, 232

USK, 36, 259–60

VAUDEVILLE Theatre, 87–91
Vaughan Williams, Dr. Ralph, 154
Verbruggen, Jacques, 134
Victoria, Queen, 29, 30
Viola player, C. as, 40–6, 48, 54, 57–8, 60–1, 64–8, 70–6, 80–91, 93–6, 100–10, 114–16, 120–8, 134–55 pass., 161, 164, 170, 223, 260, 261; as principal, 137, 138, 139, 171, 174–7, 181–2, 184–5, 187–9, 192–4, 262
Viola players, 27–8, 32, 38, 41, 43, 47, 53, 60–1, 73–4, 82–3, 86, 94, 115, 122, 126–7, 134–5, 138–9, 257

Violas and viola-playing, 32, 40–1, 60, 66–7, 81–2
Violin player, C. as, 8, 9, 28, 30–3, 37, 38, 46
Violins and violin players, 8, 28, 32, 40, 43, 46, 75–6, 85, 102, 134–5, 140, 143, 261–2

WAGNER, Richard, 63
Waldo-Warner (viola player), 126–7
Walton, Sir William, 257
War, First World, 177 *ff.*
War, Second World, 222, 233 *ff.*
Ward, Ronald, 200
Warren, Fred, 44, 45, 48, 54, 97
Warwick Evans, C., 139, 141
Washington (D.C.), 248–50
Waterfield, Mr., 31, 40–1, 54, 97
Watson, Victor, 135
Weatherly, F. E., 111, 117–20, 179, 183, 186
Weingartner, Felix, 45
Welbeck Abbey, 36
Wertheim, Siegfried, 122, 134, 138–9, 141–2
Wessely, Hans, 71–2, 80–3
White, Maude Valerie, 181
Whitemore, Cuthbert, 162, 166, 170
'Who is Sylvia' (Coates), 111, 132–3
Wiklund, Adolf, 228–9
Wilde, Jimmy, 221
'William Tell' Overture (Rossini), 141
'With a Song in my Heart' (Rodgers, arr. Coates), 218
Wood, Haydn, 181, 186
Wood, Sir Henry J., 43, 45, 47, 117, 120, 127, 132, 134–8, 141–3, 146–7, 154, 164, 168, 176, 182, 184, 190, 193–4, 206, 240
Wood, Mrs. Henry J., 117, 132
Wood, Lady (Henry), 176, 194
'Wood-Nymphs' (Coates), 187–8
'Wreckers, The' (Smyth), 152
Wright, Kenneth, 228

'YEOMEN of the Guard, The' (Sullivan), 94
'Young Idea, The' (Coward), 200
Ysaye, 41, 129, 140, 261

ZIMMERMANN, Louis, 72–3, 81–3

SELECTED LIST OF WORKS

ORCHESTRAL AND INSTRUMENTAL WORKS

1911 MINIATURE SUITE, *for small orchestra* — Queen's Hall Promenade Concerts, cond. Sir Henry J Wood
    1) Children's Dance
    2) Intermezzo
    3) Scène du Bal

SIX SHORT PIECES, *for pianoforte, without octaves*

1912 *Graceful Dance*, THE MERMAID

A LA GAVOTTE

1913 IDYLL — Queen's Hall Promenade Concerts, cond. Sir Henry J Wood

1915 *Suite*, FROM THE COUNTRYSIDE — Brighton Municipal Orchestra
    1) In the Meadows
    2) Among the Poppies
    3) At the Fair

1917 *Valsette*, WOOD NYMPHS — New Queen's Hall Light Orchestra

1919 *Suite*, SUMMER DAYS — ditto
    1) In a Country Lane
    2) On the Edge of the Lake
    3) At the Dance

1921 *Suite*, JOYOUS YOUTH — ditto / Chappell Ballad Concerts
    1) Introduction
    2) Serenade
    3) Joyous Youth – Valse

Dance Interlude, MORESQUE

1923 *Miniature Overture*, THE MERRYMAKERS — ditto

1925 TWO LIGHT SYNCOPATED PIECES — Queen's Hall Promenade Concerts
    1) Moon Magic
    2) Rose of Samarkand

Phantasy, THE SELFISH GIANT — Eastbourne Festival

Intermezzo, BY THE TAMARISK

1926 *Phantasy*, THE THREE BEARS — ditto

1927 *Suite*, FOUR WAYS — Harrogate Festival
    1) Northwards – March

    2) Southwards – Valse
    3) Eastwards – Eastern Dance
    4) Westwards – Rhythm

Romance, MIRAGE

1928 *Ballet,* SNOWDROP AND THE SEVEN DWARFS, *for twelve solo instruments* — in André Charlot revue for opening of the Cambridge Theatre, London

1929 *Phantasy,* CINDERELLA — Eastbourne Festival

    UNDER THE STARS, *for pianoforte*

1930 *Symphonic Rhapsody,* WITH A SONG IN MY HEART (on theme by Richard Rodgers) — commissioned by Columbia Gramophone Company

Valse Serenade, BY THE SLEEPY LAGOON

THREE LYRIC PIECES, *for pianoforte*
    1) Fragment
    2) Nocturne
    3) Valse

1931 *Suite,* FROM MEADOW TO MAYFAIR — Brighton Dome Concerts
    1) In the Country
    2) A Song by the Way
    3) Evening in Town

Concert Valse, DANCING NIGHTS — Eastbourne Festival

1932 *Suite from the Ballet,* THE JESTER AT THE WEDDING — Torquay Festival
    1) The Princess Arrives
    2) Dance of the Pages
    3) Humoresque: The Jester
    4) Dance of the Orange Blossoms
    5) The Princess
    6) The Princess and the Jester

1933 LONDON SUITE — BBC Orchestra, cond. Joseph Lewis (broadcast), Bournemouth Municipal Orchestra (concert broadcast, composer cond.)
    1) Covent Garden – Tarantelle
    2) Westminster – Meditation
    3) Knightsbridge – March

TWO SYMPHONIC RHAPSODIES
    1) I pitch my lonely caravan at night
    2) I heard you singing, and Bird Songs at Eventide

1934 *March,* LONDON BRIDGE   simultaneously recorded (Columbia, in Maida Vale studios) and broadcast (BBC)

1935 *Suite,* THE THREE MEN
  1) The Man from the Country
  2) The Man-About-Town
  3) The Man from the Sea

BBC Theatre Orchestra, Concert Hall, Broadcasting House, Eric Coates programme, composer cond.

SONG OF LOYALTY, *for orchestra, with solo voice obl.*

commissioned by BBC for Silver Jubilee of King George V; BBC Orchestra, composer cond. 7.5.35

1936 *Suite,* LONDON AGAIN
  1) Oxford Street – March
  2) Langham Place – Elegie
  3) Mayfair – Valse

BBC Theatre Orchestra cond. Stanford Robinson

SAXO-RHAPSODY, *for alto saxophone and orchestra*

Folkestone Festival, soloist: Sigurd Rascher

1937 *Suite,* SPRINGTIME
  1) Fresh Morning
  2) Noonday Song
  3) Dance in the Twilight

BBC Orchestra

Serenade, FOR YOUR DELIGHT

March, THE SEVEN SEAS

1938 *Ballet,* THE ENCHANTED GARDEN

BBC Orchestra, cond. Clarence Raybould, followed by first performances, composer cond. in Stockholm, Oslo, Copenhagen, Hilversum, Bournemouth

1939 *Concert Valse,* FOOTLIGHTS   BBC Theatre Orchestra, composer cond.

Romance, LAST LOVE

1940 *Serenade,* I SING TO YOU

March, CALLING ALL WORKERS	BBC Theatre Orchestra, cond. Stanford Robinson; Columbia record, Symphony Orchestra, composer cond. released same day, 1.9.40
1941 *March*, OVER TO YOU	Bristol Aero Company Works Band
1942 *March*, LONDON CALLING	for BBC Overseas Service Children's Programme
Suite, FOUR CENTURIES 1) Seventeenth Century — Prelude & Hornpipe 2) Eighteenth Century — Pavane & Tambourin 3) Nineteenth Century — Valse 4) Twentieth Century — Rhythm	BBC Theatre Orchestra, cond. Stanford Robinson
March, THE EIGHTH ARMY	BBC Northern Orchestra, cond. Maurice Johnstone
1943 *Souvenir*, FIRST MEETING, *for violin and pianoforte*	
1944 *March*, SALUTE THE SOLDIER	Scots Guards Band in Trafalgar Square, London
Suite, THE THREE ELIZABETHS 1) Halcyon Days — Elizabeth Tudor 2) Springtime in Angus — Elizabeth of Glamis 3) Youth of Britain — The Princess Elizabeth	BBC Symphony Orchestra, Bedford Town Hall, Christmas Eve
1948 *Rediffusion March*, MUSIC EVERYWHERE	commissioned by Rediffusion Ltd.
1950 *March*, HOLBORN	for the Borough of Holborn
1952 *Interlude*, THE UNKNOWN SINGER	Cheltenham Festival

1953 *March*, RHODESIA	for Central Africa Rhodes Centenary Exhibition, Bulawayo, Hallé Orchestra, cond. Sir John Barbirolli
March, MEN OF TRENT	for the City of Nottingham Police
1954 *Concert Valse*, SWEET SEVENTEEN	BBC Light Programme Music Festival, Royal Festival Hall, London
1955 *Television March*, SOUND AND VISION	
March, THE DAM BUSTERS	Associated British Pictures for film 'The Dam Busters'
1956 *Intermezzo*, IMPRESSION OF A PRINCESS	BBC Light Programme Music Festival, Royal Festival Hall, London
1957 *March*, HIGH FLIGHT	ditto Warwick Film Productions for film 'High Flight'

Except in the case of short works first given from the studio on sound radio, the foregoing orchestral works were conducted by the composer on first performance, unless otherwise stated. Eric Coates made his last appearance as a composer-conductor on 26th November 1957, at the Royal Festival Hall, London, with the BBC Concert Orchestra, conducting *High Flight* and *Elizabeth of Glamis (The Three Elizabeths)*. He died on the 21st December that year.

SONGS AND BALLADS – A SELECTED LIST

Between 1908 and 1923, over 100 songs by Eric Coates were published. After this his output of songs fell sharply. In the 30 years following 1926, he wrote 30 songs, of which all except five were written and published prior to the outbreak of war in 1939.

Year	Title	Author
1908	Four Old English Songs 1) Orpheus with his lute 2) Under the greenwood tree 3) Who is Sylvia? 4) It was a lover and his lass	William Shakespeare
	When I am dead	Christina Georgina Rossetti
	Devon to me	John Galsworthy
1909	Stonecracker John	Fred E Weatherly
1910	Lace and Porcelain	Harold Simpson
1911	Reuben Ranzo	Fred E Weatherly
1912	A Dinder Courtship	Fred E Weatherly
1913	Betty and Johnny	Fred E Weatherly
	The Grenadier	Fred E Weatherly
1915	The Mill o' Dreams (song cycle)	Nancie B Marsland
1916	Green Hills o' Somerset	Fred E Weatherly
	Sigh no more, ladies	William Shakespeare
1918	The Fairy Tales of Ireland	Edward Lockton
1919	By the North Sea	Arthur Conan Doyle
1920	Pepita	G Douglas Furber
1921	I pitch my lonely caravan at night	Annette Horey
1923	I heard you singing	Royden Barrie
1924	Sea Rapture	S G Hulme Beaman
1925	Song of the Little Folk	Jennie Dunbar
1926	Bird Songs at Eventide	Royden Barrie
1927	A Song Remembered	Royden Barrie
1928	Homeward to You	Royden Barrie
	Little Lady of the Moon	Fred E Weatherly
1929	Always as I close my eyes	Maud Handfield-Jones
1930	Summer Afternoon	Royden Barrie

1932	If Stars were Tears	Frank Eyton
	Stars and a Crescent Moon	Phyllis Black
1933	Rise up and reach the stars	Winifred May
1934	Music of the Night	Phyllis Black
1938	You are my rose	Christopher Hassall
	Your Name	Christopher Hassall
1940	Today is Ours	Frank Eyton
1942	Star of God	Fred E Weatherly
1943	A Song of Summer	Lady Joan Verney
1956	God's Great Love Abiding (hymn)	Composer's words